OP-'68

NBCL

5.00

JZC

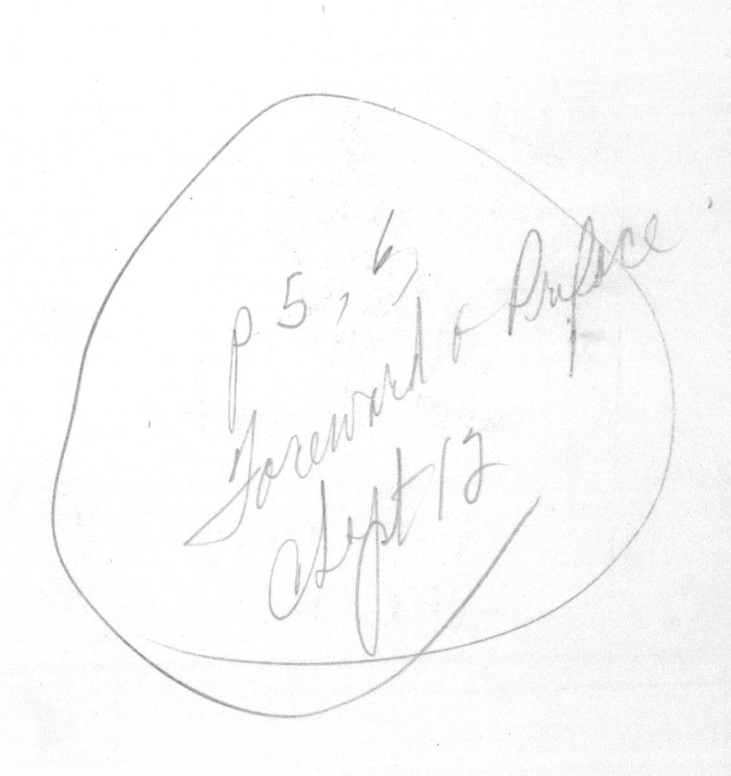

BROTHERHOOD OF EVIL

The Mafia

BROTHERHOOD OF EVIL

The Mafia

by Frederic Sondern, Jr.

With a Foreword by

HARRY J. ANSLINGER

Commissioner of the Federal Bureau of Narcotics

FARRAR, STRAUS AND CUDAHY

New York

Library of Congress catalog card number 58-12484

Published simultaneously in Canada by
Ambassador Books, Ltd., Toronto

Manufactured in the United States of America

To District Supervisors Charles Siragusa and John T. Cusack of the U.S. Treasury's Bureau of Narcotics—two of those dedicated, infinitely patient men who devote their lives so successfully to our common welfare.

Contents

Foreword

Brotherhood of Evil is a searching, exciting, and accurate book. It tells a story that every American should know.

We are engaged in a war against organized crime which involves the whole nation; in a war against an army of subtle and defiant men whose power and wickedness have grown steadily during the last decade. They poison our children and create thousands of criminals with their heroin. They exact several billion dollars every year from us by their extortion rackets on waterfronts, in warehouses, in many labor unions. We, after all, pay the infamous levy which the underworld collects. They tamper with the integrity of many local governments. Most dangerous is their corruption of our law; the outrageous use of our legal institutions, so carefully designed to protect the innocent, for their own evil purposes. They are utterly without conscience or humanity. Murder, violence of all kinds, vicious sabotage, blackmail are commonplace and natural to them.

The core of this army are the mafiosi. Like the Communists they have discipline, cohesion, and a philosophy. These are no ordinary hoodlums; they are far more menacing and have been for a long time. The Mafia is very old.

The author is qualified to tell this story. He has, for years, been close to many of us in various fields of law enforcement and been with us in many battles in its behalf. He knows what he is talking about at first hand.

Brotherhood of Evil will be fascinating reading for the general public. It should be compulsory reading for every law enforcement officer in the United States.

Harry J. Anslinger
Commissioner
Bureau of Narcotics
Treasury Department

Washington, Oct. 27, 1958

Preface

In the history of crime the Mafia is unique. There have been many secret societies devoted to evil-doing, but nothing like the strange combine of Sicilian families which forms this company of born lawbreakers, and which has produced such men as Lucky Luciano, Albert Anastasia, Frank Costello and Joe Adonis, to name only a few.

The Mafia is not a secret society in our sense of the phrase at all. It has no president, no initiations, dues, elections, or by-laws except unwritten ones. Its cohesion is guaranteed by family relationships which go back over generations and an uncodified ideology at least two hundred years old, handed down from father to son and from mother to daughter. It is a brotherhood of people trained in crime from their earliest years.

There has been much controversy over the Mafia recently, and even some disagreement over the name itself. Writers and police authorities not sufficiently informed have referred to the Mafia variously as the Unione Sicilione, the Black Hand and the Syndicate. The brotherhood has to do with all three, but they are entirely separate entities. To increase the confusion, a good bit of nonsense has been said and published about the brotherhood. It has been called by some a "hidden government" within the United States with great political as well as criminal power. Others, including some responsible newsmen and law officers, have denied its existence entirely. Actually the truth lies in between these two views.

The evidence on the Mafia, its background and operations is mainly in the files of the Federal Bureau of Narcotics, the Secret Service and the Internal Revenue Service—the enforcement branches of the United States Treasury which have had the most to do with the brotherhood. The Mafia is very real indeed, and has been for a long time, to Commissioner Harry J. Anslinger of Narcotics, Chief U. E. Baughman of Secret Service, and such veteran federal agents as Charles Siragusa, John T. Cusack and George Gafney—Narcotics Bureau district supervisors for Europe and the Middle East, Southeastern United States, and New York State. To agents Joseph Amato, Pat Ward and Martin Pera of the bureau's New York office, and to many more men in other federal units, the Mafia and its operations are as obvious and inevitable as breakfast. They live with it every day. They have testified to the reality of the Mafia over and over again before legislative committees, who frequently remained incredulous and skeptical. Finally, our lawmakers on both state and federal levels have begun to believe them, mainly as a result of the startling events at Apalachin, New York, in November 1957.

We have two main purposes. One is to tell the story, and the history, of the Mafia as it really is. To understand the brotherhood and its impact on our society one must know not only the spectacular villainies of such outstanding mafiosi as Luciano, Anastasia and the rest, but also their peculiarly Sicilian mentalities, characters, personal habits and lives. Having brought into perspective these strange antisocial men, their gangs, and the damage they do us, another duty devolves upon the writer. The mafiosi, singularly insidious though they are, make up a minute fraction of the many hundreds of thousands of Americans of Sicilian birth or extraction, the great majority of whom are honest people engaged in conventional pursuits. The reader is asked to remember that the terms Mafia and Sicilian are not synonymous. The latter group must be protected against the stigma which is growing and will continue to grow in the course of many investigations into the Mafia that are now underway. This is the second reason for writing this book.

BROTHERHOOD OF EVIL
The Mafia

CHAPTER ONE

A Grand Council Meets

Aroused federal, state and municipal law enforcement agencies have, through their systems of underworld informers, gradually put together an accurate picture of what happened at Apalachin.

On the morning of November 14, 1957, at a large and well-appointed home deep in the hills behind the village of Apalachin in central southern New York, near the Pennsylvania border, a remarkable business conference was underway. More than sixty of our most important national and international racketeers had come together for one of their periodic meetings. Some had journeyed from as far away as California, Florida, Texas, Cuba and Italy. Their host was Joseph Barbara, a wealthy merchant whose firm controlled much of the distribution of beer and soft drinks through the booming industrial area around Binghamton. Like their host, who immigrated to America from Sicily in 1920, all were of southern Italian birth or extraction—most of them of Sicilian, some of Calabrian, a few of Neapolitan background. A grand council of the two hundred-year-old society of the Mafia was in formal session.

It was an imposing gathering of power and wealth. Almost every element of the rackets managed by the Mafia in the United States was represented at high or highest level. Dynamic, chunky little Vito Genovese, who is the American underworld's greatest financier, with interests ranging from narcotics through gambling to labor extortion, was there with his two oldest friends and partners, Joe Profaci and Mike Miranda—only slightly less prominent than he. Big John Ormento, head of New York City's powerful 107th Street gang, Joe Bonanno, Carlo Gambino and a dozen other equally important top executives of organized crime were present, accompanied by their assistants and subsidiaries. The Sicilian brotherhood to which they all belong has practically absolute monopolies throughout the country of two vast enterprises: the sale of illicit narcotics and the control of large-scale gambling, both legal and illegal. Moreover, these men and their gangs (particularly in cities with large Italo-American communities which defer to the Mafia's terroristic politics) control important segments of the vending, pinball, and slot machine business, food and liquor distribution, trucking, garbage removal, building contracting, longshoring and various labor unions as well as innumerable other legitimate undertakings—and run them in traditional gangster fashion with extortion and violence. An average of the estimates made by our most experienced authorities on rackets in the United States—U. S. Attorney General William P. Rogers, U. S. Commissioner of Narcotics Harry J. Anslinger and others—establishes the annual illegal take of all these rackets at several billion dollars, of which the *mafiosi* and the other gangsters under their management get the lion's share. In the pockets of the fastidiously clothed gentlemen meeting at Joe Barbara's home was a total of no less than $300,000 in cash. A *mafioso* of any standing must have at least a thousand dollars with him at all times—for a quick business deal or a bet. Signor Simone Scozzari of Palermo, with "real estate interests" in California, who had flown over from Sicily especially for the occasion, had only a few hundred dollars in bills on his person, but he also had a cashier's check for more than $8,000. The automobiles assembled in Joe Barbara's ample parking space were all of the Cadillac class.

Inside Barbara's $150,000 main house and the roomy, glass-fronted summer house nearby, various executive committees of the brotherhood had organized their conclaves. Others were grouped around the huge stone barbecue pit between the summer house and the four-car garage, which also contains a completely equipped bar. Joe Barbara prided himself on the quality of his hospitality and had laid in several hundred dollars' worth of prime beef and a selection of choice wines. The atmosphere was much the same as it would have been on the farm of a *capo mafioso* of wealth in Sicily. The conversation was mostly in Italian, in the peculiar Sicilian vernacular. According to strict protocol, there was much bowing and hand-shaking. There were also emotional embraces as cousins and other close relatives, of which there were many, met and greeted each other. The mafiosi have been intermarrying for more than two centuries and the family relationships in the top brackets are confusingly ramified; they are also very tightly knit. Joseph Magliocco—a major New York racketeer—affectionately hugged his brother-in-law and second cousin, Joseph Profaci. Ignazio Cannone welcomed his godfather, Natale Evola. The weather at Apalachin was unusually mild for November and most of the guests were dressed in immaculate light suits of Italian silk, white on white shirts and highly polished shoes of soft leather. The majority were in their late fifties and early sixties—dignified, even pompous. All seemed to be in a decorous good humor.

To understand the Mafia, one must realize that this unique society of lawbreakers is not a rigid, monolithic organization, as most powerful secret societies of the past have been. There is no president, no formal roster; there is no initiation or oath. They are unnecessary. A mafioso selects one or more of his sons, or perhaps a favorite nephew, trains and guides him in the traditional philosophy and methods, introduces him to the right people and another mafioso is gradually created. The Mafia is, actually, a loosely knit association of such families combined by many generations of tradition and upbringing and by an antisocial ideology rooted in more than two centuries of turbulent history. The important members of these groups, the core of the society, probably number about a thousand. These are held together by the dons, the brotherhood's elders. Among them are (or have been) such spectacular figures as Adonis, Luciano, Anastasia. The prefix don is a title of particular respect for a prominent man, superior to that of signor and señor, used generally in southern Italy and Spain. But to the mafiosi it has a special meaning. Each Mafia don, according to ancient custom, is the co-ordinator of his area—it may be a section of Brooklyn, Chicago or Los Angeles, Las Vegas, Youngstown or Kansas City—and he settles disputes among the mafiosi in his territory and decrees punishment for the recalcitrant, including assassination when necessary. He is not formally elected; he is slowly recognized by the elders as the biggest, most capable man in his section. A wise and successful gang leader of Mafia origin, if he is not eliminated by rivals or caught too often by the police, eventually becomes a capo mafioso. After proving his worth as an organizer and executive on a larger scale, he finally becomes a don—in effect the head of his local Mafia complex and responsible for its peculiar welfare.

The dons arrange their meetings according to the needs of the moment, as they have for more than thirty years, and the attendance depends on the number and diversity of the problems to be discussed. Ten of them may suddenly gather in San Francisco to organize the shipment of narcotics from the Orient, a dozen may get together in Chicago to talk over new possibilities in the labor rackets, twenty may converge on New York to set up a gambling syndicate. Word is simply passed on through their amazingly efficient and secure grapevine and those who are concerned appear. This continual ebb and flow in the brotherhood's operations, the continual change of personnel in the various rackets, and the fluidity of their associations are among the factors which have made it impossible for the press, the police and the legislative committees to get a clear picture of the always writhing octopus. The convention at Don Giuseppe Barbara's was a perfect example of the fraternity's method of operation. Among those present were 19 delegates from upstate New York, 23 from the New York City and adjacent New Jersey area, 8 from the Midwest, 3 from beyond the Rocky Mountains, 2 from the South, 2 from Cuba, 1 from Italy. At the moment, ten were primarily interested in the gambling business, nine in narcotics, sixteen in the production of illicit alcohol and five in union racketeering. But the operations of all, as usual, interlocked.

A number of emergencies had arisen which particularly concerned the mafiosi of New York and the eastern seaboard. During recent months rivalries and violent disputes between powerful brethren had led to the unfortunately sensational assassinations of dons Francesco Scalici and Umberto Anastasia, the attempted murder of Don Francesco Castiglia (Frank Costello), and the killing of several less important members. The traditional unity and discipline within the society were being shaken, the elders felt, and stricter lines of jurisdictional demarcation in the narcotics, gambling and labor fields had to be drawn at once. There were other serious problems. Ever since the Kefauver and the Daniels committees of the U. S. Senate were thoroughly shocked some years ago by the testimony of Treasury Department agents concerning the Mafia's structure and its role in organized crime, Congress has become increasingly concerned with what formerly seemed a myth to most of the legislators. The prying of Senator McClellan's more recently constituted anti-rackets committee had grown embarrassing. National magazines and many newspapers had given the brotherhood much unwanted publicity. Worst of all, a growing number of big city police departments which—either for local political reasons or out of sheer ignorance—had always discounted the influence of the Mafia or denied its existence entirely, were beginning to take a closer look and to understand connections and patterns of operation which they had not grasped before. The dons liked none of this. Many of them have long enjoyed virtual anonymity and freedom from police interference. Appropriate counter measures had to be taken.

The idea of gathering at Apalachin had not been too popular among the brethren. Many thought it dangerous. The meeting would be unusually big because of the emergency. They could get to Don Giuseppe's only by car, and the sudden appearance of so many automobiles with license plates from other counties and states at a season when few tourists circulate in the isolated country area might be noticed and investigated. The dons and their staffs usually converge with great care and considerable tactical preparation. A number of them—some of whom, incidentally, were at Barbara's on November 14, 1957—were discovered in session in a hotel in Cleveland back in 1928 and arrested for carrying concealed weapons. The same happened again in Chicago a few years later. The police paid them little attention, they escaped with fines and the press failed to understand their significance. But the dons very clearly recognized the peril that they had avoided. Since then they have arrived in New York, Chicago, Hollywood (Florida), Miami Beach, Tampa—their favorite meeting places—in small groups by devious routes, and never armed. The mafiosi, however, are not wholly practical. They are sentimental in their peculiar way, and sometimes recklessly so. Don Giuseppe, despite the relatively small area which he controlled, was a capo mafioso of the first order, of unusual experience, wisdom and authority. His services as mediator and moderator—and he was brilliant as both—were badly needed for the amicable settlement of many of the issues which faced the convention. There was another almost equally compelling reason. Don Giuseppe, at 51, had a dangerous heart condition which made it impossible for him to travel to one of the usual Florida meeting places where, in the winter, the upper echelon of the fraternity likes to take the sun, spend afternoons at the races and evenings in night clubs run by friendly associates. It was therefore decided that business should be combined with a fitting tribute to their perhaps mortally ailing friend and respected associate. And so, the dons assembled.

The mightiest of Don Giuseppe's guests was Don Vitone Genovese. (Vito Genovese—born in Sicily in 1897—FBI #861267; NYCPD #B-5993; international list of the Federal Bureau of Narcotics #130.) Compact, shrewd and enormously energetic, Don Vitone is generally considered by the underworld from New York to California as one of the most capable and versatile organizers of rackets in the business. His pleasant house in Atlantic Highlands, New Jersey, is sometimes referred to by the brethren as "Fort Knox." Don Vitone's police record is a classic of gangsterdom extending over four decades. He was first arrested at the age of 20, four years after he had arrived in the United States, for illegal possession of a gun. Eleven more arrests followed over a period of years—on suspicion of assault, robbery, homicide. On many occasions he was brought in by various city and federal police agencies for questioning about an extraordinary assortment of other illegal activities. He was never convicted on a single charge. In 1934, his foot slipped for once. The New York City police and Brooklyn's district attorney had reason to believe that Genovese had arranged the assassination of a fellow mafioso, Fernando (The Shadow) Boccia. Genovese evidently thought that they had a good case and escaped to Italy. He continued his remarkable career there during the next twelve years before, during and after World War II, indulging in many types of profitable skulduggery. In 1946 the American military government in Italy, on the insistence of the New York authorities, sent him back to the United States for trial for complicity in the murder of Boccia. But the principal corroborating witness for the state was poisoned in a Brooklyn jail, the prosecution collapsed and Don Vitone was again a free American citizen. So he has remained, more prosperous than ever.

Among the other elder statesmen of the Mafia who had made the pilgrimage to Apalachin were two of Don Vitone's closest associates, of many years standing. One was Don Giuseppe Profaci, wealthy and powerful olive oil and cheese distributor of Brooklyn. To the police he is known as Joseph Profaci (FBI #4469866; NYCPD #E-14481; Narcotics list #247). The other was Don Michele Miranda, a prosperous Manhattan used car dealer. (Mike Miranda—FBI #91524; NYCPD #B-129648.) The three have been a typical Mafia clique for many years. All of approximately the same age, they were born in Sicily within a few miles of each other and came to the United States at about the same time. In their earlier days, during the era of Al Capone, they were gun-carrying henchmen to some of the foremost gang leaders. Profaci, an assistant and favorite of Lucky Luciano, was already sufficiently prominent at the age of 31 to meet with the country's top racketeers at their 1928 gathering in Cleveland. Both Profaci and Miranda were arrested with Genovese in connection with the Boccia murder, but also escaped prosecution. In the years since then, like Don Vitone, they have risen to the top bracket of the brotherhood, assumed a formidable respectability, can command the most expensive criminal lawyers, regard police and judges with contempt and almost sneeringly plead the Fifth Amendment before legislative investigating committees. Some law enforcement officers bitterly refer to this level of the Mafia as the "non-touchables" —and so they have been for a long time.

Other capi mafiosi held court from the couches in Joe Barbara's big living room, in the summer house and around the barbecue. Don Giuseppe Magliocco, New York beer distributor, was one who commanded respectful attention. The standing in the organization of Don Giuseppe Bonanno, once an associate of Al Capone and still a close friend of Lucky Luciano, also went back as far as the Cleveland meeting of

1928. Dons Carlo Gambino and Vincenzo Rao, also born in Palermo, were approximately of the same age and rank. Belonging to the uppermost families of the society, Gambino's son is married to the daughter of Don Tomasio (Three Fingers Brown) Luchese, while Rao is the cousin of the late famed Don Giuseppe (Pip the Blind) Gagliano.

In the same bracket with the beer and cheese merchants was Don Carlo Chieri (Charles Chiri), vice president of the Automotive Conveying Company of New Jersey. Automotive Conveying used more than 100 tractor-trailer units to haul new cars from the Mahwah and Edgewater plants of the Ford Motor Company to dealers in 14 states. Until a few years ago the trucking concern was owned by Don Giuseppe Doto (Joe Adonis to the underworld)—convicted gambling organizer, dock racketeer and narcotics trader. Officially, according to the Interstate Commerce Commission's files, Charles Chiri was president, Joseph Doto vice-president. In 1955 the U.S. Department of Justice finally caught up with Doto, discovered that he had been born in Italy and not in the United States as he had always claimed and began proceedings to deport him as an undesirable alien. Don Giuseppe promptly sold out to Don Carlo, at a handsome price. On the capital from this and other successful ventures, legitimate and illegitimate, Don Giuseppe now lives very handsomely in Rome. The brethren make this sort of arrangement with a minimum of formality.

Younger and of slightly lesser seniority and rank were such mafiosi as Giovanni Ormento. Big John, as he is generally known in the fraternity, is a spectacular individual regarded by the more conservative with a mixture of disapproval and admiration. He has a booming voice, an utter contempt for the law and a love for rakish clothes and diamonds. His outsized wristwatch is bordered with big stones; his belt buckle, tie clasp and fingers flash dramatically. Such ostentation is not in keeping with Mafia tradition. Other serious demerits against him, as far as the brotherhood is concerned, are three convictions for the sale of narcotics. Considering the volume of the trade which he handled as one of the principals of the 107th Street syndicate, the largest in New York and probably in the United States, his sentences were light. In 1937 he was sent to Leavenworth for three years, in 1941 for eight and in 1952 for two. Ordinarily such obvious lack of ability to avoid the law would have abruptly cut off a younger mafioso's career. But Big John has both an unusually ingratiating personality and powerful connections. Thirty years ago, at 15—he was born in New York of immigrants from Sicily—he became a messenger boy and apprentice of the Sicilian combination of gangsters who have long made their headquarters in the area of Manhattan's East 106th and 107th streets, and have been the major influence in the city's gambling, prostitution, narcotics and labor rackets. Of well-connected Mafia stock himself, he came to know such prominent men as Luciano, Adonis, Costello, Anastasia. Big John was regarded by his superiors as reliable, if not too intelligent, and he gradually rose toward the top echelon of the New York area. Only three years ago he received the final accolade. He was best man at the wedding in Detroit of the daughter of Don Giuseppe Profaci to Anthony Tocca, an Illinois power; among the guests were Anastasia, Miranda, Genovese and others equally important. Big John had reached the upper strata; he had become one of the "non-touchables."

The aggregate police record of 56 of Don Giuseppe's guests was remarkable. The 56, between them, had been arrested 275 times and shared more than 100 convictions for serious crimes ranging from homicide and armed robbery through narcotics trading to extortion and organized prostitution. Only nine of the men had no police history. The guests had countless aliases. The obfuscation of correct names is a Mafia trick of ancient origin which causes police authorities almost as much trouble and confusion today as it did two hundred years ago. The mafioso does not, like cruder criminals, simply take other names entirely. He has a number of slightly different ways of spelling his patronymic. Bonanno, for example, signs and identifies himself variously as Giuseppe or Joseph, or Joe Bannani, Bonono, or Bananni. Miranda unexpectedly becomes Mirandi, Morando, Maranda. This is not a result of illiteracy; it is a well tried system which often upsets police files and baffles newspaper reporters and their morgue librarians. Every mafioso of importance also has a nickname. It is more than a nickname, really; it is sort of a recognition signal as well. Bonanno, for example, is always referred to among the brotherhood as Joe Bananas, host Barbara as Joe the Barber, diamond studded Ormento as The Governor, or Big John.

The business of the meeting at Barbara's—according to well placed informers who have pieced the picture together for the Treasury Department's agents—concentrated on two questions crucial to the future of big organized rackets; narcotics and gambling. The dons are shrewd businessmen and, like the directors of any big corporation, try to look ahead. Large-scale trading in illicit drugs has become increasingly dangerous, not only to the dealers themselves but to the fraternity as a whole. Widespread publicity and resulting public anger over the insidious menace of heroin and the increasing crime rate attached to it has spurred legislators, police and judges to adopt much harsher measures than ever before against one of the Mafia's principal sources of income. Ten- to fifteen-year sentences are being imposed for the first time, and under the new federal law even the death penalty may be ordered under certain circumstances. Above all, however, the publicity about the drug traffic has seriously affected the accustomed anonymity of the society by drawing attention to so many Sicilian names.

Warnings to that effect began to reach the capi mafiosi of New York, Chicago and other centers months ago. Among the most compelling came from Lucky Luciano and Joe Adonis in Italy. Although spectacularly deported from the United States as dangerous convicts and undesirable aliens, they are still among the most senior of the Mafia elders. Both keep a close watch on the American underworld scene, and their suggestions, carried by a continuous stream of friends and couriers between the Continent and America, have almost the weight of orders across the Atlantic. Don Salvatore Lucania (Luciano) lives pleasantly in Naples, Don Giuseppe Doto (Adonis) in affluent luxury in Rome. Their ideas are presented at every important Mafia meeting; this time, at Barbara's, they were delivered by Don Giuseppe Bonanno, who had been in Italy just before the convention. Both Lucania and Doto apparently felt very strongly that the brotherhood should stop its narcotics activities for as long as the heat is on, despite the fact that Don Salvatore, particularly, derives most of his revenue from arranging heroin shipments to the United States. Most of the brethren apparently agreed with this attitude and there was talk of turning over the whole business, for the time being, to gangs connected with but outside the organization, thereby taking smaller cuts but maintaining comparative safety. The consensus of opinion seemed to be that intensified operations in gambling and labor rackets would make up the difference.

Another issue which had aroused intense debate at Barbara's concerned jurisdiction in the enormously lucrative gambling operation which has mushroomed in Cuba during the last two years and is beginning to surpass even that of Las Vegas. Luigi Santos Trafficanti and a partner, Luigi (Joe Rivers) Silesi, had come from Havana to establish before the capi mafiosi their exclusive overlordship, of long standing, in this domain. The Cuban government, for $25,000 a year, grants a gambling license for a casino to anyone investing at least $1,000,000 in a new hotel. Trafficanti—Señor Trafficante in Havana—and associates had set up a typical syndicate. Meyer Lansky, the big New York gambler, and a group of his friends had the necessary money and saw the financial possibilities. Meyer himself acquired the concession in the magnificent new $14,000,000 Riviera Hotel on the Malecon;

his brother, Jack, established more decorous but equally profitable gaming rooms in the older but opulent Hotel Nacional. Other tourist centers were assigned to a group of carefully selected casino executives and croupiers from New York, Chicago, Las Vegas. As is usual in most arrangements by members of the brotherhood with outside elements, Luigi Trafficanti remained essentially the chairman of the board. His political connections were formidable, reaching well into President Batista's palace. All was legal; no police could interfere; it was a racketeer's dream of legitimacy and security come true. Suddenly his position was threatened by a fellow mafioso. Don Umberto Anastasio (Albert Anastasia), one of the extremely wealthy and powerful masters of the docks and numbers rackets in New York, was sending agents to Cuba to scout for projects—without Trafficanti's permission. This was a serious breach of the brotherhood's rules, and complaints went promptly from Havana to New York. Anastasia was apparently warned by other capi mafiosi, but kept right on with his predatory plans. As a result, on October 25, 1957, Don Umberto was shot expertly through the head by two calm executioners as he sat in a barber chair in the Hotel Park Sheraton, in midtown Manhattan. The case, like most Mafia assassinations, has not been solved. Trafficanti and Silesi had been bothered by the New York police about Anastasia's murder, and Silesi subsequently sent a message to District Attorney Hogan, who wanted him for questioning, to "drop dead." Now they wished assurances from the elders that such invasions and embarrassments would not occur again.

These and other discussions were in progress in the living room and the summer house when the first warnings of disaster came. Several brethren who had been around the barbecue pit burst in breathlessly. Four men, evidently police officers, were taking down the numbers of the cars parked in front of the garage and in a neighboring field. "That's just a state cop," the host is reported to have said. "He bothers us once in a while, but he's harmless. They think this is a business convention." The mafiosi looked at each other uneasily, but shortly afterward the pickets reported that the policemen had gone away, and the meetings continued. There was noticeable nervousness, however. Every mafioso present realized the possible consequences of their being found together.

And then Bartolo Guccia burst into the proceedings. A voluble, elderly Sicilian, he has been delivering fish to the Barbaras for years. From the same section of Sicily, Don Giuseppe was his *paisan* and a *compadre*—patron and friend—who had helped him during various brushes with the law when he was a gunman. He had come that morning around noon with the three porgies and a mackerel which Mrs. Barbara had ordered for the next day, Friday. On the way back down the hill he had, to his horror, found two unmarked but unmistakable State Police cars parked to jam the road. An ex-convict himself, he grasped the situation immediately. The four grim men in plain clothes standing alert by the cars waved him and his little truck through the narrow passage without so much as a question, and he went quickly. But half a mile farther on, Bartolo Guccia's conscience got the better of him. Don Giuseppe had long been very good to him, the other gentlemen were evidently close friends and all were obviously in danger. Abruptly, he swung his truck around. He was frightened as he again approached the police. But once more they let him through without hesitation. He pounded back up the hill. "Road block," he shouted to the men around the barbecue where almost everyone had gathered by this time for lunch. "State Police! They're stopping everybody! They're all over the place!" Mafiosi put down drinks and steaks. There was panic on every face. Don Vitone Genovese, without a word, headed for his car; there was a concerted rush in the great man's wake toward the parking spaces. Don Giovanni Montana thought differently. A very wealthy and respected taxicab, trucking and real estate owner in Buffalo with important political connections, the city's "man of the year" in 1956, he saw ruin staring him in the face. In his expensive camel's hair coat, which was to get him into trouble later on, he walked quickly and then began running across the open field behind the Barbara house toward the thick woods which border it. A dozen others followed him.

About a mile down the road which is the only exit from Barbara's, in a position which commanded a view of the whole property, stood a grinning sergeant of the New York State Police, binoculars in hand. "They've fallen for it," said Edgar Croswell to his partner, Trooper Vincent Vasisko, with triumph in his voice. "By gosh, they've fallen for it. They're running. This is going to be a bad day for a lot of people," he added as he reached for the microphone of his radio to call for reinforcements. It was to be a very bad day indeed for the brotherhood; probably the worst in its long history.

CHAPTER TWO

A Detective Named Croswell

A detective sergeant of the New York State Police dealt the Mafia the most serious blow that the brotherhood has ever received.

Edgar Croswell of the New York State Police had waited 13 years for Don Giuseppe Barbara to make a serious mistake.

The detective sergeant is a tall, spare, quiet man with gray hair and a narrow face set in lines that are severe and forbidding—until he smiles. Behind the clear, penetrating eyes is an unusually shrewd, patient, precise and uncompromising policeman's mind sharpened by 19 years of hard experience.

He had been assigned as a detective of the Criminal Investigation Bureau to the Vestal substation of the State Police, near Binghamton, for only a short time before he suspected that there was a formidable adversary in the neighborhood. In the course of routine investigations into illegal gambling, the manufacture of illicit alcohol and the sale of faked rye and Scotch whisky, Croswell kept running into the name of Joseph Barbara. The shady elements in and around Binghamton—particularly those of the large Italian colony—seemed to regard him with not only respect, but awe. The sergeant grew curious about the background of the elusive, obviously wealthy man who owned the prosperous Mission Beverages Company of Endicott and the big house on the hill at Apalachin.

And then Croswell, in 1944, happened to meet Joe Barbara

personally. On a routine patrol one evening, the sergeant—he was still a trooper then—drove by a parked truck and noticed a man coming out of the bushes by the side of it who tried to run when he saw the State Police car. Suspicious, Croswell stopped him and discovered that he was the driver of the big Mission Beverages trailer. Shaking with fright at the sight of the unexpected uniform, the inexperienced thief blurted out that he had taken two five-gallon cans of gasoline from the truck's reserve and hidden them in the woods, intending to pick them up later. Croswell arrested him, took him to the station and called Barbara. A fuming, squat, bright-eyed little man arrived shortly. "I'm Barbara," he announced in a thick Italian accent. "Why did you arrest my man? He ain't done nothing wrong." Trooper Croswell tried to explain. "But, Mr. Barbara, he was stealing your gas, and it's hard to get these days." And then Croswell noticed a bulge where the little man's coat covered his hip. "Are you carrying a gun, sir?" he asked quietly. "Sure I carry a gun," was the reply. "Gotta license." Croswell stared. "May I see it, sir?" Barbara complied impatiently, producing a pistol permit issued by the ranking judge of Broome County. "Now you release my man, see?" he barked. "He ain't stole nuthin? You let him go right away."

Croswell's reaction to this scene was a lasting one. The pistol permit in the possession of a man of Barbara's reputation, his arrogance and obvious disdain of the police, the fact that he thought nothing of an employee stealing precious gasoline and his having—despite his record—a liquor distributor's license and a gun permit, made Trooper Croswell angry at first, and then patiently inquisitive. The New York State Police files led him to those of the Federal Bureau of Investigation, the New York City Police Department, the Pennsylvania State Police, and various other local and federal agencies. His thoroughness as well as his interest increased as he gradually pieced Mr. Barbara's unusual history together.

An inquiry such as this is not as simple as it would appear

from the TV and movie screens. Even a senior officer of a big city police force cannot push buttons, bark into telephones and have teletypes almost immediately chatter into action with all the desired information. The FBI's remarkable centralized identification section—continually fed information by local police forces all over the country—is able to quickly supply the record, fingerprints and picture of almost any individual who has been arrested almost anywhere in the United States during the last few decades for, or on suspicion of, a serious crime. But these records only show, in the tersest language, the date and place of an arrest and the disposition of the case. The accurate tracing of the detailed background of a criminal or a suspect is another matter. Many large metropolitan police headquarters are overcrowded, their filing sytems antediluvian and their busy officers generally have little patience with digging out old cases which do not immediately affect them. But Edgar Croswell was persistent.

Giuseppe Maria Barbara was born in 1905 in the small town of Castellamare on the western tip of Sicily, a historic stronghold of the Mafia to this day. At 16, he came to the United States with his older brother, Carlo, joined relatives in Endicott, New York, got a job in a shoe factory and settled down. The story of his next decade is hazy; the record shows only that he was made an American citizen in 1927. But, at 31, he was already known as Joe the Barber in the bootlegging, prostitution and gambling rackets of the flourishing Wilkes-Barre–Scranton–Pittston district, and as a power to be reckoned with.

There followed a series of arrests and police histories characteristic of an enforcer, as the underworld calls the skillful Mafia gunman. All of them involved disputes within the brotherhood and the punishment of those who offended against it. In 1931, bootlegger Calomare Calogaro—a Sicilian—was shot by two men in Wyoming, Pennsylvania. As he lay dying, he finally gasped that a Tony Morreale had been one of his attackers; he was apparently about to breathe the name of the other when his voice trailed away. Morreale was arrested by the State Police, but Joseph Barbara appeared promptly before the authorities to provide a seemingly airtight alibi for his old friend. After the police had added up all their information, they were almost certain that Joe the Barber had been the second killer; he also was taken into custody. The court was not convinced, however, and Barbara was released. A few months later, the enforcer had a brush with the New York City police, who found a Thompson submachine gun in his car. It was subsequently discovered by a bullet comparison test that the same gun had been used in a recent gang murder in the city. But the links between Barbara and the car—which was not his—and the weapon were legally too weak, he had a shrewd lawyer, and no indictment resulted. In 1932 he was arrested again, this time in Scranton, after two minor gangsters from New York had been mowed down on a back street, one fatally. The other, believing that he was dying, named Joe the Barber. The New Yorkers had tried, the police had reason to believe, to blackmail Barbara over a large still that he was running in the neighborhood. It looked like a strong case. But the victim-witness made a remarkable recovery, discovered that he was not going to die, and from his hospital bed steadfastly refused to identify Barbara when confronted with him. "Naw, dat ain't de guy," he said easily. "Ain't never seen him. Musta got de name wrong or somepin'."

Joe the Barber came close to disaster once more, the next year. The body of Albert Wichner, a local bootlegger who specialized in hijacking, was found by the Scranton police stuffed into the back of his own car. He had been murdered in a peculiarly cruel way; he had been forced to strangle himself by means of sashcords noosed around his neck and tied tightly to his ankles, which were doubled behind him. This is an ancient Mafia method of executing particularly hated enemies, used occasionally by Al Capone in his day and by other mafiosi before and since. It is never applied to members of the brotherhood, who according to custom must be killed immediately and without warning. The Scranton detectives worked hard, and then harder as the case became clearer and more positive. Wichner's wife, tight-lipped and savage, gave them all she knew. Her husband hijacked liquor from out-of-state gangs for Joe the Barber and two associates, Santo (King of the Night) Volpe and Angelo Polizzi—the triumvirate which ruled the Scranton rackets. He had, she knew, cheated them out of many thousands of dollars and she had warned him that they would inevitably find him out. On the night before his death, Wichner had been summoned by the bosses to appear at Barbara's house to discuss a new proposition. He went, and came home in high good humor; big things were getting started. He was to go to Barbara's again the next night to make the final deal. Something had worried Wichner's wife immediately. Barbara had cautioned him not to tell anyone, even her, where he was going the next night. "This is bad, Albert," she had pleaded. "They know. They'll get you." Albert had paid no attention. Joe the Barber, he said, was a nice guy.

Along with Mrs. Wichner, the police had found a witness whom they thought would clinch the case. A young man happened to be driving by the car in which Wichner's body was later found. It had been parked in a dark back street which was almost empty of other automobiles. He had noticed it because, as he swung around the corner near it, two men had suddenly begun walking away from the car across the roadway. His headlights caught them full on, they hesitated in his path, he almost hit them and they ran. When the driver read the account in the newspapers he had come straight to police headquarters. His identification of the car, of Barbara and Polizzi, was unhesitatingly positive. And then the usual sequence of events began which so often baffles police officers who tangle with influential mafiosi. Mrs. Wichner's memory suddenly became hazy. The young man's recollections, so clear before, also grew contradictory. The prosecutor threw in his cards; Barbara and Polizzi were discharged.

At this point, Joe the Barber decided on a change of scene. His attractive place in Old Forge was comfortable and he was making excellent money, but he knew that the Pennsylvania State Police, now convinced and infuriated, were determined to get after him. At least two prowl cars were always near his house, his visitors were often trailed and searched. His ability to operate in the area had come to an end. But the mafioso was flexible. A few months later Joe the Barber had disappeared from the Pennsylvania scene. Mr. Joseph Barbara had quietly come back to Endicott, New York, across the border. Always an extremely able businessman, he quickly did very well. For a small sum he bought a modest but lucrative soft drink bottling plant from an elderly Italian. It expanded rapidly. Despite his record he managed two extraordinary feats of legerdemain. The State Liquor Authority, usually strict, granted him a license to distribute beer, and the Canada Dry Company a franchise to bottle their products for the area. Barbara's outlets and his fleet of trucks grew with remarkable speed.

Croswell, having learned all this, settled down for his long period of watchful waiting. Occasionally he would drive up to the house on the hill or to the bottling plant and list the license plates of the cars outside. Often, at least one belonged to someone on whom the State Police kept an open file.

On one occasion, Croswell and another officer were taking pictures of the house and grounds for possible future reference. They thought that no one was at home. Suddenly the door of the main residence flew open and a furious Mrs. Barbara dashed at them, flanked by several sinister boxers. The sergeant firmly if nervously stood his ground, and thinking quickly, made the lady a respectful bow with hat in hand and introduced himself as a representative of *House and Garden*. The magazine, he said, was doing a series on the finest houses in various parts of the state. He had just been about to call and ask permission. Mrs. Barbara's angry frown vanished abruptly. The dogs also relaxed. Of course, she smiled. The gentlemen could take pictures of anything they wished.

The more Croswell saw and heard of the Barbara household, the more interested he became. The sergeant has imagination and a great curiosity about people apart from his natural policeman's inquisitiveness. He found an Old World, essentially Sicilian pattern of family and business life. Sicilians are by nature strong, hardworking, proud people. They are reserved, suspicious of outsiders and devoted to their families. Those of the brotherhood—most of them, at least—also have these qualities in addition to others all their own, which have lasted through generations and a transplantation to an essentially alien land.

The Barbaras were a typical, tight unit. In the early 30's Joe the Barber—still a gun-carrying gang boss—married Josephine Vivona. The women of the fraternity are bred and educated to understand, condone and seemingly ignore the activities of their fathers, brothers and husbands. They are usually completely reliable. No matter what the provocation of jealousy or revenge, only a few have ever given information to the police. Occasionally some of them may stab or shoot, but they very rarely appear before a district attorney or a court with any damaging testimony. They cook well as a general rule, are fastidious housekeepers and adoring mothers. The Barbaras, even after their increasing prosperity at Apalachin, hired servants only occasionally and never kept them for long; despite the size of the place, Mrs. Barbara preferred to do everything herself. She is today an attractive, poised, and well-groomed woman. Her clothes are well chosen and obviously expensive. So are her furs and jewelry. But there is no ostentation. Don Giuseppe himself, as Sicilian today as he was when he landed in this country, obviously loves his family of two sons and a daughter. Nothing is too good for them. At the same time, his imposition of paternal discipline is draconic. Joe Barbara Junior, now 21, was selected by his father as assistant and executive officer; he went to work at the bottling plant at seven in the morning and was often in his office until nine or ten at night. Barbara Senior, with the Canada Dry Company revoking his franchise as a result of the Apalachin scandal, has since sold the bottling plant for $250,000, and has placed his house and grounds on the market. The family, like others of the same kind—the Genoveses in New Jersey, the Profacis in Brooklyn, the Ormentos on Long Island—live in a queer little world of their own. Their only associations are with members of the family and old, tried friends. They trust no one else, and avoid any social contacts except those absolutely necessary for business or political reasons—and even these are seldom invited to *the house.*

Beyond the certainty born of long experience that a racketeer with Barbara's background seldom changes his thinking and instinctive methods, Croswell had little to go on. The U.S. Treasury Alcohol Tax Unit's agents in the area had reason to believe that Barbara was diverting sugar which he bought for his bottling plant to stills which he financed in the neighborhood for the production of untaxed alcohol. This sort of bootlegging is today a big if not well known business in many parts of the country. The federal excise tax on a gallon of whiskey is approximately $10.50. The racketeers, in clandestine distilleries, make a gallon of alcohol just as good in quality for $1.50, sell it for five dollars—with a $3.50 profit—to another echelon of bootleggers who cut and flavor the alcohol—using excellent modern chemical processes—into acceptable rye and Scotch which is poured into used bottles of the real product, with their authentic labels intact, and sold for another 200 to 500 per cent profit. The proceeds for all involved are substantial. And a few years ago Pasquale (Patsy) Turrigiano of Endicott was arrested after a raid by government agents on a large bootleg plant near Binghamton. In one of his pockets was a voucher which indicated that a Joseph Barbara had just paid a $277 instalment on a loan to Mr. Turrigiano by the Industrial Bank of Binghamton. During the time that Turrigiano was under indictment, tried, and served his sentence, Mr. Barbara continued the payments. But Croswell's suspicion, well founded as it may have been, that the $40,000 still—they are expensive—actually belonged to Don Giuseppe could not be proved in court.

Wiretaps, on a court order, were placed on the telephone lines of several top Binghamton racketeers. The information gathered led to the arrest and conviction of a number of them. Barbara's staccato voice had been heard frequently, apparently giving orders in the Sicilian dialect which is practically a code, but again the legal links were not strong enough for an indictment. Croswell also knew that the $15,000 which Mr. Barbara officially drew as salary from the bottling company was not nearly enough to maintain his establishment. Investigation revealed that ever since he left the Scranton–Pittston area, he had received a loan every year of between $25,000 and $50,000 from one of his old friends in Pennsylvania—without interest or security. Only two of these obligations, over a ten-year period, were ever paid off. This is one of the methods of private banking common in the fraternity, and it is brilliantly simple. It is predicated, of course, on the fact that a mafioso's word and handshake is as good as a bond. One racketeer sends the proceeds of his illegal operations, which he cannot declare and explain without the danger of eventual police reaction, in cash to a trusted friend of the same echelon. The second—in Barbara's case generally a wealthy Pennsylvania coal miner owner also Sicilian by birth—puts down this money in his returns as earned from one of his own legitimate enterprises, pays the tax on it and returns the balance to his friend in the form of a loan. Since tax fundamentally has been paid on the income, no matter what its source, the Internal Revenue

Service—an enforcement agency of which every gangster has lived in almost superstitious fear since the crashing collapse of the great Al Capone—is usually not too anxious to begin one of the expensive and difficult investigations, requiring many agents and many months in order to trace the details of such transactions. This is the sort of frustration which confronts so many dedicated policemen, and which often gives them ulcers. Sergeant Croswell had ulcers, and they were at least partially brought on by his frustration over Barbara.

In October 1956 a peculiar incident occurred. State Trooper Leibe was driving a routine patrol of Route 17 near Binghamton. He stopped a speeding car in the town of Windsor. He at once, with a policeman's instinct, disliked the looks of the three occupants. In accordance with the strict New York State Police rules he was scrupulously polite, but he carefully examined the operator's license, which the driver produced after some fumbling with various coats. It was made out to a Joseph di Palermo of New Jersey, but the description of hair, eyes and other physical characteristics on the permit did not tally with those of the man at the wheel. If Trooper Leibe had known who was in the car, he might have been nervous. The driver was Carmine Galente, one of the underworld's top powers in gambling and narcotics from Canada and the United States to Cuba, Italy and France and, by his record, an extremely dangerous man with knife and gun. With him in the car was Joseph di Palermo, whose license he had borrowed. Palermo had been Galente's assistant and torpedo for many years, a convicted bootlegger, counterfeiter and narcotics trader, and an equally ugly customer. Neither of them, particularly at that moment, wanted police or public attention. If Trooper Leibe had not stopped them on a busy thoroughfare, he might very well be dead today.

"This is not your license, sir," he said.

There was electric tension in the car. Three pairs of eyes glared at the man in the hated uniform.

"Oh," Galente finally growled. "I guess I looked in the wrong coat." There was more fumbling.

"I ain't got mine with me. Musta left it home. But look. I'm in a hurry. Can't we make a deal?"

"Get out of the car," snapped Leibe, with his hand close to his holster. "You're coming with me." He pointed at di Palermo. "You follow my car to the station."

It was the sort of moment that every policeman dreads. He is not sure whether he is detaining completely innocent people and inviting complaints and rebukes from his superiors, or whether he is in imminent danger of his life.

Galente hesitated for a moment, thinking. Then he nodded to di Palermo. "O.K.," he said. "You know what to do." Without another word, he climbed into the State Police car and was driven to the substation at Binghamton.

At the substation he faced the cold eyes of Sergeant Croswell. "Look," rasped the chunky little man. "This is a lotta crap. So I don't have my license with me. So I pay my fine. O.K.—let's get it over. I can make a lotta trouble, ya know." This last remark was a mistake for Carmine Galente and eventually for the Mafia as a whole. An idea, or rather a hunch, began forming in the sergeant's mind. The names of both Galente and di Palermo seemed vaguely familiar to him from FBI, Treasury Department and other police circulars. There was also something else.

"I'm sorry, sir," said the sergeant. "I'm afraid that you'll have to stay here until we find out about your driver's license. It's just routine, but that's the rule." A snarling Galente was searched; $1,815, mostly in hundred-dollar bills, was found in his pockets and he was taken to a detention room. The moment he was out of Croswell's office, the sergeant went into action. Troopers began checking all hotels and motels in the neighborhood. The teletype brought in the bare facts on Galente—15 arrests, one on suspicion of killing a policeman; a twelve-and-a-half-year sentence for shooting a detective and two children during a holdup. And a few hours later a trooper came up with the news which Croswell had expected. Galente, di Palermo and at least two prominent New York City racketeers—Frank Garofola and John Bonventre—had spent the previous night at the Arlington Hotel in Binghamton. Joseph Barbara, as host, had stayed with them and signed the check for all, a considerable one, in the name of the Canada Dry Bottling Company.

Croswell consulted his superiors and it was decided that Galente should be held, investigated further and prosecuted. The sergeant at this point knew very little about the Mafia or its operations. He had read about it, but like most police officers who have not had direct contact with a sufficient number of the brotherhood to form a picture of it, thought that it was largely a creation of newspapermen's imaginations. He was to change his mind. Within 24 hours a strong wind was blowing in Albany. A battery of important lawyers with connections were telephoning a number of powerful assemblymen about what could be done for Galente. Exactly what went on has not been established and probably never will be, for compelling political reasons, but it is quite clear that heavy pressure was brought to bear. (Three state legislators—one Democrat and two Republicans—later disclosed that they had been asked to intercede on behalf of Galente. All three said they had refused when they learned of Galente's past activities.) Unfortunately for Galente, his criminal record was a little too unsavory. He was just too hot to handle. When the usual strings would not pull, the section of the brotherhood interested in Galente tried the direct approach.

One afternoon two out-of-state policemen appeared at the Binghamton substation. They were Captain Chris Gleitsmann and Sergeant Peter Policastro of West New York, a town in New Jersey across the Hudson River from New York City. Law officers like to drop in on each other and talk shop with understanding colleagues, and Sergeant Croswell was cordial. The captain seemed a genial man, asked about the weather and places to visit in the neighborhood. It was a friendly chat until, suddenly, the captain's tone of voice changed. "What about this Galente case?" he asked. "He comes from my town, you know. He's not a bad guy." Croswell's eyes narrowed. "Well, what about the Galente case?" The sergeant's back had begun to prickle in expectation of what might be coming. The captain squirmed slightly in his chair. "Well—now look. I've been sent by my commissioner—Modarelli. I'm not supposed to use his name, but you should know. Galente ... runs the Abco Vending Company and is a very good friend of the Commissioner's. We'd like to see Galente ... well ... kind of excused. It wasn't really a bad violation. We'll pay the maximum fine. Can't we get him out of a jail sentence?" Croswell slowly shook his head. Reaching into a desk drawer he pulled out Galente's identification card with his criminal record on it and handed it to the captain. "Look," said the officer, "there'll be considerations." Again the sergeant shook his head. "The answer is definitely *no*." Smiling, the captain significantly held up one finger. "Is that supposed to mean a thousand dollars?" asked Croswell. His eyes had turned to agates and the knuckles of his clenched fists were white. "Yes," the captain replied quietly. "And if you think I'm kidding, here it is." A roll of bills with a rubber band around it was in his hand. He misinterpreted the look on the sergeant's face. "If that isn't enough," he added hastily, "I'll have to use your phone for a few minutes." Croswell turned pale. "Now don't be foolish," the captain added, "we cops should take the opportunities that come our way. We should decide whether a case gets quashed." The sergeant had risen slowly from behind his desk and was leaning over it. "You put that money back in your pocket." His voice was low, flat, and threatened violence. "And get out of here—fast." Captain Gleitsmann got out.

Carmine Galente was duly tried in Broome County court for speeding and fraudulent use of an operator's license, found guilty, fined $150 and sentenced to thirty days in jail. His defense was conducted by Donald W. Kramer, mayor of

Binghamton, who advised Galente to plead guilty. The judge, with full knowledge of the defendant's record and what had happened since his arrest, imposed the maximum sentence.

The episode would not leave Edgar Croswell in peace. He kept reconstructing it in his mind. It didn't seem to make sense. Why was it worth someone's while to draw up the heaviest political guns and then to spend several thousand dollars if necessary over Galente's relatively minor offense which—if all the dust had not been raised—would probably have been settled with a $50 fine? The answer was, of course, that this was one of the brotherhood's occasional outbursts of hysteria. Don Giuseppe Barbara, particularly tense and nervous as a result of his physical condition, had pulled the fire alarm in New York City. It was essential to keep the meeting at the Arlington Hotel quiet. Some well-informed police officer or reporter might put the names of Barbara, di Palermo, Galente, Garofola and Bonventre together, remember other gatherings of the sort and draw embarrassing conclusions. Brooklyn and Jersey had responded to the alarm with all available apparatus. When it was realized that the Albany contacts would not respond, Director of Public Safety Ernest W. Modarelli of West New York dispatched his captain of detectives and $1,000 in cash to see Croswell. This didn't work, either, and a typical fraternal decision was made—more than probably by a group of capi mafiosi over pasta and Chianti in a New York restaurant. Galente was to serve his sentence in the Broome County Jail and then leave the country for his foolishness. Di Palermo had also outlived his usefulness, was under investigation by the Federal Bureau of Narcotics and meant nothing but trouble as well. Both are now fugitives as a result of cases since developed by the FBI and the Treasury. They are probably in Italy, although the Italian police have been unable to find them. But it was an expulsion order from a Mafia council primarily that made them run; such orders are far more rapidly and drastically enforced than those of a United States commissioner.

Much of this was still in the back of Sergeant Croswell's mind when he and his partner, Trooper Vasisko, stopped by the Parkway Motel in Vestal late one afternoon on November 13, 1957, to investigate the report of a bad check which had been cashed there. They were talking to the proprietor's wife when a Cadillac pulled up to the door. Croswell happened to look up, glanced through a window and saw who was getting out of the car. Without a word he grabbed Vasisko by the arm and pushed him into a lounge off the entrance hall, out of sight of the desk. Joseph Barbara Junior, cocky and pompous at 21—he looks and acts much like his father—strode in. "We want three double rooms for two nights," he announced. "The best you got. I'll take the keys with me; the people may be late." The proprietor's wife, though irritated, was polite, produced the keys and asked whether he would register the visitors now so that they would not have to be bothered when they arrived. "No," said young Barbara irritably. "I don't know exactly who they'll be. We're having a convention of soft drink people. We'll fix everything up tomorrow." The Cadillac departed.

Good policemen develop an instinctive something that they themselves often cannot explain. A bell began to ring for Croswell. "Come on," he said to his partner, "I've got a feeling. Let's check the bottling plant." The sheds in Endicott showed no unusual activity. The Barbara house was next. Four big cars were parked in the driveway. One belonged to Patsy Turrigiano, the convicted illegal still operator from Endicott. One was from New Jersey, one from New York, one from Ohio. Croswell jotted down the numbers. "Let's go back to the station and find out who these people are," he said. "Something's going on. I'm sure of it." The bell kept ringing, louder. The teletype did not respond immediately from Trenton, Albany or Columbus. The sergeant telephoned two old friends in Albany, agents Arthur Rustin and Kenneth Brown of the Alcohol Tax Unit of the U.S. Treasury Department, with whom he had often worked before, and told them what he suspected. "We'll be there right away; as fast as we can drive," was the answer.

Croswell has been accused subsequently by officials and newsmen of not reacting with sufficient speed during the next 24 hours and not calling for sufficient help. These accusations stem from hindsight and ignorance of accepted, practical police procedure. A call for help that proves unnecessary may mean a bad mark on an officer's record. As a matter of fact, from that moment on Edgar Croswell began sticking his neck out to a degree that today makes him shiver to recollect. But all his subsequent moves were to add up to one of the most telling blows ever dealt the Mafia and organized crime in the United States.

The State Police teletype had still not reported on the Ohio, New York or New Jersey cars at Barbara's. Impatient and jumpy, Croswell drove back to the Parkway Motel. The Ohio car was parked outside one of the sections. "There are two of them," reported the proprietor. "They just went to their room without registering. I'll have them make out the registration cards right now." Croswell nodded. In a few minutes the proprietor was back, both angry and obviously nervous. "They won't fill out the cards. They're very tough guys. They said Joe Barbara would take care of everything in the morning, and they didn't want to be bothered. I don't like their looks. I think we ought to throw them out." If the two ex-convicts, Giuseppe DiMarco and Giuseppe Scalish, could have heard what followed, they would not have been there the next morning or have slept very well. "No, no," said the sergeant. "Leave them alone and don't say anything, please. Just treat them as though I hadn't asked."

Finally, at 3 A.M., Croswell went to bed, tired and disappointed. There had been no further activity either at the motel or at Barbara's. His hunch, he felt, had probably been wrong. He said as much when he called Inspector Robert Denman in Sidney, New York, his immediate superior, to report the next morning. Neither knew of the extraordinary meeting of the clans that was already under way. Five blue-jowled but immaculate gentlemen descended from a Mohawk Airlines flight from Newark at Binghamton Airport, to be whisked off in Barbara's Cadillac. All had given assumed names for the ship's manifest. Three were part of the New Jersey delegation, another from Illinois, one from Colorado—Larasso, Olivetto, Riela, Zito and Colletti were their real names, all to be conjured with in their underworld areas. The roads to Barbara's were also discreetly busy; but no one was exceeding the speed limit. "It may not amount to anything," said the inspector, "but you'd better keep at it just in case."

Croswell, Vasisko and the two federal agents who had joined them started with the motel. Four more of Barbara's guests had arrived very late at night, it seemed. They were already gone. The bottling plant in Endicott was tried next. No activity. But as Croswell's car climbed the rise up to Barbara's, his heart suddenly leapt. There were a dozen Cadillacs, Chrysler Imperials and Lincolns on the apron in front of the garage and 25 more in the field, many with the special license plates which denote political influence. "Those aren't salesmen's cars," remarked Vasisko. "No," said the sergeant quietly. "I don't think they are salesmen's cars. Let's get their numbers down as fast as we can."

As it happened, the garage and then a wing of the house screened Croswell and his colleagues from the gay and busy company around the barbecue pit until, notebooks in hand, the policemen were almost finished; at this moment a group of strollers, talking animatedly, came around a corner of the garage. Seeing strangers, they stopped in their tracks. For a moment they exchanged glances. Then shouts in Italian and excited gestures brought a dozen others. They, too, stopped and stared. There were more shouts followed by a general panicked retreat. It was clear to Croswell, Vasisko and the treasury agents that they had come across a rather unusual convention. "So what do we do now?" one of them asked. "We have no authority, no warrant, no nothing."

Croswell's mind had been racing. He knew now that he had been right. "We have plenty of authority," he said, "off Barbara's property; on the public highway." Tactically, it was fairly simple. Only one road from Don Giuseppe's house led to U.S. Route 17 and away; two others were impassable because of bridges destroyed by floods. The sergeant knew the area intimately.

A mile down the hill from Barbara's, the state and the federal cars drew up on opposite sides of the road, leaving only a very narrow passageway. Croswell, on the radio, called his superior. He needed more men, he said. Within the next hour Zone Commander Lieutenant Weidenbarner at Horseheads, Chief of Area Inspector Denman at Sidney, and Superintendent of State Police McGarvey in Albany all had the same feeling as Sergeant Croswell. State Police cars began pulling out of barracks at Binghamton, Whitney Point, Waverly and Horseheads and heading at high speed for Vestal and Apalachin. Much had happened in a short time at Croswell's road block.

A few minutes after Bartolo Guccia, the little fish peddler, had discovered the road block, the first big car came down the hill at a moderate pace. Russel Bufalino was driving; next to him sat Don Vitone Genovese. They and the other three with them were tense as they got out of the automobile. So were the police officers. But everyone was very polite. White-faced but smiling, Don Vitone produced a driver's license when asked for identification and uncomplainingly allowed himself to be searched. "You have all been at Mr. Barbara's?" asked Croswell. Don Vitone nodded. "What were you doing there?" Don Vitone looked sad. "He is very sick, the poor man. We just came to wish him speedy recovery." And then, gently—"But I don't have to answer these questions, do I?" No, Croswell answered, he did not have to answer any more questions. "Thank you very much," said the don with just the trace of a sneer, ordered his companions who had also been identified and searched into the car and drove off.

By the minute, the sergeant's tactical and strategic problems were growing. He knew now what he had in his hands. He knew also that one serious slip could cost him his career. He made a decision and braced himself. Several cars full of troopers had arrived. From where he stood, he could see that a dozen or so men were running from the Barbara house across a field to the woods behind it. Other cars were piled up in front of the road block. "All right," said the sergeant, "let's bring them all in to Vestal. Get those guys out of the woods. Don't let anybody get away." Only a few did.

By five o'clock in the afternoon some 60 of the brotherhood had been detained and packed into various rooms of the small Vestal substation. None of the troopers who were there will ever forget the scene. By that time they knew that their prisoners were probably the biggest collection of dangerous people that had ever been found together outside of a penitentiary. The teletype had been chattering and telephones had been ringing, bringing in their records from various parts of the country. The Apalachin guests themselves were very quiet. The Mafia always is when at bay, and it had not been so cornered in a hundred years. The men were obviously stunned. There was no conversation. One might have thought none of them knew each other. Their faces were white and stony. They smoked incessantly. Several of the dons watched the ash trays and carefully emptied them into wastebaskets when they became too full. No one complained; no one even asked for coffee.

One by one they were summoned to Sergeant Croswell's office, gave their names and addresses, took off their shoes, emptied their pockets as troopers searched and watched. Most of them had been through this rigidly careful procedure before, some a good many times, and knew what was expected. "All right," Croswell would say. "Please count out your money." Simone Scozzari from Palermo laid only $602 in cash on the sergeant's desk, but then also a cashier's check for $8,445 more. The officers stared wonderingly as one after the other, with few exceptions, pulled out rolls of hundred-dollar bills and counted them off as the sergeant noted the amounts. "O.K. Please put it back in your pocket." What was Mr. Scozzari's occupation? "I have been unemployed for 20 years," replied Mr. Scozzari sadly. "Would you mind telling me what you were doing at Mr. Barbara's?" asked Croswell. "Not at all," said Mr. Scozzari. "I knew that poor Joe was sick and I decided to come up and see him." "What, all the way from Sicily," asked the sergeant. "Oh no," said Mr. Scozzari. "Just from California. That's where I been recently." The sergeant smiled bleakly. "But what were *all* of these people doing there at the same time?" Mr. Scozzari shrugged a wonderful heaving Italian shrug. "I guess we all just happened to have the same idea at the same time."

In long procession one after the other repeated the formula —"I just come up to see how Joe is"—with variations as they produced driver's licenses and imposing wads of currency. It is standard operational procedure that no letters or documents except a license are ever carried on the person. Everyone—and this is also characteristic—described his position most modestly. Charles Chiri, the big trucker, said simply that he was "in transportation work." Joseph Bonanno was "retired"; so were many others. Still others, also with thousands of dollars on them, blandly announced themselves as clerks and minor assistants.

Gradually, singly and by pairs, the dozen guests at Barbara's that Croswell had seen so hurriedly taking to the woods were being brought in by troopers who had found them lost and disconsolate in thickets and behind trees, surroundings which were so unfamiliar. They were a sorry, almost pathetic lot. Their fine shoes were covered with mud; thorns and burrs were clinging to their once immaculate clothes; collars were wilted by sweat. Nevertheless, they stuck to their surprising stories. Most of them had been "looking at real estate." Two maintained stoutly that they had been "walking to the railroad station." Croswell smiled. "What railroad station?" he asked. "The same one we got off at. The Pennsylvania Railroad one near here," was the reply. "Well," laughed the sergeant, "it's only about 70 miles away. You must be pretty good hikers."

The most curious story of all was that of John Montana, Buffalo's man of the year. Two troopers had found him deep in the woods behind Barbara's, trying desperately to extricate his expensive, tailor-made camel's hair topcoat from a barbed wire fence in which it had become hopelessly entangled. The officers helped him politely and then took him to the Vestal barracks. An impressive man and a power in state politics, he had himself well in hand by the time he faced Sergeant Croswell. He was naturally distressed at having been brought to a police station but, being a good citizen —and, as he added pointedly, a rather prominent one—he would be delighted to tell the sergeant anything he wanted to know and give him any help in his power. Croswell, rising to the situation, was equally suave. He was puzzled by this congregation of people with police records at Mr. Barbara's. Could the councilman help him? (Montana had been a Buffalo councilman for a number of years.) A frown of concentration was on the councilman's face as he began his narrative.

He had been driving that morning, Mr. Montana explained, from Buffalo on his way to business appointments in Pittston, Pennsylvania, and New York City, when the brakes of his new Cadillac began acting peculiarly. A thought occurred to him. Joe Barbara, an old acquaintance—although neither a close friend nor a business associate, he hastened to point out—lived only about 20 miles away, had a fleet of trucks and would probably have a capable mechanic on hand. "But why didn't you stop at one of the garages closer by?" Croswell asked gently. "Not everybody can fix a Cadillac," replied the don with hauteur.

The tale continued. Mr. Montana had arrived at Barbara's only to find that some sort of a business gathering was going on in and around the summer house. He recognized no one that he knew, so he went to the main house and rang the bell. Mrs. Barbara answered, and in her usual pleasant way offered him a cup of tea and invited him to wait until Joe was finished with his guests. Mr. Montana accepted and was chatting with the lady when there was suddenly some sort of a commotion outside—some sort of an argument or something. In any case people had begun abruptly getting in their cars and driving off. He had thought of leaving also but realized that with his brakes not functioning the drive down the hill in such traffic might be dangerous. He had therefore gone for a walk instead to wait until everyone had left and gotten lost in the woods. And that was all there was to it, he said with a final wave of the hands. Sergeant Croswell nodded gravely.

While all this was going on, Croswell and his superiors up the line had been racking their brains for something they could do about the extraordinary assemblage. The attorney general's office in Albany went into high gear. But there was absolutely no ground for arrest or even fingerprinting. They were certainly not vagrants. And after the last of the police reports had come in, it was clear that only one—a parole violator from New Jersey who should not have left the state—was wanted anywhere. The New York State law on the unlawful gathering of persons of ill repute did not apply because such a gathering, to be illegal, must be in a public place. None carried guns; all, with one exception, had given their correct names. Under New York law they could be held on suspicion for only a "reasonable length of time," and the interpretation of that length of time by New York judges is invariably strict.

It was decided by Croswell and his superiors that there was only one thing to do. That was to turn the fullest possible glare of publicity on Barbara and his guests and let public opinion do the rest. Reluctantly the sergeant freed them by batches; they went quietly but very quickly.

CHAPTER THREE

Sequel in Albany

The Watchdog Committee of the New York State Legislature ran into some ancient methods and rules of the brotherhood and could do little about them.

Reporters and feature writers swarmed over Vestal and the Apalachin meeting was a nine-day front page wonder all over the country. The Mafia, which many people had never heard of before, was prominently mentioned. Every article on the subject, however, presented a different picture of the brotherhood. In some it was correctly called the Mafia; in others the fraternity was the Black Hand, the Unione Sicilione, or The Syndicate. To the public and government officials alike it was all very confusing. It was clear, however, that some sort of organization must have been behind the extraordinary convention. Various hitherto unbelieving law enforcement agencies quietly began thorough investigations within their jurisdictions. A number of political leaders saw immediate possibilities—with either real public service or vote getting kudos, or both, in mind. Gangbusting had made Thomas Dewey a governor and almost president of the United States. With its great popular appeal and newsworthiness, criminal investigation and prosecution has done almost as much for quite a few others.

In Albany there was considerable consternation. If a congress of criminals had taken place in New York City and been discovered, the state capital would probably have paid little attention. But this was different. The meeting had been in a rural area. The upstate and downstate counties take such things for granted when they happen in the City, but not in their own territories. Assemblyman William F. Horan of Tuckahoe, chairman of the legislature's Watchdog Committee—officially the Joint Legislative Committee on Government Operations—sensed that something should be done, and quickly. Subpoenas were prepared for the 34 Apalachin delegates who lived within New York jurisdiction. Only 11 could be served. Most of the gentlemen had left earlier than usual for their winter headquarters in Florida and Las Vegas. Nevertheless, on December 12, 1957, the committeemen began open hearings which were to prove far more important than they themselves realized.

Sergeant Croswell led off with a modest but graphic description of his raid and its background. There was considerable squirming when the sergeant reviewed the arrest of Carmine Galente the year before and the efforts made in high places for his release. He was treading on dangerous ground, and he was gently but firmly pushed off of it. Various other police officers followed. Then came the bombshell.

John T. Cusack does not look at all like the Hollywood conception of an agent of the Federal Bureau of Narcotics. A mild-mannered, pleasant-faced man in his thirties, he has more the air of a bank teller than of what he is—one of the bureau's most brilliant policemen. His investigations, both here and abroad, have led to convictions of several of the biggest narcotics dealers in the country. (One trip to Paris almost cost him his life when, posing as a heroin buyer from New York, his true identity was discovered by the gang he was negotiating with.) As a representative of the bureau, he has earned a reputation with federal attorneys and judges for the careful preparation and usually incontestable accuracy of his testimony. Now he was appearing before the Watchdog Committee as head of the Bureau of Narcotics unit on the special staff of the U.S. attorney for the Southern District of New

York, which also has men from the Customs Service, Internal Revenue Service and other agencies.

District Supervisor Cusack (he had just been made head of the bureau's southeastern area) soon had the legislators' complete attention. He read his 15,000-word report on the operations of the Mafia, carefully compiled from the bureau's files by himself and other experts on organized crime, in his usual measured, incisive way. The Narcotics Bureau was interested in the Apalachin affair, he said, because at least five of Barbara's guests were intimately connected with the national and international traffic in narcotics. (He described Big John Ormento as "one of the most active and important narcotic violators" in the country.) "We are convinced," said Mr. Cusack, "that there was a prominent place on the agenda at Apalachin for the discussion of the manufacture abroad [and] the importation and distribution of narcotics in the United States." Then he recapitulated the known underworld meetings of the past—Cleveland in 1928, Florida in 1952 and 1953, Chicago in 1954, Binghamton in 1956 and Apalachin in 1957.

"We of the Federal Narcotics Bureau call these Mafia meetings," said Supervisor Cusack. "The Narcotics Bureau has been interested in the Mafia, as such, for approximately eighteen years. . . . We consider the Mafia a well-organized secret fraternal order. . . . Its members with few exceptions are all of Sicilian origin and are located in every prosperous city in the world, principally those of Europe and North and South America, where profits in crime are most lucrative. The business of the Mafia is what we term commercial crimes that prey on man's human weaknesses, such as the illicit narcotics traffic, organized prostitution, counterfeiting, bootlegging, organized gambling, loan sharking and extortion."

The supervisor kept looking at his audience to see how they were responding. There were four state senators and four assemblymen present. All were listening carefully, but in the faces of some was blank incredulity. Cusack continued patiently. He and many another federal agent had met such looks before.

"When the opportunity presents itself, the Mafia moves into legitimate business, selecting ventures where their strongarm tactics and cash resources will quickly bring large profits.

"Our extensive narcotic investigations of various members of the Mafia fraternity during the past have repeatedly shown a pattern of either infiltration or complete domination of several legitimate fields including organized labor with the follow-up of labor management ventures; the distribution of beer, liquor and soft drinks; the importation and distribution of Italian olive oil, cheese and tomato paste; the control of wholesale fruit and vegetable produce markets; the baking and distribution of Italian bread and pastries; vending machines of all types and juke boxes; the operation of night clubs, restaurants and bars. Their night clubs are frequently complemented through their interests in model and theatrical booking agencies and in musical recording companies.

"Mafia members use 'front people' who are completely trusted in the community to own and operate these various legitimate interests. Legally a 'front man' could eliminate the actual owner, but this is seldom if ever done as these 'front men' are usually Mafia brothers of minor rank and ability.

"In order to further their legitimate enterprises and cloak their illicit operations, Mafia members conduct a well-planned program of ingratiating themselves with people of all walks of life. Their modus operandi calls for interest and activity in community and church affairs, generous contributions to charities and ostensibly respectable family lives. They are always ready to entertain and do favors for the right people."

Cusack went through the history of the Mafia from its beginning 200 years ago in Sicily, its ancient code of behavior, its role here and abroad, using individual case histories to prove his points.

"We have seen such a phenomenon as this, for example," said the supervisor. "At certain times during the past seven years the French underworld, which is controlled by Corsican gangsters, has had a monopoly on the illicit heroin manufactured in Europe. The French gangs wanted to ship and distribute their heroin to the United States independently. They couldn't do it. The Mafia racketeers in Italy and America control distribution in this country to such a degree that the French could not move without them. And today the sale and smuggling of almost all French heroin to the United States is controlled through Mafia groups which negotiate with the French sources in Paris and Marseilles for the shipments of narcotics to the American continent."

Supervisor Cusack wound up with his conclusion. "On the basis of our official investigations that extend over a 30-year period, we have amassed conclusive evidence of the existence of the Mafia, and consider this secret international society a threat. . . ."

If any doubt remained in the legislators' minds, it should have been dispelled by the events of the next days. Supervisor Cusack had given them the background which enabled them to understand the subsequent operation so typical of the brotherhood. The mafiosi were ready for the contest. All were equipped with skillful lawyers. Each had his strategy firmly in mind.

Mr. John Ormento was the first to be called. Big John, hulking, beetle-browed, his diamonds flashing, took the witness chair, lounged back, stared arrogantly at the legislators and set his ugly blue jaw. After some hesitation he gave his name and address. "Where were you born," asked Committee Counsel Arnold Bauman. "I decline to answer," rumbled the recognized chief of the 107th Street mob after a nod from his attorney, "on the grounds that it might tend to incriminate me." Assemblyman William F. Horan, the committee's soft-spoken chairman, frowned. "I direct you to answer the question." Big John almost snarled, his shoulders hunched in fury. Another glance at his lawyer. "I decline to answer . . ." The chairman warned him of the possible consequences. Big John sneered. "I decline to answer . . ." For several hours that day and the next, looking bored as he stared alternately at the ornate beamed ceiling and the onyx paneled walls of the Senate chamber, he struggled with the legal formula for pleading the Fifth Amendment of the Constitution no less than 83 times. He kept having particular difficulty with the word "incriminate." He would not admit to such matters of positive record as his having been at Apalachin, knowing any of the others who had been there, owning a trucking business in the New York City garment district or indeed having been convicted and imprisoned three times for trading in narcotics.

Chairman Horan and Counsel Bauman kept on doggedly with their questions although they knew that none would be answered. The State Police, who had been working day and night, had supplied them with every available detail of the criminal histories and connections of the Barbara guests. It was a question of getting these details into the public record. With calculated patience the legislators used their unanswered queries to put down the story of John Ormento so that it could be used against him at a future date.

The brotherhood continued to thumb its nose at the Watchdog Committee. Signori Profaci, Guarnieri, Falcone, Carlisi, Maggadino, d'Agostino, Evola, Castellano, Miranda, Valenti, Bufalino, Riccobono, Rao—all sat in the witness chair in much the same way. Immaculately trousered legs were crossed easily; fingernails were polished on sleeves; yawns were stifled. Most pleaded the Fifth Amendment from start to finish, giving only their names and addresses. An interesting version of the formula was delivered by Mr. Joseph Riccobono, once a member of the notorious Lepke extortion gang. "I refuse to answer," he said solemnly in reply to the counsel's questions, "on the grounds of not to testify against myself. Whether it means the same thing or whether it doesn't, I am not in the position to know." The committeemen gaped at the witness. There were other memorable performances when a few witnesses answered some of the questions put to them. The fish peddler, Bartolo Guccia, who had given the alarm at Barbara's, was asked why he had turned around after passing Sergeant Croswell's road block and gone back up the hill. The old Sicilian's act was a masterpiece. Hands and expression illustrated the distress that he had experienced on suddenly remembering, after he had gone down the hill, that he had not asked the Barbaras what kind of fish they wanted *next* week. That was the reason for his going back. "I grow old and forgetful," he said sadly. "There is always the telephone," remarked one of the committeemen drily. But Bartolo chose not to hear. Even better was Anthony Maggadino, an undertaker by profession in Niagara Falls. He came to the United States from Sicily 22 years ago, and his command of the English language had been more than adequate when Sergeant Croswell questioned him at the Vestal substation. He had been somewhat out of breath after his forced march through the woods behind Barbara's and his subsequent apprehension by troopers, but his English had been not only fluent but colorful.

Mr. Maggadino, a nervously smiling little man of 60, approached the witness chair with a characteristic mortician's soft step, clasped hands and soberly respectful attitude, bowing to the committee. Having looked to see whether the chair was quite clean, he sat down, adjusted his position to an attentive pose, and waited. As the first question came, his forehead wrinkled and he shook his head. Haltingly, he gave his name and address. After that he could understand nothing, announced that he was unable to "speak the English," and asked for an interpreter. Chairman Horan almost lost his temper, but he succeeded somehow in holding himself back. "All right," he snapped, "we'll go along with this mockery." And a mockery it was. Counsel Bauman would ask a question. Mr. Maggadino would look respectful but blank. The question would be translated into Italian. Mr. Maggadino would listen, furrow his brow and purse his lips in thought. Then he would say, in Italian, "Fifth Amendment," and the interpreter in English would intone the correct formula. "All right," the chairman finally barked. "That's enough. You may step down." Mr. Maggadino waited for the translation, stood up and bowed once more. "*Gracia tanto,*" he said with a little smile.

The most magnificent performance of all, however, was that of John C. Montana of Buffalo. Silver haired, impressive in a beautifully tailored double-breasted blue suit and matching tie, the tall, dignified businessman strode firmly to the witness chair with the air of a solid citizen about to do an important public service. His initial testimony, delivered in a hearty and compelling tone, surprised legislators, public and newsmen alike. Not immodestly but with weight, he described an unusual career. Giovanni Montana was born in Sicily 64 years ago. Emigrating with his family when he was a small boy, he began working in a Buffalo candy factory at 14 and sold popcorn on the side. By the time he was 20 he owned a fleet of six trucks. A year later he set up the taxicab company which has a virtual monopoly of the business in Buffalo today. For the last 30 years, Mr. Montana has been one of the city's leading and most philanthropic citizens. At Thanksgiving and Christmas hundreds of his turkeys are dispatched to the needy. In the summer his cabs and trucks are always at the service of any organization that wants to take orphans or crippled children on an outing. President of the Van Dyke Cab Co., parent company for a string of subsidiary enterprises, president of the big Frontier Liquor Corporation and the Montana Race Horse Stables, he also became prominent in state politics. He was a city councilman for four years and served on a series of important civic committees. In 1954, an impressive dinner given in his honor was attended by more than a thousand of Buffalo's principal citizens, including the mayor.

Mr. Montana had even heavier shot in his locker. Back in 1955, he said with a flourish, he and his wife had been the guests of Governor Harriman in his New York City home at a luncheon for the Italian prime minister, Mario Scelba. In 1956, during the presidential campaign, Mr. Montana had been the chairman of the reception committee which welcomed Vice-President Nixon to Buffalo. "I know Mr. Nixon very well," he announced gravely. (Both the Governor's Mansion and the Office of the Vice-President speedily stated that neither the governor nor the vice-president had the faintest idea who Mr. Montana was.)

Mr. Montana did not use the Fifth Amendment once. With hearty candor, he elaborated on the story which he had told Sergeant Croswell. He had been on a two-day business trip to Pittston, Pennsylvania, and New York City for a meeting of the Cab Research Bureau, of which he is a director. On the way from Buffalo to Pittston, near Ithaca, his brakes and the left-hand windshield wiper of his new Cadillac Sixty Special had developed trouble. It was raining hard and he had to drive slowly. Then he remembered Joe Barbara. Had Mr. Barbara ever done business with Mr. Montana? Counsel Bauman asked. Yes indeed; Barbara in 1934 became a beer distributor for Montana, who then owned the Buffalo Beverage Corp. Anyway, Mr. Montana had driven to Barbara's to have his brakes and wiper fixed. From the breakfast room of the main house, where he was having a cup of tea with Mrs. Barbara, he saw that Joe was having "some kind of party," but he hadn't asked what it was and had not been invited to join it. There were, he estimated, between 20 and 40 people. No, he had not recognized anyone. He inferred that he did not approve of Joe's friends as a rule. About 15 minutes later, still sipping tea, he had noticed some sort of disturbance outside; someone had shouted "Road block," and there was a general exodus. He had been much distressed. "It was just human nature," said Mr. Montana with outspread hands and a pleading look at the committee, "that I would say to myself: what am I doing here? I didn't want to be any part of that other thing, and if there was any trouble, I didn't want to be any part of it." Mr. Montana had thereupon taken to the woods.

(Law officers have speculated on what the councilman meant by "that other thing." Most of the mafiosi present were simply alarmed at being found together, but some definitely thought that they were being raided by other gangsters in a sort of super St. Valentine's Day Massacre.)

Mr. Montana's testimony had been rather convincing, but he had made one very serious mistake. "You arrived at the Barbara house, you say, sometime between two and two-thirty," said Counsel Bauman in a casual tone, "and you stayed about twenty minutes?" Montana frowned. "Yes," he answered. "You are sure of that?" asked Bauman. "Of course," answered Montana. The witness was excused after another series of questions which he answered easily and with conviction. "Thank you, gentlemen, thank you," he said as he left the stand. There was a gleam in Bauman's eyes. Sergeant Croswell, notebook in hand, was summoned back to the witness chair.

During the next few minutes Mr. Montana found he had little to be thankful for. "When did you set up your road block?" Bauman asked Croswell. "At twelve-fifty, exactly," answered the sergeant. "No one could have gotten by it without being noticed?" asked Bauman. Croswell shook his head. "No sir; not possibly." Bauman smiled. "And this road was the only way to Barbara's?" The ordinarily dour sergeant grinned. "Yes, sir, it's the only way."

Despite everything that had happened and what had been rubbed under their noses, the Watchdog Committee issued a report which was a masterpiece of understatement. Its *Conclusions* were as follows:

1. The Apalachin meeting of November 14, 1957, is strong evidence that there exists in this country an active association or

organization of criminals whose operations are nationwide and international.

2. Discovery of the Apalachin meeting was the direct result of the superior work of Sergeant Edgar D. Croswell of the State Police. But for his alertness, competence, and devotion to duty, this meeting would probably have passed unnoticed and become no more than another rumor in law enforcement circles.

3. Nevertheless, the incident reveals a serious defect in the state's law enforcement apparatus. . . . The Apalachin meeting emphasizes the need for a bureau of centralized police intelligence and continuous investigative action directed at organized crime and racketeering on a state-wide basis....

Assemblyman Horan was not only in poor health at the time (he died of a heart ailment a few months later), but he was also politically nervous. At a press interview (which this writer attended), Horan showed his reluctance to discuss the committee findings. "You be careful," he said, pointing a minatory finger at us. "There are lots of things here that you don't know about, and have no business knowing about." We were standing in the Watchdog Committee's file room and he gestured toward the rows of cabinets. It was clear that we were to get nothing. "But why?" we asked. "The press can do a lot to help an investigation like this. The federal law enforcement agencies have trusted us for a long time." The assemblyman stared at us, then pushed an elegant brown homburg back on his head. "Listen," he said, "you don't know what you're tackling." We replied that we thought we did, that some of us had known about the Mafia for quite a few years and about its part in organized crime in this country. There was newsworthy information here that could be reported with maximum advantage for the law enforcement agencies that had been fighting the brotherhood. Assemblyman Horan surveyed us with shrewd, clear Irish eyes—cynical, a bit puzzled, but not hard. "Well," he said, smiling, "I wish you luck." Then the expression on his face changed. "But you can't see any of our files, you understand. You're not going to get anything except the records of the public hearings." We said as politely as possible that if necessary we could probably get along without the committee's files, that many of us had been working on the subject far longer than the committee and had access to far more detailed and better organized records. The assemblyman did not care for that. "Ok," he snapped, "but the open hearings are all you get, and that's that." As matters turned out, we could get in only one day's work even at these records, although they should have been entirely public. For by the next morning they, too, had been closed to the press at Mr. Horan's orders. Fortunately, we had been able to transcribe the exact words of many of the witnesses and had obtained the gist of most of the rest.

Assemblyman Horan reacted as he did for a variety of reasons. He was a man of integrity but governed, as are so many others, by certain political axioms. The Italian vote in New York is a peculiar and very powerful factor not only in the city but in many other metropolitan areas of the state, such as Utica and Buffalo; it is highly organized and very obedient. Although almost all Italo-Americans hate the brotherhood, the Italian vote reacts violently against any politician who brings up what it considers its disgrace.

"I know that the Mafia exists," a prominent, absolutely trustworthy, Italo-American businessman of Sicilian birth said to us. "I know that it is a disgrace to us that so many Italian names appear in the leadership of organized crime. But we do *not* like to be reminded of it." He pounded his desk and scowled. "Do you realize what harm you are doing hundreds of thousands, perhaps millions of decent, hardworking people by writing this book of yours?" he shouted. We said that we fully understood the dangers of misconstruction and misinterpretation. Why, we asked, if so many people of Italian birth and extraction were exercised about the brotherhood, didn't the various Italo-American societies with all their political power and contacts take a spearhead position in the current drive against it? Our friend hesitated. "How could *we* do that?" he asked. By setting up "action committees" in the societies all over the country that would gather information, plague the authorities and the newspapers, we suggested. He looked at us and frowned. "You are not naive usually," he said slowly. "Do you realize the personal danger that would shadow the life of any Sicilian, or any Italian for that matter, who undertook such a thing? I know that there are many federal and local policemen and officials who cross swords with the Mafia. That is different. The police are too dangerous to touch, and law enforcement is their business. But a man like me, a private citizen?" He snapped his fingers. "Like that!" He bent his forefinger, put it in his mouth and clenched his teeth over it. "Do you know what that means?" he asked. We knew the answer but we wanted to hear him say it. "That means, my friend, when a mafioso does it, that *you* will be dead tomorrow."

The brotherhood has traded on all of this for a long time. It has shaped political power, wealth and physical menace into a remarkable apparatus. It all began approximately 200 years ago.

CHAPTER FOUR

How the Mafia Came to America

More than 200 years of bizarre history lies behind the brotherhood—behind the lives and habits of such men as Capone, Luciano, Costello, Anastasia—behind the Apalachin meeting—behind the Watch-dog Committee's hearings.

The origin of the Mafia and its name has been a matter of controversy among Italian historians for a long time. Legend has it that both go back to the 13th century. In the spring of 1282, according to a typically dramatic story which has been passed down through generations of Sicilians, a French soldier, one of the bodyguard of the hated Angevin prince who then ruled the island, raped and killed a young woman of Palermo on her way to church for her marriage. The bridegroom hunted the soldier down, hurled himself on the murderer screaming, "*Morte alla Francia,*" only to meet his own death. All Sicily boiled over as news of the sacrilegious killing spread, and the French were cut down wherever they could be found. It was one of the bloodiest massacres in the island's bloody history—this much is a historical fact—and the young bridegroom's cry is said to have become, "*Morte alla Francia Italia anela*" ("Death to the French is Italy's cry"). From the initials of this slogan, the word Mafia is supposed to stem.

Modern Italian historians discount this as pure fable. Actually, the Mafia began taking concrete shape around the middle of the 18th century. It was, to begin with, an underground political resistance movement. Sicily was writhing in the grip of its Bourbon rulers who taxed, tortured, imprisoned and executed with a brutality unusual even in that age. It was every man for himself. The only refuge was the family—whose loyalty could be trusted. Out of this grew an extraordinarily tight family relationship. In their world of violence and chaos, a man in order to prosper and even to survive had to be always cautious, ruthless, quick to seize an opportunity and able to avenge wrongs committed against himself or his family. An individualist of this kind was admired and came to be known as a mafioso—an old Sicilian phrase which meant, roughly translated, shrewd man; the word also connoted that he was skillful with a gun. The mafioso inspired a combination of fear and respectful regard.

For many years the original mafiosi—the ancestors of the Profacis, Bonannos, Ormentos who met at Apalachin—fought their Austrian, Spanish and French rulers, terrorized their tax collectors and murdered their police agents. A code of behavior gradually took shape, and came to be known in the brotherhood as *omertà*, which can be translated liberally as "conspiracy of silence." There were five cardinal commandments—as compelling today, incidentally, as they were then. A mafioso must come to the aid of a brother in trouble with every means at his command, even at the risk of life or fortune. A mafioso must obey implicitly the orders of a council of brothers senior to him. A mafioso must consider an offense by an outsider against a brother as an offense against himself and the entire brotherhood and be ready to avenge it at any cost. A mafioso may never, under any circumstances, appeal to the police, the courts or any other governmental authority for redress. A mafioso, on pain of death, may never admit the existance of the brotherhood, discuss any phase of its activities or reveal the name of a brother.

These were the fundamentals. Over the years, corollary by-laws were added, also as alive today as then. A mafioso is always polite. "They give you the willies," as one federal agent said not long ago. "You arrest them, and they just smile and bow and ask you how you are. They're amazing people." We have seen this happen on various occasions. Self-control, particularly difficult for the volatile Sicilian temperament, is a very strict rule. Ostentatious display of wealth or power is generally frowned upon in the brotherhood. Big houses such as Joe Barbara's are rare. A mafioso may have a substantial fortune tucked away, as a good many have, but the ancient tradition requires him to live an outwardly modest life. He has his Cadillac or Chrysler Imperial, bought for cash, and almost always at least one mistress; the number depends on his standing in the brotherhood. Home, however, is often a two-family house with overstuffed furniture, antimacassars on the chairs, five-and-ten ceramics and all the other trappings of a stuffy middle-class European household. Here he is the soul of respectability—an affectionate husband, a kind father, usually temperate and a faithful worshiper at his church.

In the 1860's, with the unification of Italy and Sicily under an Italian king, the character of the Mafia changed abruptly. There was no longer any need for a patriotic underground society to combat a foreign tyrant. But the mafiosi were most unwilling to give up their privileged positions as the island's heroes and men of power. They had unusual skills in murder, kidnaping, robbery, extortion, espionage and lesser skulduggery. They had also added another commandment to their unwritten code, still effective today. A mafioso does no manual labor unless absolutely necessary; he lives off others. During the next decades, the Mafia established in Sicily the most remarkable secret criminal government within a government in history.

Police Prefect Cesare Mori, who tried to smash the Mafia in Sicily in the 1920's, and probably came to know more about the brotherhood's origins than anyone else, wrote a book, *At Crossed Swords with the Mafia,* in which he described the phenomenon.

"The Mafia," he wrote, "was the ruler of almost every segment of society. It had its chiefs and assistant chiefs. It issued its orders and decrees in the large cities as well as in the small centers, in the factories as well as in the fields. It regulated agrarian and urban rents, could intervene in almost any sort of business, imposing its will by fear and with threats and eventual punishment imposed by recognized Mafia officials. Its commands were literally law. Landholders and businessmen considered it worth their while to insure their properties and persons by paying regular tribute to the Mafia. The security gained from such insurance was far greater than anything the state and its agencies could guarantee. It was better, for example, for one who traveled by night with money—and even by day in many places—to have two associates of the Mafia at his side than two or more officers of the police."

Prefect Mori had this to say about its basic organization and philosophy (we have paraphrased in part from the original involved and ebullient Italian):

"I have often been asked," the prefect wrote, "what signs of recognition the mafiosi had among themselves, how their hierarchy was designed, their rules of admission, the appointment of its heads, its statutes, methods of administration, allotment of its funds. Actually, surprisingly enough, none of this exists. The Mafia is as much a philosophy as it is a society. It is a peculiar mental affinity that essentially joins the mafiosi, and forms them into a caste. They have no sign of recognition; there is no need of it. The mafiosi know each other automatically by their way of speaking, in part, and by intuition —scent, if you please. They have no statutes; the traditional law of *omertà* suffices. There are no elections; the capo mafioso arises by self-designation and self-imposition. There are no rules for admission; when a potential member shows the desired qualifications, he is simply absorbed. When his qualifications are no longer satisfactory, he is expelled, either by murder or a form of enforced retirement.

"The most salient and perplexing factor in the psychological makeup of the typical mafioso is his conviction that he is doing no wrong. As long as he obeys the rules of *omertà*—whether he extorts, steals or even murders—he is, to himself as well as to his brethren, an honorable man. His conscience is at peace."

The Mafia discovered America in the 1880's. The few mafiosi among the Sicilians who joined the great Italian emigration at that time soon found splendid opportunities for their traditional occupation. The new immigrants, bewildered by the strange land, its language and customs, naturally huddled together in the Little Italys of New York, Chicago, New Orleans and many other cities and towns across the country. For the inherent organizing talent of the mafiosi, they were easy prey. The members of the brotherhood had brought all of their talents and philosophy with them. Word of the bonanza of course quickly reached Sicily and more were on their way.

The Black Hand came into being. There has been much confusion about it. It was never a society in itself. Mafia extortion gangs simply used the imprint of a hand as a signature on their warnings, ransom notes and other demands. In Sicily for decades they had signed with a skull, a dagger or a hand. In America they discovered—and they have always been clever psychologists—that the hand was for some reason the most effective symbol. The first targets of the brotherhood were prosperous Italian farmers and merchants, who understood the Mafia's capabilities. A Long Island truck farmer would receive a notice to leave a hundred dollars in cash in a certain place, or else. The note was written in the unmistakable Mafia style of the Sicilian dialect and signed with The Hand—the *Mano Nera*. If he failed to meet the deadline, a stenciled black hand would appear on a fence or on the side of the house. That was the final warning.

"Then my father would pay," an elderly Italo-American vegetable grower near New York City, who was brought over from Sicily as a child, explained to us. "He would say, 'Giuseppe, you see, it is the same as at home. The Mafia is always with us.' Then I would plead with him to go to the police. After all, we were in America. 'No, Mother of God, no,' he would shout. 'The police here cannot do even as much as the police at home. They do not know the Mafia. We get put out of business or killed and no one will know why. They do not understand the mafiosi and they never will.' " Italian merchants and manufacturers in the Italian districts of New York, Chicago, San Francisco felt the same way. They paid, and the mafiosi prospered.

The first American policeman to cross swords with the Mafia and to begin to understand the strange brotherhood was Chief David Hennessey of New Orleans. The year was 1890, the pattern of its criminal activity startlingly similar to that of New York City in 1958. A group of mafiosi had taken over control of the New Orleans docks. The city and its harbor had become the center of the country's rapidly growing fruit trade from Latin America. No banana freighter could be unloaded until a fixed tribute was paid by the importer to the firm of Antonio and Carlo Matranga, originally of Palermo. No Negro or Italian longshoreman would move unless he had his orders from one of their appointed bosses. The importers were complacent, dock racketeering was common—as it is today—all along the seaboard, and there were no complaints.

Suddenly a series of particularly brutal murders shook the city. One Italian had his throat cut and was dumped into a canal. Another, almost decapitated, was found with what was left of his head stuffed into his own roaring fireplace. Shotguns, bombs and daggers—the traditional Mafia methods—were accounting for several murders a week. Chief Hennessey was an honest, intelligent, imaginative policeman of a kind most unusual in his day. His investigation, most of which he conducted by himself, was thorough. The more he found out, the angrier he became. He ran head on into the system which the capi mafiosi of New Orleans had created. Most of his own policemen, many of them Italian, were suddenly deaf, dumb and blind; so was the Italian colony. But Hennessey was a stubborn man. He was warned time and again to lay off; financial proposals were made. He ignored both threats and bribes. Gradually he pieced together the details of the mechanism with which the formidable Matranga family ruled the New Orleans docks. The murders, he discovered, had been the result of a typical Mafia feud between the Matrangas and the Provenzano brothers who had tried to move in on their territory. It was hard going for the chief in those days—70 years before Senator Kefauver and Sergeant Croswell—with no FBI or Treasury Department to help. Nevertheless, Hennessey put together an accurate picture of the mafiosi's operations and, finally, was ready to present it to a grand jury. The brotherhood decided that he had moved in too close and knew too much. A few days before he was to testify, as he was walking home from police headquarters one evening, a salvo of shotgun blasts cut him down. He was terribly wounded, but he managed as he staggered and fell to pull his service revolver from its holster. Heaving himself up in a last gesture of defiance, he emptied the gun. A detective who happened to be nearby and heard the shooting dashed up and found the chief sitting on the stoop of a house, gun still clutched in his fingers. Hennessey identified his attackers as the "dagoes" before his head fell forward between his knees and his revolver clattered on the step. A few hours later, after a number of violent struggles in the hospital against the paralysis that prevented him from speaking, he was dead.

The New Orleans Police Department at the beginning was not too energetic about investigating Chief Hennessey's death, but the anger of the citizenry could not be ignored. One grand jury, after hearing the testimony of a number of the chief's more loyal assistants, returned a presentment that might have been written today. "The existance of a secret organization known as the Mafia has been established beyond doubt." The jury spelled out the details. It found, officially, that "the society" was composed of Italians and Sicilians who had left their country to avoid punishment for crimes they had committed there. Althought the jury had never heard the word *omertà* and would not have known what it meant, they catalogued some of its rules clearly. ". . . strangely difficult, almost impossible to discover the perpetrators of these crimes or to secure witnesses. . . ."

Under increasing public pressure the police was compelled to go to work. Indictments were returned and nineteen Sicilians finally went to trial for the Hennessey murder as principals and conspirators. It should have been a simple case for the prosecution. Fear of reprisal by the Mafia had gradually been overcome by the intensity of public opinion and almost 60 witnesses were ready to testify against the defendants. Some had seen and could identify four who had been running from the scene of the killing. There was overwhelming corroborative evidence. The verdict, according to the New Orleans newspapers, was a foregone conclusion.

But the Mafia, as subsequent investigations showed, had also been at work. The mafiosi of 1890 were as determined as their offspring of 1957 at Apalachin to protect the brotherhood's anonymity. Money flowed into New Orleans to hire the best legal talent available. Thomas J. Semmes, a spectacular attorney who was considered one of the country's greatest criminal lawyers at the time, headed the defense. A battery of five others, all with Anglo-Saxon names, assisted him. (This has long been the standard operational procedure of the brotherhood; with few exceptions, a mafioso is rarely defended in court by an attorney with an Italian name.) At least half of the jurymen were both intimidated and handsomely bribed. On the guilt of three of the defendants the jury could not decide, the rest were held innocent.

Mayor Joseph A. Shakespeare of New Orleans made a report to his City Council which sounds very similar to the recent writings and speeches of Senator Kefauver and Attorney General Rogers 70 years later. "A decent community cannot exist," the mayor wrote, "with such a society in its midst. The society must be destroyed or the community will perish. The Sicilians who come here must become American citizens and obey the law of the land, or else there is no place for them in our country."

The mayor was angry. He had admired his chief of police despite the political trouble which the often tactless Hennessey had caused him. The city was even angrier. As in Chicago in the 1920's under the rule of Al Capone, the people were afraid of the mafiosi; they were also ashamed of themselves. Although Shakespeare was a reform mayor, New Orleans at the time was probably one of the most corrupt cities in the country. But the brotherhood had gone too far. Two days after the verdict on the Sicilians had been brought in, New Orleans erupted into one of the most horrible mass lynchings in our history.

A protest meeting called by a group of the city's leading people, with the approval of Mayor Shakespeare and the editorial encouragement of the *Picayune* and the *Times-Democrat,* began peacefully enough but suddenly turned into a roaring, bloodthirsty mob of several thousand who marched on the jail and battered down its gates. The mafiosi after the conclusion of their trial had not been released, but had been taken back to the Parish Prison to await completion of various legal formalities. Self-appointed execution squads searched the building for the Italians as deputy sheriffs discreetly disappeared. Two prisoners were dragged screaming into the street in front of the prison, ropes materialized, nooses were fashioned and men hoisted them onto lamp posts. A group of armed citizens carefully riddled each with bullets as they swung, kicking. Nine more mafiosi were discovered and lined up in front of a prison wall. Another firing party with rifles, pistols and shotguns methodically cut them to pieces.

The press in this country and newspapers abroad—including the stately *London Times*—discovered the Mafia for the first time. Some editors approved, some disapproved of the action of the New Orleans mob. It immediately became an international incident. The irascible James G. Blaine was our secretary of state. The Marquis Rudini, the Italian foreign minister, was no more tactful. A series of extremely vituperative messages was exchanged by Washington and Rome. The marquis inferred that we were barbarians incapable of enforcing our own laws and Mr. Blaine replied sharply that although we were a relatively young country, we did not have the criminal societies which seemed to flourish in Italy. The Italian ambassador was withdrawn from Washington. President Harrison decided that the trouble was not worth the bother and he authorized the payment of some $30,000 as an indemnity. The Italian government was placated, King Umberto sent a flowery message, relations between the countries returned to normal, and the existance of the Mafia was forgotten for a time.

The brotherhood, its ramifications and some of its activities were discovered again just after the turn of the century by a tubby, shrewd detective of the New York Police Department—Lieutenant Joseph Petrosino. Born in the coastal town of Salerno, near Naples, the stocky little man had heard much about the Mafia from his parents. As the brotherhood began to flourish in New York—it came to be known then as the Black Hand—Petrosino with his background and knowledge made it his specialty. A systematic man, he built up a file on the dock racketeers, brothel owners, fish and meat market gangsters and other mafiosi of that day. He was brilliant in the organization of the cases which he developed and several hundred Italians, especially Sicilians, who had neglected their naturalization procedures were deported as undesirable aliens. It became almost an obsession with Petrosino. He felt very deeply that the Mafia's abuse of American freedoms and process of law was not only an outrage to himself as an American citizen but a disgrace to the parent country which he loved. In 1909 he talked Theodore Bingham, one of New York City's few great police commissioners, into an unusual operation. A secret service unit, officially known as Italian Squad of the Police Department, was to be created to combat the Black Hand extortions of the Mafia. The Board of Estimate was unimpressed and refused to appropriate money for the purpose. Bingham, however, was well informed, convinced and determined. Private funds were raised, as they were years later in Chicago to destroy Al Capone and his mafiosi. Petrosino was authorized by the commissioner to go on an unprecedented trip. The lieutenant was to contact Italian police chiefs—particularly in Sicily, Calabria and Naples—and set up arrangements with them for warning the New York City Police Department whenever an important criminal left for the United States. This was unheard-of at that time. It was years before the establishment of Interpol, the International Criminal Police Organization, which functions so efficiently today, and the law enforcement agencies of Europe and the United States very rarely even corresponded with each other. The State Department as well as foreign governments were inclined to frown on the international cooperation of policemen, which the diplomats regarded as an uncouth and embarrassing crew in any case. Commissioner Bingham dispatched Petrosino anyway.

The lieutenant, fully aware that he was attacking a very formidable enemy, was careful. He traveled under an assumed name and in Rome went directly to the minister of the interior. His excellency was sympathetic. Petrosino was equipped, surprisingly enough, with credentials from the ministry which made him practically an Italian policeman of high rank. A few weeks later he set out confidently for Palermo to begin his investigations. That was as far as he got. On the morning of March 13, 1909, while on his way to the Questura—the city's police headquarters—he paused in the Piazza Marina to watch the colorful scene and people. Two men came up behind him. Unhurriedly, they drew revolvers from under their jackets and fired four bullets point-blank into his back and head. Petrosino, like Hennessey, had gone too far into the affairs of the brotherhood, and somewhere along the line the news of his presence and the nature of his job became known. He was dead when he hit the pavement; his executioners mingled with the excitedly gathering crowd, walked away and were never found. Cables and letters again went between Rome, New York and Washington. The Italian government offered an lire reward for the arrest of the criminals, Commissioner Bingham in New York used harsh words—all with little result. The body of Lieutenant Petrosino was in due course shipped home. His widow was granted a pension, he was given an impressive funeral by the Police Department and tributes to his work came even from the White House.

Lieutenant Petrosino's knowledge of the Sicilian brotherhood, unique at that time, was buried with him. The New York Police Department's special squad of detectives, which he had organized, went out with Commissioner Bingham. The Italian vote made such activity embarrassing politically to the new city administration. Petrosino and his special squad might have done much over the next few decades against the almost incredible rise of the brotherhood in the United States and the foundation it built for the organized crime of today. Dozens of capi mafiosi of the future, who were to control bootlegging, gambling, prostitution and other racketeering in the roaring twenties, were growing up in various parts of the country. They were eventually to cause us untold damage, financially and particularly morally. But no one was to know for a long time still who they were and how they were connected.

In 1925 another wave of Mafia immigration began. Benito

Mussolini had decided that Sicily was to be the political and intellectual center of his Fascist empire of the Mediterranean. Before this could be done however, the dictator realized, the brotherhood's rule of the island had to be broken. For the difficult job Mussolini picked the able and energetic questore of Milan, Colonel Cesare Mori—a professional policeman who had come to hate the Mafia and its works as much as Petrosino and Hennessey ever had. Mori was given extraordinary powers and over a thousand picked policemen. He descended on Sicily like a cyclone. His preparatory intelligence was fairly good. Whole families of mafiosi were arrested, given drumhead trials and deported to the penal colonies of the Lipari Islands and the island of Ustica.

For the time being, the activities of the Mafia in Sicily ceased almost entirely. Those who were sent to the islands pretended profound penitence and expressed enthusiastic support of Il Duce and the new Fascist way of life. Many were released as a result. Others escaped with the help of fishermen who knew that the Mafia would show its gratitude. Those who had not come to Mori's attention—and these included some of the most dangerous—simply stopped operations. The extortion rackets, robberies, smuggling, feuds and murders dipped sharply. In 1928 Prefect Mori reported to Mussolini that the Mafia had been so disrupted that it would never function again. Through an intensive psychological campaign, he said, he had convinced the Sicilian people that the brotherhood was a disgrace to them all. They had responded, even to the children in the schools. The Mafia was dead.

The prefect was mistaken. Some of the mafiosi either by choice or from lack of means lived more or less honestly for several years until the collapse of Mussolini's regime in World War II gave them their next opportunity. Many, however, managed to come to the United States by devious means without immigration formalities, as merchant seamen or across the Mexican and Canadian borders, to join friends and relatives already established in this country. (Several of the Apalachin delegates stemmed from this era.) They were easily absorbed by the brotherhood. By 1925 the Mafia in the United States was reaching new and undreamed-of heights of wealth and power as a result of Prohibition and the organizing genius of Al Capone in Chicago and Charlie "Lucky" Luciano in New York. It happened in six years. . .

The year 1919 had seen the Mafia in the United States an element in the underworld, an important but not dominating one. The mafiosi were, as usual, neatly organized in every city in which they operated. Every group had its territory and its activities well defined, its capo mafioso who represented it in the council when there were quarrels. In Chicago, for example, Don Giuseppe (Diamond Jim) Colosimo and his executive officer, Johnny Torrio, controlled a very lucrative section of the city's gambling, prostitution and corrupt labor unions, and were absolute political masters of the First Ward. There were many other well organized gangs, predominantly Irish and Jewish, in the city. The mafiosi had made no attempt to move in on their territories. The Mafia policy was then one of peaceful coexistence. This was to change radically in Chicago, New York and elsewhere within a year.

In January 1920, the Eighteenth Amendment to the Constitution and the Volstead Act—probably the most unenforceable legislation ever approved by the Congress—came into effect. Colosimo and Torrio in Chicago, with a farsightedness unusual in the underworld of those days, had anticipated the results of the new and obviously unenforceable laws and were ready for them. Torrio, the executive of the partnership, had discussed the matter with brother mafiosi and had made plans. Several thousand Sicilians in and around Chicago prepared to produce alcohol in their kitchens and beer in their garages. This was the kind of thing they understood and liked. Then hell broke loose in the underworld. Every gang in the city, realizing how immense this new source of revenue would be, tried to seize as much control of it as possible. Even traditional Mafia cohesion and discipline were collapsing under the weight of the golden flood. Diamond Jim Colosimo—the sacrosanct capo mafioso—was riddled with bullets in his own café, from which he had ruled the area for so many years, by mafiosi from Detroit who wanted to move in. Torrio, as the don's second in command, found himself in charge and in a critical position. He was an able executive with an orderly mind, imagination and an intuitive flair for picking competent men. Torrio sent for Al Capone, a youngster of 21, who was running a chain of Colosimo-Torrio brothels in the Chicago suburbs. Capone became the new don's executive officer and a fabulous era in the Mafia's history began.

CHAPTER FIVE

The Grand Design of Alphonse Capone

The underworld's greatest genius made the brotherhood what it is today.

Alphonse Capone, unquestionably the greatest organizer of crime in his or any other era, was born in Naples in 1899. A few years later his parents brought their three young sons and a daughter to one of the poorest Italian immigrant sections of Brooklyn, New York. Young Al grew up on the streets while his father dug ditches and his mother worked in sweatshops. He left school after the fourth grade and graduated to a Brooklyn poolroom, headquarters of a group of minor racketeers. He also organized a gang of his own to terrorize the other youngsters of the neighborhood and collect tribute from a number of grocery and fruit stand operators who preferred paying a small fee to having their produce ruined. In the early 1900's it was not called juvenile delinquency, but the pattern was not very different from that of today. Young Al developed a great admiration for Johnny Torrio, a rising mafioso who specialized in extortion and gambling. Torrio recognized the boy's qualities. He was unusually shrewd, fearless and utterly unscrupulous. The only trouble with him was that he was a Neapolitan, and had a Neapolitan's temper. It was this temper that got young Al, in his teens, the deep perpendicular slash on his left cheek which gave him the nickname of Scarface.

There is Mafia lore in this little story. Young Al had set up the mafioso Torrio as his idol. He ran errands, found women, did everything and anything for his boss, and listened carefully to his every word. He wanted to be a mafioso too. He couldn't, because he was a Neapolitan. The brotherhood is adamant about that to this day. A Neapolitan may sit in with the highest councils and his opinions are respected, but the Sicilian brothers never take him completely into the fraternity. He, they consider, does not have the self-discipline which *omertà* demands. Young Al did not understand that. He wanted his hair cut in the long, peculiar fashion which the mafiosi had affected for decades. An elderly Sicilian barber in Brooklyn thought this sacrilege on the part of a Neapolitan and refused. Young Al, already a hulking, powerful bully, swept a rackful of the old man's precious shaving mugs to the floor. The barber had a razor in his hand.

Torrio moved to Chicago in 1915, but he never forgot young Al. As the Colosimo-Torrio kingdom began to grow, Torrio sent for Capone. The fantastic rise of the young man who arrived in Chicago as an almost penniless hoodlum is history. By 1925, after Colosimo's death, Torrio and his protégé Capone were splitting—according to a subsequent and careful estimate of the Bureau of Internal Revenue—not less than $100,000 a week. In January of that year Torrio was almost killed by the O'Banion gang, whose leader had been assassinated by Torrio-Capone gunmen some months before. Torrio, after he was able to leave the hospital, wisely decided that he had a sufficiently substantial income for the rest of his life, handed the kingdom over to Al Capone and retired.

The reaction of the always flexible Sicilian mafiosi who had formed most of the Torrio-Capone staff, and on whom the new leader would have to rely, was typical. The capi mafiosi in Chicago and neighboring areas decided that they would go along with Capone, Neapolitan or not. They had watched his operations, had faith in both his imagination and executive ability. Their confidence was well placed. In the next few years he and the mafiosi who worked with him not only took over bootlegging, prostitution and gambling in Illinois and neighboring states but also laid the foundations for the nationwide syndicates as we know them today. For the first time, at Capone's behest, mafiosi in Chicago were in touch with brothers in New York and San Francisco to arrange, for example, for the smooth importation of whiskey from Great Britain and its distribution to mafiosi throughout the country. New channels of communication and cooperation were opened.

The story of the Battle of Chicago, which took more than 500 gangsters' lives in less than five years, has been told often and in detail. Capone with the Mafia at his back marched into every ward in the city with Napoleonic precision and thoroughness. One by one the O'Banion gang, the Bugs Moran group and the others were decimated by sawed-off shotgun slugs and .45 caliber Thompson submachine gun bullets fired by expert Sicilian marksmen from fast, always black cars. Many of the lethal techniques used seemed new. Actually, most of them were ancient Sicilian methods adapted to modern tools. The handshake assassination, for example, is as old as the Mafia. Dion O'Banion's gun hand was firmly gripped by one Capone torpedo, to prevent his grabbing any one of the three revolvers he always carried, even in his florist shop, while his partner carefully blew the Irish rival's head apart. To the mafiosi there was nothing new about the "Saint Valentine's Day Massacre" when a group of Capone's executioners dressed in police uniforms stood six members of the Moran gang against a wall of their garage headquarters to be searched, as they thought, and mowed them down with machine guns. Many mafiosi in Sicily for generations had uniforms of the *Carabinieri,* the national constabulary, for the same sort of purpose.

The bomb has also long been a traditional instrument of the brotherhood. In Chicago the Mills hand grenade of

World War I, the "pineapple," became standard equipment for attacks on recalcitrant stores and speakeasies. The Capone mob was working out refinements for booby traps years before these devices were resorted to by the military in World War II. One neat device could be hooked to the ignition system of a car in a matter of seconds, to explode at a touch of the starter. In Sicily a mechanism which went off when the wheels of the cart to which it was attached began to turn had been used for many years.

Capone learned much from the Mafia, and the mafiosi learned as much from him. The pasty-faced, powerfully built, enormously energetic little man had administrative capacities which might, if his path and instincts had been different, have made him the head of one of our biggest legitimate corporations. It did make him the head of the largest illegitimate one we have ever known. His organization, which eventually netted over 20 million dollars a year, was a model of efficiency with skillful deputation of authority to department chiefs who knew the value of teamwork. Internal Revenue estimates that he took out and carefully invested in blue chip securities some 50 million dollars. For the Mafia he did much more. He, the Neapolitan, with two dramatic strokes organized the brotherhood into what it is today.

Capone himself, with all his wealth and power, and much as he always wanted to, could not be a capo mafioso or a Sicilian don. He designated the dons, and his selections were generally approved by the brotherhood. Capone had a mortal enemy in the New York Mafia, a powerful capo mafioso named Giuseppe Aiello. Aiello hated Capone personally; he envied him for his growing control of Chicago, his ability and the fact that a Neapolitan should be giving orders to mafiosi. The gunmen who shot down and almost killed Torrio had been dispatched by Aiello, from Brooklyn. Another Aiello team, operating in broad daylight a few months later at one of Chicago's busiest intersections, made big holes with dumdum bullets in the head of Antonio Lombardo, a prosperous merchant of Cicero whom Capone had elevated to the top of the local brotherhood. A third team, shortly afterward, paid a call on Pasquale Lolordo, Capone's next appointee. This was an assassination more in the traditional Mafia style. Three men arrived one afternoon at Lolordo's well-appointed apartment and introduced themselves, with impeccable credentials, as associates of one of his New York friends. They were unquestionably mafiosi—the members of the brotherhood can recognize each other almost on sight—and the capo was cordial. Signora Lolordo brought wine, and after she had disappeared into the kitchen and shut the door, as the wives of mafiosi always do, the men indulged in pleasant conversation. Suddenly revolvers barked, Don Pasquale was on the floor with his head in pieces and the visitors were gone. The Chicago police say that the signora, in her original agony, immediately and positively identified one of Aiello's men from his picture in the rogues' gallery as one of the murderers. Later she became vague, and finally withdrew her statement entirely. *Omertà* had taken hold; it is respected by the mafiosi's women as well as by the brothers themselves.

Aiello mapped his final move against the hated Neapolitan. He had been able to infiltrate the Capone organization and corrupt two of his most trusted advisers—Giovanni Scalice and Alberto Anselmi. There developed the kind of devious conspiracy which the mafiosi love. Scalice and Anselmi had been Capone's most able gunmen; he felt he had them in the palm of his hand for murders they had committed; they knew all the ins and outs of Mafia organization, policy and personalities. When Scalice and Anselmi suggested their good friend Giuseppe Guinta as the new figurehead chief of the Chicago Mafia, Capone agreed. He was a New Yorker, an outsider, and could be handled. Aiello had not, however, reckoned with Capone's superb intelligence system.

From the beginning—and this was another lesson which the Mafia learned from him—Capone insisted on a highly efficient information network. It could have been a model for any government espionage agency. Barbers, manicurists, bartenders, hotel clerks, doormen, shoeshine boys all over Chicago knew the number to call when they had heard anything that might interest the Boss. So did certain key personnel in various city departments, including the police. So, also, did officers in other cities. Information that proved of value was well rewarded. The imaginative Capone was also well aware of the advantages of wiretapping, a generally unknown practice in the twenties; he hired a compact crew of experts to tap lines and protect his own. The organization's G-2 was an important factor in Capone's success and safety.

Automatically, as routine as a personnel investigation by the FBI of an applicant for a government job, Giuseppe Guinta's background and character were examined by Capone's counter-intelligence unit. Within a few days Capone knew that the supposedly innocuous Sicilian was one of Aiello's most dangerous henchmen, with the sworn purpose of eliminating the Neapolitan by gunfire and taking over the middle western empire, henceforth to be ruled from New York.

Capone thought the matter over and decided on a classic, grisly performance which has few equals in underworld history. His unsuspecting disloyal paladins, Scalice and Anselmi, with Guinta were invited to a gala dinner to celebrate the latter's installation as Chicago's capo mafioso. The banquet room of the restaurant-cabaret was packed with Chicago mafiosi. They had their orders. The local grand council of the brotherhood didn't like the threat of invasion from New York any more than Capone did. After a huge meal had been eaten, with gallons of the best Chianti, the little Neapolitan rose with a glass of champagne in his hand, apparently to drink a toast. He had been a most gracious host all evening, with smiles and handshakes for everyone, particularly for Guinta, Scalice and Anselmi. He bowed to the new don, who was flanked by his two sponsors. As he raised his glass, the smile suddenly disappeared and his whole face was transformed. It grew white as the jaw muscles clamped, the scar on the cheek reddened. "Traitors," he screamed in Italian. "Filth! Dogs!" With one quick movement he hurled his goblet into Don Giuseppe's face. With another he reached under the table for the heavy baseball bat which lay at his feet. The Chicago mafiosi had their guns out, trained on the three plotters—the guests of honor—who sat riveted to their chairs by sheer terror. Unhurriedly, like a medieval executioner, Capone walked around the table until he was behind Scalice, who knew what was coming and crossed himself. The club in the Neapolitan's beefy hands came down with tremendous force and Scalice toppled forward, brains spilling onto the tablecloth. Anselmi was next; then Guinta. Capone threw the bloody bat on the floor, spat, waved an order to have the bodies removed and stalked out. Anselmi and Guinta, not quite dead, were then riddled with bullets to make sure. The three mangled corpses were found the next day by the Indiana State Police across the state line in a roadside ditch. Although the whole underworld and the Chicago police knew within hours what had happened, no indictments were ever even sought, let alone obtained.

By Mafia standards it had been an impressive performance indeed, quite justified by the brotherhood's rules and an indisputable decision by a council with proper jurisdiction. A few weeks later Capone issued invitations to the senior capi mafiosi of Chicago, Detroit, New York, Philadelphia and several other big centers to meet in Atlantic City in May 1929. Almost all of them accepted. It was not the first interstate meeting of the brotherhood. One, and probably the first big one, had been held the year before in Cleveland. (Embarrassingly enough, an alert hotel clerk grew suspicious of the 21 guests who dressed and acted so similarly, and informed the police. Profaci and Magliocco—who were to be caught almost 30 years later in a similar situation at Apalachin—and many of the others were found carrying guns. They were fined $50 apiece and given suspended sentences.) But it was the Atlantic City gathering that made underworld and Mafia history. In the Treasury Department's files is a series of fragmentary accounts of the convention from various informers which, when put together, made a fascinating picture. The mafiosi arrived, suspicious, flanked by bodyguards, revolvers handy in shoulder holsters and waistbands. But the chunky Neapolitan was both a politician and a diplomat of unusual ability—a statesman in his way. Within a few days he had put together a number of formidable and friendly combines. The Sicilians listened, fascinated, as Capone explained a project on which he had been working for some three years—a nationwide syndicate and organization, not only for bootlegging but gambling, prostitution, labor racketeering and various kinds of extortion as well. The Neapolitan was coolly farsighted. He sensed that Prohibition would end before too long and was beginning to think about the consequences. At Atlantic City a series of peace treaties for the Chicago, New York and other areas was hammered out and ratified—without documents and signatures but with a validity that lasted a long time. It was the fundamental design and unwritten constitution of the modern American Mafia.

On his way home, in high good humor from the great success in Atlantic City, Capone had a peculiar accident which should have been a warning to him. He stopped over in Philadelphia between trains and went to the movies. On his way from the theater to the depot two detectives on routine patrol saw and recognized him. A quick frisk, right on the street, revealed a beautifully built-in shoulder holster and a loaded automatic. The raging master of Chicago produced a pistol permit from that city. "I'm sorry," grinned one of the detectives. "That's no good here, mister. You're under arrest." Philadelphia's director of public safety couldn't resist the temptation. He had the great Capone brought to his office. The Neapolitan, out of sheer anger, had one of his rare lapses of judgment. He spoke to the crusty, elderly police chief—who was also a retired West Point colonel—

as though he were one of his Chicago servitors. The colonel was amazingly polite. Capone, relaxed, explained that he had actually given up the rackets several years before. That he had accomplished his ambition of many years to retire to his home in Florida, peacefully, for the rest of his life. He carried a gun, he said with a show of great candor, because he had naturally made enemies years ago who might have grudges against him and his family. The colonel smiled and nodded through Capone's whole recitation. Much relieved, Capone finally with an air of complete assurance got up to shake hands and leave. The colonel shook hands cordially, then turned to a policeman who had been standing by. "Lock him up," he said quietly, and went back to some papers on his desk. Within twenty-four hours the czar of the underworld had been tried before a Philadelphia magistrate who hated gangsters, had been given the maximum sentence under Pennsylvania law for carrying a concealed weapon and was in the penitentiary at Holmesburg for a year.

The whole underworld was appalled. It seemed incredible that the great man should have been struck down by the law in such fashion. The mafiosi around him apparently learned a number of lessons from the incident. No senior mafioso was ever again caught illegally carrying a gun. Capone himself lost considerable face among the brotherhood; such lack of judgment was considered dangerous.

The Neapolitan's empire still seemed not only secure but invulnerable. During his incarceration—he was prison librarian during most of it—his orders were relayed to his brother, Ralph Capone, who acted as an able viceroy. When he was released in March 1930, after his term had been reduced to ten months for good behavior, he was welcomed home like returning royalty by cheering crowds and many of Chicago's principal officials. The income of the various Capone combinations in which he had a finger had risen to staggering totals. Internal Revenue's rough estimate later placed it at approximately $25,000,000 from gambling, close to $10,000,-

000 from organized pro... out the same from narcotics distribution and ov... 0 from bootlegging.

But Capone's days were n... e Secret Six, a group of Chicago's most promine... had organized to protect themselves against the ... ion by Capone's mafiosi of legitimate business... eing and landering industry, trucking, restau... nd food distribution. While even they did no... y to match the more than $15,000,000 a yea... apolitan's groups were doling out to the police ... nd state officials, they did hire a team of c... s who helped gradually put the Capone pictu... eventual presentation in court. The federal g... also finally gotten started. Skilled squads from ... epartment of Justice and the Treasury Department began a careful, thorough, three-pronged attack to establish tax evasion, conspiracy to violate the prohibtion laws and to close down Capone's sources of beer and liquor. The first two objectives were extraordinarily difficult. Capone's organizations dealt almost entirely in cash; few checks were exchanged; there were no detailed records to be seized. Jacob (Greasy Thumb) Gusick, the combine's general manager and the Boss's minister of finance, had a genius for concealing the origin and distribution of even the largest sums of money. It was equally difficult to prove any connection between the Neapolitan and his Mafia henchmen. No informers could be bought and it was impossible to infiltrate the brotherhood.

The operation most immediately successful, which dug the pit for Capone's eventual destruction, was the drying up of his sources of supply. Eliot Ness, a brilliant Justice Department agent with a small but relentless squad, undertook the extremely hazardous task of finding and closing, one by one, the dozens of clandestine breweries and depots of the Capone organization scattered over the city. They had against them not only Capone and his thugs but a large part of the Chicago police itself. One of Agent Ness's men was murdered, and it was a miracle that he himself escaped with his life. He was threatened daily by telephone and letter, received offers of substantial bribes, was almost run down several times by gangster cars that were aiming at him, and, on various occasions, was shot at. His tactics were radical and spectacular. In a powerful truck specially reinforced with a huge, massive bumper of solid steel, he would ram the gates of a brewery and be inside, his men with their sawed-off shotguns ready, before the first mafioso could reach for a tommy gun. Ness was not primarily interested in the enforcement of the Prohibition laws; his real job was to break Capone and the Chicago Mafia. Within a year the agent and his little band of federal desperados had crashed into more than 30 big plants and warehouses, destroyed millions of dollars' worth of irreplaceable equipment and impounded no less than 50 big trucks—a large part of the syndicate's lifeline. The Capone treasury began to feel the strain, and bribe money as well as beer deliveries had to be curtailed more and more. The intricate machine began developing serious engine trouble. Agent Ness, a graduate of the University of Chicago and a highly intelligent man with imagination, was also fighting a shrewd campaign of psychological warfare against the mafiosi and their leader. Through underworld contacts he leaked out convincing stories that showed the government operation as far larger than it really was and subtly began putting the mafiosi on their guard against Capone's possible crash. His campaign was effective, and dissaffection grew in the ranks as well as on the periphery. One of Ness's most memorable performances was a spectacular parade that he led up Michigan Avenue one morning past the Lexington Hotel, where Capone had his fortresslike headquarters in the three top floors. To make sure of a large audience the agent spoke to the Boss himself on the telephone and told him that something was going to happen in front of the hotel at eleven o'clock. Capone's curiosity was piqued. He knew that he would be perfectly safe behind the loopholes of steel shutters many stories above the street, with the lobby and pavement below guarded by dozens of gunmen. He summoned his principal aides and waited. Precisely at eleven an impressive procession passed slowly by—45 of the organization's huge confiscated trucks manned by armed government agents. Ness had the satisfaction of learning soon after from a reliable informer that the Neapolitan had screamed with rage, upset furniture, smashed vases, shattered chairs and ordered the immediate assassination of Ness and his assistants even if it had to be carried out on the steps of City Hall.

Capone was not to have his way; there was no murder. The mafiosi evidently sensed that a crash was imminent. Ness's parade had impressed them deeply; it was the kind of performance they understood. It was obvious that the government was ready to attack. A mafioso knows what that means and is ready to bow to the wind. Only a crazy Neapolitan would think of killing a federal officer. They wanted no part of it. Ness and his men without knowing it were quite safe from that moment. The judgment of the brotherhood, as so often, was good.

The government's main attack came from a different and entirely unexpected direction led by a quiet, modest, methodical man with steel-rimmed spectacles. Frank J. Wilson, an agent of the intelligence unit of the Bureau of Internal Revenue, after several months of work in Chicago in 1928, had pretty well decided that a case could not be made against Capone. Obvious as the archracketeer's income was, it could not be proved in court. By the same methods that are used today cash was simply passed to him as he needed it. There seemed to be no records, no witnesses. But then, by a fortunate accident, Agent Wilson did find records—the books of a gambling establishment in Cicero called The Ship which did a $3,000,000-a-year business. They had been seized during a raid but never examined. The investigation which followed is one of the most extraordinary in the history of the Treasury Department. For months Wilson checked the handwriting in the ledgers against the caligraphy of hundreds of known Chicago gangsters obtained from police and court records, voting registers and banks. Finally he had luck. The handwriting in the books tallied exactly with that of Louis Shumway, one of Capone's bookkeepers and couriers. Wilson gave Shumway the choice of quietly becoming a witness for the government—to be suddenly produced at Capone's trial and then locked up in safety until the racketeer was securely in prison—or being arrested with fanfare and then released, with intimations to the underworld which would bring about his immediate execution. Shumway chose the former alternative and, under a security wrap which rivaled any spy's in a world war, was spirited from place to place. But Shumway was not enough. Wilson had to be able to prove that undeclared money actually reached Capone. Many more months of exhaustive inquiry followed before Agent Wilson discovered Fred Ries, who used to take The Ship's tremendous profits to the Pinckert Bank of Cicero in canvas bags and have the banknotes converted into cashier's checks—the favorite currency of racketeers to this day—and deliver them to the Boss.

After three years, the federal government had a copper-riveted case. In June 1931 the whole underworld shook when a grand jury handed down indictments against Alphonse Capone, his brother Ralph and 68 others for income tax evasion. The Neapolitan was liable to thirty years in prison—in effect, a life sentence.

Fantastic as the investigation had been, the trial was even more so. Capone's attorneys tried every conceivable dodge. They offered the government $5,000,000 for settlement of the tax claims and—a thing that a mafioso very rarely does—information against the codefendants in exchange for a light, two- or three-year sentence. Apparently still not understanding that they were dealing with federal and not state authorities, counselors Teitelbaum and Ahearn had their client confidently plead guilty to the charges. They had not reckoned with U.S. Attorney George E. Q. Johnson or Federal Judge James H. Wilkerson. It had always been so easy before. This time it wasn't. Neither Johnson nor the judge were prepared to make any kind of a deal at all. Then a new approach was tried, and almost succeeded. Capone's influential protectors were able to get at almost every one of the jurors with bribes, threats or both. Fortunately, Agent Wilson found out about it just in time and went to the judge with his story. The jurist immediately thought up a wonderful plan. He pretended up to the last minute that he was going to conduct the trial with the rigged jury. Then, suddenly, he excused them and rammed an entirely new panel into the box. Capone couldn't understand it and neither could his expensive lawyers as he was briskly tried, convicted and sentenced (in October, 1931) to 11 years in a federal penitentiary. A few years later the onetime undisputed boss of the second largest city in the United States died slowly and painfully of paresis, the syphilis which had been gradually eating away his system for a long time. He was only 48 years old.

The Treasury Department had achieved its immediate objective—the destruction of Al Capone. The Capone empire as a whole, lacking a crown prince, fell apart. None of the men who had been closest to the Boss—his brother Ralph, Jacob "Greasy Thumb" Gusick, Tony Accardo—had the ability necessary to manage the huge and intricate complex. But a criminal syndicate, still known as the Capone mob out of deference to its founder and still a great power in the underworld, continued to exist. But what is most important to us today, as Senator Kefauver first brought to the public's attention in 1951 and Senator McClellan has recently confirmed, was the heritage that the extraordinary Neapolitan passed on to the Mafia. The mafiosi had learned much from him to supplement their ancient traditions and bring them up to date. He had in effect laid the foundation for their virtual control of the American underworld today. He had taught them that nationwide cooperation within the brotherhood had great possibilities in every field of its traditional operation. If a brothel operator in New York, for example, was in trouble he could be useful in Detroit until the heat was off. If a narcotics merchant was discovered in San Francisco he could move to New Orleans under the shield of the brotherhood. Labor racketeering was fast becoming an interstate proposition. The mafiosi had also learned four principles from the Capone era which were practically incorporated into the code of *omertà*: 1. Always have a good lawyer. 2. Never plot or carry out violence against a federal officer. 3. Pay federal income taxes. 4. Never trust anyone except a real Sicilian mafioso.

The repeal of Prohibition in December 1933 hit the underworld hard. From one day to the next, all over the country, the big profits for the principal bootleggers and the jobs for their gangsters vanished. The mafiosi with their flexibility were the first to recover. The upper echelon of the capi of the Midwest and dons from other parts of the country met in Chicago for a conference of much the same pattern as the Apalachin gathering, almost 25 years later. The accounts of this congress, gradually collected from informers and pieced together, are fragmentary. But the formal establishment of new policies and attitudes is unquestionable. No one carried a gun. The unanimous purpose was to find, peacefully, fields of endeavor which could be substituted for bootlegging and make them, if possible, equally profitable. All phases of gambling, legal and illegal—from slot machines and casinos to the big numbers games and racetrack operations—were already stock in trade to the brotherhood. So was large-scale extortion in industries which employed a large number of Italo-Americans who knew what the Mafia was and feared it—particularly the garment makers, truckers, longshoremen and food suppliers. It was just a question of exploiting these and other rich fields more thoroughly. The meeting, after certain territories had been assigned, closed on this note. The Mafia had reached an important milestone.

Despite the economic depression which had gripped the country, most of the capi mafiosi still had important money. The Sicilians have an innate love of gambling, but are an essentially thrifty and careful people. Many large fortunes had been built up by bootlegging during the Capone era and prudently socked away. Joseph Barbara, the Apalachin host, had enough capital to buy a bottling plant and set up his legal beer and liquor distributing organization in southern New York and Pennsylvania. Joseph Profaci, in Brooklyn, established the lucrative Mama Mia Olive Oil Company and a cheese industry. Frank Costello, along with his many other business interests, was able to buy the building at 79 Wall Street which he later sold at enormous profit. Joe Adonis bought into the trucking business. The Mafia had plenty of capital to work with.

And a new sphere of activity, with the possibility of enormous profits, had opened for the brotherhood: narcotics. The demand for heroin, cocaine and marijuana had risen sharply in New York, Chicago, Los Angeles and other big cities, and was still rising. It was decided at the Chicago meeting that this was a market worth exploring and exploiting. The importation of illegal narcotics into the United States and their distribution involved foreign connections, skillful smuggling operations on a large scale and a tightly organized distributing setup. The brotherhood was eminently qualified in all three.

The subsequent organization and expansion of the illicit narcotics trade is undoubtedly the most insidious and destructive crime ever committed against the American people and their social structure.

After a year of intensive investigation in 1955 of the illegal narcotics traffic in the United States, a subcommittee of the Senate's Committee on the Judiciary presented a report to Congress which should have commanded the attention of the nation. It was a shocking indictment of the public's lethargy and the inertia of most of our legislatures and courts—federal, state, and local—toward one of our country's most serious and disgraceful social ills. It also pointed a finger directly at the Mafia.

Senator Price Daniel and four colleagues established the startling fact that in many of our cities addiction to narcotics is directly responsible for approximately one-half of all the crimes committed, and for roughly one-quarter of all reported crimes in the land. The Daniel Committee was not guessing. The first congressional group to undertake a nationwide survey of the problem, the legislators questioned more than 300 witnesses—ranging from law-enforcement officials and medical experts to dope peddlers and addicts. They also compiled the answers to their questionnaire of some 2,000 chiefs of police, sheriffs, prosecutors and judges. The resulting picture was very clear.

With the exception of gambling, the "junk business" is the American underworld's most lucrative organized racket, and it is certainly by far the wickedest. Addicts pay upward of $300,000,000 a year for heroin alone. (Heroin, the opium derivative most generally used by the American addict, is the most virulent and destructive of all the habit-forming narcotic drugs.) The large majority are under the age of 30; one in ten is under 21. Formerly concentrated among the underprivileged elements of the Negro, Puerto Rican, Mexican and Chinese communities of the big cities, addiction has gradually spread during the last ten years to an increasing number of smaller metropolitan areas and taken in youth of every race and condition.

The effect of heroin on addicts and the reason for its unfortunate popularity have been much misinterpreted. It is not a stimulant. It is actually, in medical language, a depressant. After sniffing the white powder through the nose or cooking it into a liquid and injecting it with a hypodermic needle into a vein, as advanced addicts do, the user goes into a state of luxurious lethargy. All tensions, all troubles are brushed away. When under the influence of the drug, the addict never commits a crime. He can't. He hasn't the energy or the desire. It is the reaction from the drug after its effect has worn off that causes the trouble. He has to have more and he will beg, borrow, steal, and even murder for it. The agonies of an addict forced or trying to get away from "the habit" are indescribably horrible. The expression, "kicking the habit," which means trying to break the addiction, has a very real meaning. One of the symptoms of withdrawal is an agonized kicking.

"Addiction is bad enough in itself," said Senator Daniel, "but with it goes crime—every kind of crime, committed to pay for the habit. Worst of all, this combination of addiction and crime is a very communicable disease." Over and over, testifying before the committee, police officers and addicts alike from cities all over the country told the same story.

In Philadelphia, attractive, 25-year-old June Gibbons gave the senators a detailed account of the seven years she had experienced since "a friend" had persuaded her to take the first dose of heroin. As the amount of the drug she needed increased, she turned first to shoplifting, then to prostitution. The cost of her habit gradually rose to $10 a day, then to $30. Finally she became a peddler of heroin herself, earning $60 a day when she was arrested. The senators wanted to know what sort of people her customers were. "One was a diamond setter," said Miss Gibbons. "Another had a dry goods store. Another worked in a formal rental—you know, they rent tuxedos and other formal wear. Another was a hairdresser." Senator Daniels wondered whether any of these people could pay the $140 a week which they needed as confirmed addicts out of honestly earned incomes. The witness shook her head. "Of course not," she said.

A Texas lawman, with particular eloquence, reported the male equivalent of June Gibbons' case. A boy of 19, of a decent family, was snared by a pusher who gave him a trial capsule of heroin free and taught him how to use it. Within a few weeks the boy was a confirmed addict, his craving for the drug rapidly increasing. At first, to pay for his habit, he began stealing from his own family. Then he took accessories off cars parked in the neighborhood and sold them. His costs were mounting toward $20 a day. He began stealing automobiles for a fence among the shady friends he had acquired. Finally arrested and sent to prison, he started his real criminal career. After his release he went on to burglaries, muggings, holdups. Only 27, he had become an incorrigible criminal fit only for the penitentiary. And along the way, as usual, he infected others. One was a hard-working, promising college student who became an embezzler to satisfy the craving his friend had taught him. Another was an attractive girl from a normal home who, like June Gibbons, turned to shoplifting and then prostitution. There were probably more, not known to the police.

Many thousands of such cases go into police department files all over the country every year. Details vary, but the fundamental pattern of the addict's creation and subsequent behavior is almost always the same. "We see this sort of thing every day," a Boston judge said to us. "So much so, that we take it for granted." In New York's Court of General Sessions, which tries the city's huge load of felony cases, every judge receives a complete report on the history and background of the defendant whom he is about to sentence. Accurate statistics are available as a result and show that at least 30 per cent of the city's robbers, burglars and other dangerous offenders are drug addicts. In the courts dealing with lesser criminals—pickpockets, shoplifters, petty forgers and the like—the percentage is considerably higher. The total shows one addict in every two criminals in the city of New York. (To satisfy their habits, they rob other New Yorkers, in one way or another, of no less than *$150,000 a day.*) Nor is this peculiar to our biggest metropolis. The head of the Houston, Texas, police informed the Daniel Committee that addicts in one year committed approximately 75 per cent of the city's serious burglaries and well over half of all offenses ranging from petty pilfering to automobile theft and armed robbery. Chicago, Detroit, Los Angeles, Cleveland, Philadelphia, San Antonio, Washington and 40 other city authorities reported similar situations.

The narcotics underworld from which this insidious, crime-creating poison flows comprises some 500 racketeers, many of them mafiosi, with an army of assistants and street peddlers under them. At the top are usually some 20 prime movers—concentrated in New York, with junior partners in Chicago and on the West Coast—who control the smuggling of illicit drugs from abroad and their distribution over the country. Almost all of these are mafiosi. They are known in the trade as "kilo-men" because they handle nothing less than a kilogram (approximately two pounds) of heroin at a time. The profits of the kilo-men are enormous. A New York "importer," for example, buys two pounds of almost pure heroin from his French supplier in Marseille or his Italian contact in Naples for $1,500. The courier who smuggles it into the United States gets $500 for his services. The "importer" then makes three pounds out of the two by adulterating the original heroin with milk sugar and sells the lot to a major "distributor" for around $18,000 at the present market. The "distributor" cuts the drug once more and makes a similar profit from smaller merchants in, perhaps, Detroit, Memphis and Oklahoma City. It is not unusual for a kilo-man to average an income of $100,000 or more a year. The mafiosi feel that this is worth taking chances for.

For one thing it makes possible the retaining of legal counsel of a caliber which can do extraordinary things. Niccolo Impastato, for example (born in Palermo in 1900, emigrated to the United States in 1927 without benefit of the usual immigration formalities) was arrested by agents of the Bureau of Narcotics in 1943 as second in command of the largest heroin syndicate then operating in the country. He was sentenced to two years. Shortly after his release the government's principal witness against him, Carolo Carramusa, was assassinated in Chicago by two blasts from a sawed-off shotgun. (Impastato's official underworld nickname was "Killer.") By 1951 Impastato's reputation had become such that the Bureau of Narcotics and the Department of Justice felt that his deportation was warranted. Through a series of legal maneuvers, his attorneys were able to hold up his expulsion for four years. And then, to cap the climax, two senators introduced a private bill (S. 212) before the 84th Congress in 1955 to prevent his deportation entirely. Fortunately, an excited Kansas City press, which had followed their principal gangster's activities for years, reached the national news wire services with such effect that the special legislation was killed in committee, and Impastato was sent back to Italy. But it was a near thing.

When Big Sam Accardi—also a mafioso from Sicily and Impastato's principal assistant—was arrested in 1955 in New Jersey for running the largest narcotic ring in that area, a federal judge set bail at $75,000. Bond was made immediately; Big Sam's credit was more than good enough with the local bondsmen to produce even that substantial sum, and he was promptly released. "The judge thought that seventy-five was enough to hold him," a federal narcotic agent on the case said wryly. "To somebody who has made as much as $50,000 in a month quite often, mostly tax free, that's not very much." Big Sam had plenty of time to make up his mind about what to do. The trial—although probably a year or more away—would, he knew, be rough on him. So, quite calmly, he decided to return to Italy. He obtained a passport under a false name—as so many mafiosi seem to be able to do without much difficulty—packed up his family and belongings, and went home. By the time that officers came looking for him in Newark he had been long established in southern Italy as an increasingly affluent manager of a chain of laundries which he had set up in partnership with another former American gangster. Being, in his way, an honest mafioso, he managed to pay back his bondsmen in Newark all of the $75,000 to which they had staked him. The Italian police see no reason to be angry with him; he is now a respectable Italian citizen, and will probably remain so.

Under the kilo-men are three more categories of traders—the quarter-kilo-men, the ounce-men and the deck-men—who cut and resell also with very large profits until the heroin is finally in the hands of the street peddler who dispenses a one-grain package for a dollar. The heroin, originally about 80 per cent pure, is now about 6 per cent pure. The total profit all down the line is approximately 50 times the cost of the original heroin in France or Italy. "They're not only the world's filthiest racketeers," as one police officer put it, "but the biggest gyps as well. And they sell their stinking poison in cold blood." For addiction among the mafiosi themselves is a serious offense and calls for immediate expulsion from the brotherhood.

Here, then, is the basic social and economic background of the Mafia's greatest single source of income. There is no question that the brotherhood is mainly responsible for the growth of this terrible social cancer. It also may be the fashioning of the Mafia's eventual doom through an outraged public opinion.

CHAPTER SIX

The Remarkable Mr. Anslinger

From here on the brotherhood had a fearless and relentless enemy.

From a modest office on the top floor of an elderly building on Pennsylvania Avenue in Washington, an unusual policeman directs a unique police force with duties not only all over the United States but around the globe. Harry Jacob Anslinger, commissioner of the Bureau of Narcotics of the United States Treasury Department, is a stocky, powerful man of 66. His Pennsylvania Dutch heritage shows in the broad face and the firm chin, the clear, shrewd eyes that can twinkle with humor and turn cold as ice. The voice is always measured, the speech precise. Four presidents and nine secretaries of the treasury have kept him at his job without interruption for almost 30 years. He has known the Mafia for almost as long, hates it and its works and has fought it with a methodical, unrelenting anger.The mafiosi return his sentiment and regard "that bastard Anslinger," as he is generally known in the underworld, as their principal and most effective enemy.

When President Herbert Hoover appointed him in 1930 as the first commissioner of narcotics, Harry Anslinger had already had a rather spectacular if anonymous career. After taking his law degree at the Washington College of Law, he set his sights for the Foreign Service, made it and was sent just before the close of World War I as an attaché—actually an intelligence officer—to the American Legation at The Hague. When Germany collapsed quite suddenly, our Legation in the Netherlands unexpectedly became the focal point of negotiations for the armistice and the fate of Kaiser Wilhelm II. The Legation was understaffed and young Anslinger abruptly found himself in the middle of a maelstrom of important and intricate international politics. He did so well, although he was only 26 and had little experience, that the State Department in its peculiar and unchanging way put him in its special category of people marked for unusual duty. In 1921 he was sent as vice consul—actually again as an intelligence agent—to the German port of Hamburg, where the postwar surge of Communism reached a bloody climax during his two years' tour. Anslinger's reports, in the opinion of State Department undersecretaries, were concise, clear and accurate. He never got excited, but he moved fast.

After Hamburg came jobs as consul in Venezuela and then Nassau, in the Bahamas. In the latter post Harry Anslinger again found an opportunity of using his peculiar talents. Nassau had become the largest transfer point for liquor from Europe bound for the Rum Rows along the Atlantic coast of the United States. It was also the teeming headquarters of gangster-smugglers—many of them mafiosi—that he was going to meet again, later, doing the same with narcotics. Anslinger couldn't help investigating. He was never actually in favor of the Prohibition laws; he found them foolish and dangerous. But enforcement was second nature to him. The intelligence system that he set up in Nassau to track the smuggling operations was so successful that the bootleggers suffered a major crisis and had to change their routes entirely. The Treasury Department was impressed and asked the State Department to loan Anslinger to them, temporarily. It was to become very permanent. He was made chief of the Treasury's Division of Foreign Control, which dealt with foreign governments in the suppression of smuggling of all kinds. In the meanwhile the rising traffic in narcotics from Europe was becoming a serious problem. At the suggestion of the Treasury Department, legislation was passed and the Bureau of Narcotics was created in 1930. Harry Anslinger became its first head.

"I knew right away that we had to have unusual men," the commissioner had said, "to deal with a peculiar and very agile type of criminal." His first 150 agents were handpicked by Anslinger himself and he has carefully ridden herd over their selection ever since. The requirements for appointment as an agent in any of the Treasury Department's enforcement services—Secret Service, Bureau of Narcotics, Alcohol and Tobacco Tax Division, Internal Revenue and Bureau of Customs—are very demanding. Character, background, education, prior legal or police experience must prove a man to be able to handle himself in any of the difficult situations which Treasury agents so frequently face. To this Anslinger has added a formula of his own. "We need all kinds," as he puts it, "and they all have to be good. We have to pick by feel."

A narcotic agent working in the field must be able to appear as a gangster himself on occasion, and convincingly if he is to stay alive. Undercover espionage in the underworld is one of the Bureau's most important operations—the most important, in fact. The agent has to command the jargon, the psychology, manners, habits, dress and attitudes of a dozen different criminal brackets. He must not only look and talk but also think as a racketeer when necessary. Many policemen work harder than the public realizes, but the Bureau of Narcotics is particularly demanding of its men. A Treasury Department directive puts the "description of work" this way: "Performance of duty may require work at irregular hours, involve personal risks, exposure to all kinds of weather, arduous physical exertion under rigorous and unusual environmental conditions, and considerable travel." The commissioner remarks that this is, in practice, an understatement.

Commissioner Anslinger is not a harsh taskmaster, but a compelling one in his own fashion. "He rarely tells you exactly what to do," a district supervisor has told me. "He gives you the general idea. The rest is up to you. He takes it for granted that you know your business and grasp what he wants. If you make a bad mistake, ball up important evidence or something, you get holy hell privately in a quiet sort of way. If you pull off something good, you get a blast of approval whether you're in San Francisco or Beirut. Sometimes he seems pretty far away. Actually he's right there all the time. We find that out. We like it."

There is very little turnover of personnel in the Bureau of Narcotics. One reason for this, perhaps, is the respect—occasionally almost awe—with which the narcotic agent has come to be regarded by other law-enforcement officers; even by the special agents of the majestic Federal Bureau of Investigation. The nine-pointed gold and blue enameled shield with AGENT, TREASURY DEPARTMENT, U.S., BUREAU OF NARCOTICS under the traditional eagle has become a badge of police aristocracy along with the venerable stars of the Secret Service and the postal inspectors, the oldest of the federal law enforcement agencies. Narcotics is as modest as its seniors. The Bureau, working at the very center of the underworld, often runs into information which involves cases outside its own jurisdiction—counterfeiting, extortion, labor racketeering, illegal gambling, as well as bank robbery, burglary and other crime. It has always been the commissioner's policy to quietly turn over such leads to the law agencies involved, federal and local. (This is, unfortunately, not common practice.) Even in its own field of narcotics prosecutions the Bureau, in hundreds of instances, has prepared a case with its usual meticulous thoroughness, handed it to local city or state officials to make the arrests, prosecute and get the credit while the federal men vanished from the picture before the newspapermen got there.

This was the small, compact force that was to meet the

Mafia head-on and first discover its character, size and power. Commissioner Anslinger knew very little of the brotherhood when the Bureau first began to feel its way into the new field. He had heard vague rumors of it during his Prohibition enforcement days but dismissed them as newspapermen's imaginings. "We knew that there were very powerful Italian gangs, of course. They seemed to have an extraordinary cohesion. But none of us were aware that they were predominantly Sicilian or what that meant. It took us a while to find that out. But we certainly did. We've gotten to know the mafiosi very well."

At the time that the capi mafiosi decided at their Chicago meeting to turn to narcotics on a large scale, the control of the traffic in New York, which was and still is its center, was mainly in the hands of a number of largely Jewish gangs in Greenwich Village, Brooklyn and the Bronx. The brotherhood in such cases applies an interesting philosophy and method of operation, typically Sicilian in their flexibility and ingenuity. It has a way of taking over prosperous groups of other racial or ethnic extraction almost without their knowing it. There was no forcible, gunpoint eviction which would have led to bloodshed and publicity. The formidable Sol Gelb and his associates, who controlled a large part of the New York market, found themselves surrounded by a number of very friendly, quite humble Sicilians who had money to invest in occasional deals. The Sicilians proved themselves to be financially reliable to the penny, extraordinarily discreet, invariably fair by underworld standards, with an amazing discipline in the police station and the court. It was a very gradual, cautious, thorough process. But the underworld noticed that more and more foreign sources and outlets in this country were coming under the control of such mafiosi as Lucky Luciano, who until this time had been primarily interested in organized prostitution. As the Bureau's growing intelligence system gradually penetrated the workings of the narcotics traffic, Commissioner Anslinger began to perceive a pattern. The Bureau started its special file on the Mafia, which now consists of more than a dozen closely guarded large folder books on the general background, and hundreds of others on the individual members.

Grimly, doggedly the commissioner and his dedicated men fought on against discouraging odds. He warned and pleaded at every session of Congress. Some state and municipal authorities awakened slowly under his personal prodding and began to take some of the burden of battling the army of street peddlers and minor merchants from the Bureau's shoulders, allowing it to concentrate on cutting the traffic's big arteries. The biggest stumbling blocks in the commissioner's way were the federal laws and courts themselves. The Boggs Act of 1951 finally stiffened the archaic Harrison Narcotic Act of 1914 to the point of authorizing a sentence of from two to five years for a seller of narcotics for his first offense. "When you think," the commissioner once said to me, "that a man who robs a United States post office almost automatically gets fifteen or twenty years, this doesn't seem to make much sense. An armed robber may jeopardize the lives of a few people for a few minutes. The narcotics seller literally murders hundreds on the instalment plan." And the general attitude of the federal courts made even the comparatively mild provisions of the Boggs Act hard to enforce.

One case the commissioner will probably not forget was that of Joseph Bearer, a member of a syndicate of mafiosi in New York, with four narcotics convictions under the wrist-slapping Harrison Act on his record. He left LaGuardia Airport—this was in 1951—for Washington, D.C. with a quarter of a million dollars' worth of heroin in his suitcase. A kilo-man, he rarely carried contraband himself, but this was an emergency. A Washington gang wanted "junk" urgently, no courier was available, and the buyers offered a high price. An informer notified the New York office of the Bureau of Narcotics, word was flashed to the capital and Mr. Bearer was met by agents at Washington Airport. Having had no time to obtain a search warrant from a local federal judge, Anslinger's men had to ask the gangster most politely whether he would open his baggage for inspection. Bearer did some fast and skillful legal thinking. He could refuse to submit to a search and walk away. But he knew also that the agents would follow him, make his delivery impossible, might obtain a warrant in the meantime and arrest him. If he agreed to the search, he would lose the heroin but would, himself, be almost certainly safe from prosecution. He took the latter course; and he was right. A federal judge held, a few days later, that Bearer—despite his consent—had been illegally searched and that the heroin found in his possession could not be used as evidence against him. He was released.

Decisions of the U.S. Supreme Court inadvertently made the task of a narcotic agent in organizing a case a more and more complicated legal maneuver. He could not use wiretapping under any circumstances, even to develop leads. He could not search or arrest without a warrant, of course, and such warrants were extremely difficult to obtain. The agent had to swear before a federal judge that the suspect to be arrested or searched had actually sold narcotics to him, and that he had seen evidence that the suspect had more to sell. Worst of all, many judges in trying narcotic trading cases seemed so frightened of reversal by a higher court that they acted more like defense counsels than magistrates.

The trial of Wady David—front man for a group of the brotherhood who controlled the traffic in New England—in the federal court of Boston, Massachusetts, in 1955 was an example. For 15 months the Boston office of the Bureau of Narcotics had been working to make a case against David and had finally been able to arrest him in the act of selling heroin. The proof against him was airtight and U.S. Attorney Koen asked for the maximum penalty under the Boggs Act—a total of ten years under two counts (possession and selling) of five years each. The trial judge was Charles E. Wyzanski, Jr.—an overseer of Harvard University, a trustee of the Ford

Foundation and considered one of the most brilliant legal minds in the country. In sentencing David to three years' imprisonment, Judge Wyzanski made the following extraordinary statement: "While I in no sense look on this as a trivial offense," he said, "it is to me exactly the same as bootlegging except instead of liquor it happens to be in drugs, and I have no more moral view with respect to drugs than with respect to liquor." The judge was and is a very sincere and dedicated man. He simply did not know about narcotics.

Many other federal judges had similar attitudes. They seemed to fail in differentiating between the addict—always a pathetic creature who belongs in a hospital rather than in prison—and the merchant of narcotics, who definitely does belong in jail. Even under the Boggs Act, the chances were that if a big heroin merchant were caught he would get no more than two years as a first offender, and probably serve little more than half of that before being paroled. He rarely was caught again. Not that he stopped trafficking; he simply used front men who had no prior record to sell for him. If they were arrested, they were merely first offenders and were treated accordingly. In New York City, the fountainhead of the whole traffic, where judges should have been particularly aware of its viciousness, only 28 of the 1,120 narcotics sellers convicted in federal courts over 18 years received sentences of more than five years. That made their chances pretty good, and the mafiosi were very happy about the whole thing. No sooner had Anslinger's agents found and broken up one combine when another would take its place. The U.S. Customs Service, which has always worked very closely with the Bureau of Narcotics, was hopelessly understaffed for the job of stopping the actual smuggling of narcotics off ships and planes.

In all of this the public displayed little interest or understanding. Smuggling meant bringing in furs, jewels or paintings from abroad, and as far as crime stories were concerned, newspaper editors found the neatly wrapped up descriptions of bank robberies and kidnapings solved by the FBI much more readable copy than the complicated business of Anslinger's Bureau with all its ramifications. The commissioner has always had a peculiar and difficult problem with his public relations. An extremely modest man, he hates personal publicity with a sincerity rare in Washington. He cringes when a newspaperman uses the phrase "super-sleuth" or anything similar to describe him. His interviews with newsmen are very few and always very short. "They'd love to make a Dick Tracy out of me," he says disgustedly. "Well —I won't have it. We get our work done without it." Even stronger than this personal feeling is his conviction that the narcotics problem in the United States must be presented to the people in only the most sober, factual way. "Any sensational treatment by the movies, on television or in the press just makes more addicts. We know that." Countless movie companies and TV producers have approached the commissioner with propositions for glamorizing the narcotic agent and his job. He turns dour and the answer is always an emphatic *no.*

Commissioner Anslinger from the start tried to choke off the sources of the flow of narcotics by agreements with the governments of the various European and Middle Eastern countries from which most of it came. In 1931 he went as the United States delegate to the opium conference in Geneva to sign an international convention that was to limit the manufacture of narcotic drugs to the legitimate needs of the medical professions of the various countries. In the following years, as an observer in the League of Nations Opium Advisory Committee, he succeeded in negotiating direct arrangements with a number of governments. He was to learn that such a treaty is worth precisely as much as the will of its parties to observe it. France and Italy for example, which were among the main manufacturers, had negligible addiction in their own countries. Publicly they had to make gestures of morality and international cooperation, but actually they had little interest in making life difficult for the narcotics smugglers. If the Americans were fools enough to want to buy the poison, why shouldn't they? The taxes from the chemical companies were welcome and so were the dollars. This was the general attitude of the French and Italian police which Commissioner Anslinger by tireless effort over many years has only recently been able to change. The Balkan and Middle Eastern poppy-growing countries—Yugoslavia, Bulgaria, Turkey, Syria, Lebanon, Iran, India—which produced the crude morphine base that was converted into heroin and other drugs by the Italians and French felt the same way.

With the coming of World War II, the disruption of communications and transportation stopped the brotherhood's operations in their tracks. The mafiosi turned temporarily and with typical flexibility to the black market, the counterfeiting of ration stamps and the various other kinds of criminal activity that flourished during wartime. The Bureau's agents, with their unusual abilities, experience and languages, were in great demand by the military intelligence and military police organizations; many of them went into uniform, and the Bureau marked time for the next few years. Commissioner Anslinger suspected that this interlude would not last much longer than the war, and that afterward he would have redoubled difficulties. He was right. Within little more than a year after the end of the global hostilities, the conflict between the Bureau and the Mafia had begun again on a more massive scale than ever. A new factor entered the struggle. Don Salvatore Lucania went abroad. Probably the shrewdest and most imaginative of the big organizers of the American underworld after Al Capone, a capo mafioso of the highest rank born in Sicily of an old Mafia family, Charlie "Lucky" Luciano—as he preferred to be known—began an internationally organized narcotics attack against the United States which dwarfed everything that had gone before.

CHAPTER SEVEN

The Versatile Don Salvatore Lucania

The strange man who was and still is Commissioner Anslinger's most powerful foe.

On a cold February evening in 1946, the S.S. *Laura Keene,* a tired Liberty ship, was making ready to sail from New York for Italy. It was a historic evening for the brotherhood, one which no one who witnessed it will ever forget. Charlie Lucky Luciano, former overlord of New York City's rackets and organized vice, was being deported by the United States government. No departure of royalty could have been more impressive. In front of the entrance to the pier in Brooklyn at which the *Laura Keene* was berthed stood a double row of burly longshoremen shoulder to shoulder with bailing hooks hanging like policemen's sidearms from their belts; they were the guard of honor. When Charlie Lucky arrived he was surrounded by a phalanx of agents of the Bureau of Immigration and Naturalization who had brought him over from Ellis Island, where he had been held for several days. It seemed that the heavy federal bodyguard was there more to protect him from the press than to prevent his escape. The big longshoremen scanned the official party, permitted it to pass. There were shouts of "You'll be back, Lucky"—"You keep punchin', boss." Then the ranks closed again to prevent newsmen from following.

What happened during the next few hours before the ship sailed still seems incredible. Big cars kept arriving with members of the top echelon of the brotherhood. Their bodyguards lugged out great baskets of wine and delicacies which grinning stevedores wheeled carefully onto the pier. Frank Costello and Albert Anastasia came to pay their respects to Don Salvatore and wish their old *compadre* well. There were others of almost equal underworld rank including prominent Mafia satellites such as Meyer Lansky, the great gambling organizer, and Joseph (Socks) Lanza, boss of the Fulton Fish Market and the Lower East Side docks. Tammany Hall was also prominently represented. The party aboard—with champagne, caviar and lobster, as reported by a federal agent—was very gay, while the longshoremen and their bailing hooks, city police and dock patrolmen kept newsmen and all others at bay. Finally the *Laura Keene* blew her whistle, an impressive group of cheerful gangsters gathered on the pier to wave and shout a last good-by and Don Salvatore was on his way to Italy, a new life and, supposedly, oblivion.

From Washington the infinitely patient Commissioner Anslinger had watched the whole bizarre business of Charlie Lucky's parole and deportation with misgivings. Don Salvatore, even after nine years in prison, was obviously still a capo mafioso of great influence. The files of the Bureau of Narcotics on important criminals are unusual in their attention to basic traits of character. From the record the commissioner was pretty sure that he would hear from Charlie Lucky again.

The early career of the extraordinary gangster who was second only to Al Capone in organizational genius has been told many times with varying degrees of accuracy. But in even the most factual, well-informed accounts he has never been shown as the mafioso of the purest water which he is. He is and always has been the personification of the brotherhood of evil, in American dress, with all of its ruthlessness, savage cruelty, sentimentality and peculiarly twisted ideology toward God and man. He is a modern mafioso—like Adonis, Costello and the rest. But he might as well have lived in Sicily a hundred years ago—as might all of his old friends who were snared at Apalachin.

Salvatore Lucania was born in 1897 in the little Sicilian town of Lercara Friddi near Palermo. His father, Antonio, was a hard working, thrifty laborer in the sulphur pits close by. When Salvatore was nine, Antonio Lucania had saved enough to realize his ambition of years—America. By the time he was ten, young Salvatore was on the streets in the toughest section of New York City, the Lower East Side around Brooklyn Bridge. The teeming tenement district where hundreds of thousands of recent immigrants huddled in poverty and squalor was the city's center of vice and crime. Both of the boy's parents worked long hours and had little time for him, he disliked school intensely, was often a truant and a criminal career began. At 15 he was already a petty thief, an expert gang fighter with knife and stone and chief runner for an important narcotic peddler. He was caught delivering a parcel of heroin and served six months of a year's sentence in jail. This made him eligible for underworld promotion. He applied to the Five Point Gang which terrorized Little Italy around Mulberry Street, for admission. They had been watching him. Young Lucania was small for his age, with delicate hands and feet, but he was very quick, shrewd, hard and always seemed to use his head. His application was accepted.

From here on, others far more important began to watch Salvatore Lucania. One in particular, a capo mafioso named Giuseppe Masseria, saw the young man's possibilities and qualifications. First of all, he was born in Sicily, and this is still important in the brotherhood's upper echelon. Various reporters have written that this tradition has long since been wiped out; that the old "mustache Petes" have disappeared. This is not true, as the Apalachin meeting conclusively proves. They don't wear handlebar mustaches any more, but the mentality of the mafiosi has not changed a bit. To this day they regard the *paesano*—the fellow countryman—as the most reliable associate. Secondly, young Salvatore had convincingly demonstrated on many occasions the cardinal virtues of the true mafioso: he had an iron self-control. No matter what the provocation or the emergency, the hoarse voice never rose in pitch; the cold, seemingly unblinking eyes showed no emotion whatever. The sensitive hands might flutter slightly, but that was all. Always penetratingly alert to the emotional reactions of others, he was an underworld diplomat of the first order who believed in using brains and mediation first, guns only when absolutely necessary. Even as a junior member of the Five Pointers he had been able to calm down the explosive young hoodlums, and the older ones as well, who liked a fight for the battle's sake, and without seeming to, had begun to guide them into disciplined and lucrative racketeering.

By the early 1920's, Salvatore Lucania had emerged as Giuseppe Masseria's chief of staff and, at a remarkably early age, a power to be reckoned with in the grand council of the brotherhood in New York. A few bloody years followed, as in Chicago, while the bootlegging empire of the eastern seaboard was being organized. After at least a hundred murders and untold mayhem of various kinds, Giuseppe Masseria was established as the area's principal capo mafioso and Lucania as his crown prince. It was a powerful team. The squat, crude, older man with little pig's eyes, who could consume three heaping platters of spaghetti at one sitting, had great seniority in the brotherhood and a fearsome reputation for ruthless and efficient killing that went back to 1905. Young Salvatore became his brains, his memory and his constant companion—but always, as far as the police and public were concerned, in the shadows. Very few, even in the underworld's upper reaches, knew of the great influence that he was beginning to exert on the New York mafiosi's thinking and operations. Like Al Capone, he was a businessman of crime and a superb executive. He had the same sense of tidy organization and orderly chain of command. But unlike the noisy Neapolitan, the basically austere Sicilian preferred anonymity—not only for business reasons but from personal preference.

With the weight of Don Giuseppe Masseria's influence behind him and his own uninhibited imagination, he—again like Capone in Chicago—started a gradual expansion of the brotherhood's activities from bootlegging into other fields which he also sensed would remain after the inevitable end of Prohibition. He had two friends who were also growing powerful, Joe Adonis and Albert Anastasia, the coming boss of Murder, Incorporated. The three Sicilians had all sorts of projects for organized gambling, a chain of brothels, large-scale narcotics peddling, "protection" extortion on New York's docks, in the garment industry and the big food markets. The aging capo, Masseria, didn't like it. He thought that the boys were going too far too fast and said so with all the authority of a don. They refused to obey and he began putting obstacles in their way. The inevitable happened.

An ancient rule of the brotherhood requires a capo mafioso to step down when age impairs his initiative. If he retires gracefully, as many have, he can look forward to a peaceful twilight of life with the position of a respected elder statesman who is consulted by the new executives and often acts as impartial arbitrator in their disputes. If he does not withdraw voluntarily, he is traditionally given one warning—the assassination, generally, of a minor assistant. Don Giuseppe had his late in 1930 when one of his bodyguards was cut down in an ambush from which he himself could not have escaped if his death had been decreed. But the capo was stubborn; he had no intention of laying down the reins. One day in April 1931, therefore, Charlie Lucky invited him to dinner at Scarpato's, an excellent Italian restaurant in Coney Island. The capo liked plenty of food and wine; it was late before they finished and the dining room was almost empty. Charlie

Lucky went to wash his hands. He was unquestionably and provably in the men's room when three men materialized behind the tiddly don's chair, methodically emptied their revolvers into him and as rapidly disappeared. By the time Lucania dashed out, as he told the police a few minutes later, the killers were gone and his beloved old patron was very dead. None of the restaurant's staff could give even the vaguest description of the men. All they did know, and very definitely, was that Mr. Lucania had been in the washroom. It was the perfect example of a Mafia execution carried out in the traditional manner. By ancient custom a ranking mafioso when condemned by his own brotherhood must be killed, if at all possible, humanely and unexpectedly, and preferably after plenty of food and wine. It has always been so, and still is.

Salvatore Lucania by succession was now a capo mafioso of the first class. His extraordinary rise to racketeering and political power during the next years was less spectacular than that of Capone in Chicago had been, but it was more careful and thorough. With the flexibility of a new generation of mafiosi which had grown out of American influences on the brotherhood's original exclusiveness, Charles Luciano, as he now began to call himself, realized that he had to work out a system of peaceful coexistence with the non-Italian gangs of New York; until they could be subjugated or suppressed, that is. Various reporters who have written about the brotherhood believe that the Mafia as such came to an end during this period; that its membership became simply a part of a nationwide syndicate of criminals of all races and kinds. This seems, on the basis of much evidence, an incorrect assumption. The story of organized crime in the United States from Luciano through the Apalachin meeting up to this writing indicates that the brotherhood has not deviated from its essential principles by a degree. Capone and Luciano changed its methods, modernized them, but basically Salvatore Lucania was just as much of a mafioso as Giuseppe Masseria of the previous generation.

Before long Charlie Luciano had working arrangements not only with his fellow mafiosi, but also with such un-Sicilian associates as Louis (Lepke) Buchalter, dictator of the garment center rackets; Meyer Lansky of New York gambling; Longy Zwillman of various New Jersey gangs and very powerful; the Scalici brothers of the Brooklyn docks (they were Sicilians) and others. It was the first of the big racket syndicates perfected by Luciano in the post-Capone period. Its members quickly realized the advantages of this sort of arrangement and subscribed to it. In New York the destructive internecine warfare stopped abruptly. The idea of large-scale underworld communications and consultations, with their economic dividends—developed by Al Capone and worked into a permanent pattern by Salvatore Lucania—spread through the country's racket combines from coast to coast. Meetings of gang leaders not only of states but from whole sections of the nation became increasingly frequent; so did long distance telephone calls, as recent investigations have shown.

Many writers have lumped these groups together and called them The National Syndicate or just The Syndicate. Actually, what Capone and Lucania inspired by their examples is a number of syndicates, all continually in touch with each other. On careful examination, one finds that almost every one of them is either dominated or strongly influenced by a group of mafiosi. Senator Estes Kefauver after many months of investigation wrote that "the Mafia is the cement that binds organized crime." And the men who perfected this peculiar kind of cement were Capone and Lucania.

Salvatore Lucania made another important contribution to the top bracket of the brotherhood and its associates. He radically changed their dress and their manners. He became the underworld's exemplary Beau Brummel, in a quiet way. His suits were conservative and well tailored; his shirts, ties, shoes and accessories were expensive but not ostentatious. The wide-brimmed fedoras and odd overcoats which had been the mafioso's uniform for so long had already begun to disappear, and the quietly elegant Mr. Luciano carried the trend further. Everybody who worked for him, as he is reported to have once said to his immediate staff, "has to look legit." This precept has been maintained by the brotherhood ever since. He influenced the brotherhood's manners in the same way. Under his chairmanship a meeting of the heads of various cartels at the Waldorf Astoria—where, as Mr. Charles Ross, he lived for a number of years in an apartment suite—became a far more austere gathering than a convention of industrial executives in the same hotel might have been.

The detailed story of the rise and fall of Charlie Lucky Luciano—his nickname stems from his extraordinary luck in gambling with cards and horses—has been told so often that only the barest chronology of it seems necessary here.

By 1935, "Mr. Charles Ross" in his elaborate headquarters in the Waldorf Astoria was one of the most powerful capi mafiosi which the brotherhood has ever produced. He was master of the most lucrative of the New York rackets. No gambling operation, no important dock or garment extortion could be organized without his permission and a provision for his cut. He had ironclad protection from Tammany Hall which extended from New York City to Albany. Frequently, members of the New York judiciary and sachems from the Hall would attend his morning levees, which, as the hotel staff later testified, had a regal air. Don Salvatore had reached the pinnacle. He might have stayed there for quite a while had he not made, despite all his caution and perspicacity, two very serious mistakes.

Prostitution has been a specialty of the Sicilian brotherhood for two centuries. It is regarded by the mafiosi as a business as inevitable and reliable as that of the mortician, in which they have always been interested. Charlie Lucky as a youngster on the Lower East Side had been, besides thief and narcotics runner, a messenger and solicitor for a number of brothels. He had learned the business from the ground up, its economics and personnel problems. As he rose to the New York overlordship, he realized that organized prostitution could earn almost as much as gambling, narcotics or extortion. With three stalwart mafiosi as field generals, he put together the largest combine of brothels in the history of this or probably any other country. At the height of its operation, more than 200 madams and well over 1,000 girls were paying tribute to Charlie Lucky's organization from a business which grossed approximately $10,000,000 a year. Charlie Lucky, however, was too greedy. The madams had to pay too much for protection, and the girls had little take-home money. The strong-arm methods of Davey Betillo—Charlie Lucky's executive officer for this division—which produced brutal beatings and slashings for the slightest defection or failure to pay was finally more than the girls could take, and rebellion began to simmer. "Mr. Ross" in his luxurious eyrie at the Waldorf, surrounded by obsequious assistants, did not sense the growing unrest and its menace. "Whores is whores," he said on one occasion over a tapped telephone. "They can always be handled. They ain't got no guts." This was his first mistake.

Charlie Lucky liked the company of prostitutes and constantly had them in his entourage. That was his second mistake. He regarded all of them as "dumb broads" and thought nothing of making telephone calls and conducting business with his assistants in their presence. Unfortunately for him, several women like Nancy Presser, Cokey Flo Brown and Mildred Harris were neither stupid nor without courage. He had abused them all, finally, with contempt. Their peculiar prostitute's pride was offended. They all had excellent memories.

In 1935 New York City went through one of its infrequent revulsions against chronically inefficient and dishonest government. A special grand jury brushed aside the regular district attorney and demanded a special prosecutor. Thomas E. Dewey was appointed. He soon found that Charlie Lucky Luciano was his main objective; that almost all of New York's organized crime stemmed from the sleek, apparently untouchable Mr. Ross of the Waldorf. Dewey's brilliant investigation and prosecution of the great capo mafioso is history. Charles Lucania was indicted for the crime of compulsory prostitution, tried in General Sessions Court and found guilty on sixty-two counts. The prostitutes that Charlie Lucky had regarded as such harmless trash were superbly convincing witnesses. Dewey could also have prosecuted for narcotics trading and extortion on a huge scale, but the white slavery charge was the easiest to prove, aroused the greatest public indignation and would bring the most severe penalty. Before pronouncing sentence Judge McCook fastened the cool, immaculate don with his eyes. "You are," he said quietly but with venom, "one of the most vicious criminals that has ever been brought before this court. It is the sentence of this court . . . 30 to 50 years. . . ." The judge thought that he was handing down the equivalent of a sentence for life. He did not reckon with the don's ingenuity, lawyers, connections—or his position as a capo mafioso.

Charlie Lucky disappeared from public view in the State Penitentiary at Dannemora, a maximum security prison known to New York felons as "Siberia." It is an interesting fact that a big-time racketeer maintains his prestige and certain privileges even behind the walls. Many chores are done for him by fellow convicts, he becomes an arbiter of disputes, his advice far more sought than that of the chaplain. "He practically ran the place," a guard who saw much of Charlie Lucky told us once. "He used to stand there in the yard like he was the warden. Men waited in line to talk to him. Charlie Lucky would listen, say something and then wave his hand. The guy would actually *back* away. It was something to watch. The real mob boys when they were about to be discharged would always have a last talk with the Boss, as they all called him. He was sort of philosophical about the whole thing. He thought he was going to be there for a long time and tried to make the best of it." The coming of World War II did not excite Charlie Lucky. He had no idea of what it was going to do for him or that it was going to make him, at least for a while, an asset to the United States government.

The value of Don Salvatore's war effort has been the subject of much controversy. Some writers have claimed that it was outstanding, others that it was negligible. The truth seems to lie in between.

In 1942 an unusual group of men gathered in the headquarters of the Bureau of Naval Intelligence for the 3rd Naval District, which covered New York, New Jersey and the largest and most important eastern seaports. Among them were former prosecutors, FBI and Treasury agents, city detectives—all handpicked for the almost superhuman job of protecting the miles of docks which were the anchor of our lifeline to Europe, and of stifling the sources of information which Hitler's intelligence services had set up in the New York area. Sabotage on the piers was increasing. The huge French liner *Normandie,* which was being converted into a troopship capable of carrying an entire division, burned and sank at her Manhattan berth. Accurate information on sailing dates and cargoes of ships leaving New York was reaching the cordon of German submarines which then virtually controlled the eastern seaboard and sank our and British shipping almost at will. At a meeting of the harassed Naval Intelligence staff at 90 Church Street one day, someone advanced the idea of enlisting the tightly organized New York-New Jersey dock underworld in the struggle. The Annapolis men present thought it unorthodox and dangerous. The professional police officers saw the possibilities at once. No force could patrol the vulnerable piers and ships as effectively as the tough, alert longshoremen, truckers and watchmen who knew every inch of them. The waterfront prostitutes and their pimps could be a counter-intelligence corps, if properly organized, of the first order. An unusually shrewd and courageous officer, the late Lieutenant Commander Charles Haffenden, USNR, appointed himself coordinator of the whole extraordinary operation.

It was not easy to pick an underworld autocrat of the caliber that the Navy needed. He had to be a patriotic, reliable crook. Haffenden and his staff finally chose Joseph (Socks) Lanza, an immensely energetic organizer whose predominantly Italian gangs controlled the huge Fulton Fish Market and the docks on Manhattan's Lower East Side. Lanza, who was under indictment at the time for extortion, accepted and proceeded to do an excellent job. Longshoremen, under orders from Lanza, became among the Navy's most vigilant patrolmen and agents. The fishermen who supplied the market and knew the offshore waters as only they can, formed a first-class observer corps. The organization was so successful that Haffenden wanted to expand it to the critical piers of Brooklyn, the West Side of Manhattan and Jersey across the Hudson. Here, however, the planners at 90 Church Street ran into a wall of underworld suspicion and resistance. Even Lanza, with all his power and connections, was unable to breach it. The racketeers in control, many of them mafiosi, regarded the Navy—war or no war, and despite the fact that they hated Mussolini—as part of government and law, and therefore anathema. Lanza had a suggestion. There was only one man who had sufficient authority to solve the problem—and that was Charlie Lucky Luciano. The more conservative elements at 90 Church Street had misgivings, to say the least. The idea of the United States Navy approaching the exwhoremaster-general of New York—in prison at that—seemed too fantastic. It was done nevertheless.

Most of the details of what happened from here on are still classified information in unapproachable Pentagon files. An angry Senator Estes Kefauver, with all the authority of a congressional investigating committee behind him, tried to get at the facts in 1951. He had little success. The Navy, members of District Attorney Hogan's office and everybody else who really knew anything were and remain vague for a good reason. It was a very embarrassing business.

The main features of the story are clear enough. At the Navy's request, Charlie Lucky was suddenly transferred from Dannemora, in the farthest corner of New York State, to the equally secure but more accessible Great Meadows Penitentiary just north of Albany. Every few weeks a small group of naval officers in civilian clothes headed by his old friend and lawyer, Moses Polakoff, would go to visit him. These conferences were arranged with utmost caution and secrecy. Various writers have published quotes from the conversations—all entirely spurious. But there is no doubt that Charlie Lucky unlocked doors for 90 Church Street. A few words from the capo mafioso to such mighty *compadri* as Joe Adonis, Vincenzo Mangano—dictator of the Brooklyn docks—and Albert Anastasia of Murder, Inc. would have brought immediate compliance. Most of these messages were probably carried by Counselor Polakoff, who has long occupied a unique position of trust among New York's racketeers, having defended the most prominent of them over three decades. Others went out over the extraordinary communications system which powerful gangsters seem to be able to maintain with the outside in even the most closely guarded prison. The details are conjecture and always will be. In any case, the arrangement seems to have been effective. There was surprisingly little sabotage or any other trouble on the docks of the 3d Naval District during the remainder of the war. Various Nazi intelligence officers interrogated in Germany after the war, incidentally, commented on the extreme difficulty which their agents had in doing any damage in New York at all. They had thought that the teeming port would be an easy sabotage target, with plenty of American *Bund* members to place incendiaries and delayed-action bombs. It wasn't. According to the German chiefs, some of whom we interrogated, their men were discouraged by the vigilance of a very tough and violent, as they put it with amazement, group of Italians.

Don Salvatore's contribution to our invasion of Sicily, on the other hand, was probably negligible. The details, again, are buried in the Navy's "red files." But it is a safe assumption that he would not have been trusted with even the slightest intimation of our war plans. The Sicilian Mafia, as it happened, was of solid assistance to our forces. They supplied reliable fishermen as scouts, skilled and secure villains of every kind, "safe houses" from which advance agents could work. But the capi mafiosi of New York had nothing to do with it.

In 1945, counselors Polakoff and Wolf brought the case of Charles Lucania before the New York State Parole Board. It was a long and difficult hearing. The witnesses—racketeers, law officers, lawyers and Charlie Lucky himself alike—were all amazingly mute when it came to details. Finally, however, the board came to several conclusions. Charles Lucania had definitely made a contribution to the war effort. It was customary in New York to deport a criminal alien after he had served a substantial part of his sentence, and that under the circumstances nine years should be regarded as such. And finally, the board thought, Charlie Lucky exiled to Italy for life could do no further damage to the United States. Governor Dewey, although as district attorney he had convicted Charlie Lucky in the first place and should have known his character as well as anyone, concurred. The governor granted parole and the federal authorities ordered deportation. Charlie Lucky, like many mafiosi, had never bothered to become an American citizen.

In thinking that Don Salvatore could do no more damage, however, the Parole Board and the governor were very much mistaken. In Italy, the don behaved himself very quietly at first. He was properly deferential to the Italian police who ostentatiously ordered him at once to his birthplace at Lercara Friddi, where he was welcomed as a returning hero.

There are reports in the files of the Rome Questura of the exuberant celebration which drew mafiosi from all over Sicily to drink to the health and success of the don. Luciano stayed in the dusty little town for only a few weeks, however; he had no intention of becoming a Sicilian country squire. Government palms were crossed with dollars and before long Don Salvatore installed himself with the full approval of the Questura in a modern apartment on the banks of the Tiber in Rome.

The attitude of most of the Italian police toward Don Salvatore has, essentially, been much the same ever since. "What real crime has he ever committed?" an irritated questore once shouted at us. He brandished a sheet of paper. "Look. Here is his FBI record in America. As a boy he is once arrested for selling narcotics—just a little bit. Then nothing, for years. Then this outrageous sentence for compulsory prostitution. What is compulsory prostitution, I ask you? There is no such thing. A woman is a prostitute because she wants to be. This Lucania was simply catering to popular demand. I see no wrong in that." We tried to point out that conditions and mores in the United States are somewhat different from those in Italy; also that Charlie Lucky had committed and instigated many crimes of other kinds. "You have proved no others," snapped the questore. "As far as I am concerned he is an innocent and persecuted man. If he commits a crime under Italian law, we will arrest him. But why should I plague myself with American problems?" he concluded, shrugging his shoulders.

Barely a year after Charles Luciano was deported from New York, a Salvatore Lucania arrived by air in Havana, Cuba. His Italian passport and Cuban visa were in perfect order. Preparatory to finding a suitable house, he rented the penthouse suite of one of Havana's finest new hotels, paid several months' rent and proceeded to make a series of telephone calls to New York and other cities in the United States. An impressive list of capi mafiosi headed by Joe Adonis (he had not yet been deported to Italy) and satellites such as Meyer Lansky began to appear in the Cuban capital. At the same time Charlie Lucky, with his usual foresight and skill, was entrenching himself in Cuban politics. Legislators, judges, police chiefs came to Signor Lucania's elaborate and carefully organized parties; they and their wives received expensive presents from an always open hand. It looked as though Signor Lucania was on the way to becoming a power in Cuba.

Unfortunately for Charlie Lucky, Commissioner Anslinger in Washington was watching every move. Two narcotic agents had been dispatched to Havana and several employees of the Hotel Nacional were temporarily on the Treasury Department's payroll—an elevator man and a telephone operator among others. The Bureau had good sources of information in Rome which had reported Charlie Lucky's departure for Cuba. They had reason to believe that before leaving Italy he had set up an extensive organization in that country to smuggle narcotics into Cuba which he would then send to the United States. Anslinger proceeded to play a waiting game, to find out as much as possible about his contacts and method of operation.

The plan was almost wrecked by an incident which produced one of the more amusing reports in the Bureau's somber files. A well known Broadway and Hollywood star, an old friend of Charlie Lucky's, went to Havana to see him. The don gave a party in his apartment to celebrate the reunion, which lasted late and grew somewhat abandoned. Early the next morning a terrible thing happened. A group of Girl Scouts, well scrubbed and enthusiastic, arrived at the hotel to see the star, who was one of their idols at the time, and get his autograph. His arrival had been announced in the morning papers. Somehow, through a series of disastrous mistakes by various personnel, the eager girls, shepherded by a nun, were herded into an elevator and taken up to the penthouse. A door was ajar. Beyond it was rather ribald chaos.

There were bottles on the floor, lingerie hung from wall brackets and a number of people lay sleeping where they had collapsed. The Scouts were marched back into the elevator very quickly by their white-faced leader. The sister reported at once to her mother superior, the mother superior to her bishop. Frenzied narcotic agents reported to Washington that there would undoubtedly be publicity which would ruin all their schemes. Publicity, by almost superhuman effort of the Bureau, was suppressed, Charlie Lucky never knew of the early morning visitation, and the surveillance continued.

The Cuban press eventually of course discovered who the wealthy and generous Signor Lucania was and the news was sensational. But the public reaction was not what Commissioner Anslinger expected. No one seemed disturbed by Charlie Lucky's presence on the island. Quite the contrary. By this time Anslinger had found out everything he wanted to know, realized that the first big shipments of narcotics via Cuba to the United States had been organized and now wanted the channel blocked.

When the Bureau of Narcotics informed the Cuban government through the State Department that they would appreciate his being sent back to Italy, there was considerable indignation. The Havana authorities demurred. It finally took the combined pressure of the State and Treasury departments to persuade them that Charlie Lucky would be a constant source of embarrassment between the two governments. But it was not until Washington threatened to cut off the shipment of all legitimate medical narcotics that the Cuban government at last reluctantly took action. When a polite squad of detectives of the Cuban Federal Police arrested him Luciano showed, as usual, no emotion at all. "Be seeing ya," he said curtly to his two bodyguards, who had been eating with him, and departed ringed by policemen. A few weeks later he was on a ship back to Italy.

The failure of the Cuban venture was a heavy blow to Don Salvatore and the other members of the brotherhood who had

The Barbara estate, scene of the Apalachin conference. The barbecue pit can be seen between the summer house (lower left) and the garage.

UPI

Vito Genovese, one of the leading figures at the Apalachin meeting, photographed at the time of his arraignment, July 8, 1957, on a charge of trafficking in narcotics.

UPI

Both Vito Genovese and Russell Bufalino (above) appeared before the McClellan Committee. Bufalino respectfully declined to answer 93 questions about his activities and associates.

UPI

"Big John" Ormento, another participant at the Apalachin meeting, has a record of three convictions for dealing in illicit narcotics.

UPI

Albert Anastasia (dark suit) and his attorney. Anastasia was murdered in a hotel barbershop three weeks before the Apalachin meeting.

Santos Trafficante, pictured here at the bar of his gambling concession in the Sans Souci Hotel in Havana, is alleged to have quarreled with Albert Anastasia over gambling rights in Cuba.

UPI

Vincent (The Chin) Gigante was tried for the attempted murder of Frank Costello. Costello, who was shot from in front, professed never to have seen Gigante before, and the verdict was "not guilty."

UPI

UPI

UPI

Frank Costello in two moods. *Top,* before the Kefauver Committee in 1951. *Bottom,* after being sentenced for contempt of court during the trial of Vincent Gigante.

Top, Frank Scalise (left) with Lucky Luciano and Igea Lissoni, Luciano's constant companion until her death in 1958. *Bottom,* Charles Siragusa of the Federal Bureau of Narcotics (center) with Lt. Gen. Fornara of the Guardia Finanza (left) and Lt. Gen. Morosini of the Carabinieri.

been in on it with him. Substantial money had been invested. Besides, from the purely personal point of view, Havana might have been such a pleasant and understanding headquarters. But the mafiosi are flexible.

The don undoubtedly knew that he faced a rough few months. But he was quite cheerful when he came down the gangplank of the wheezing old freighter which had very slowly brought him across the ocean, to be received by the chief of the Genoa police—personally—and taken to a cell in the city's Questura to be questioned and held until the authorities in Rome decided what should be done with him. Rome again decided that he should be exiled to his birthplace in Sicily. This time Don Salvatore stayed only a few days in Lercara Friddi before returning to the capital, his pleasant apartment and his attractive mistress, Igea Lissoni. But the friends in the Ministry of the Interior and the Questura were nervous. An order of exclusion against the don was imminent, which would bar him from Rome. Charlie Lucky anticipated the move. He had plans, and Rome was not the place for their fruition. Neither was Palermo. In Rome, even if he could buy his way out of the order, he would be under constant surveillance. In Palermo there would be too many mafiosi to pester him and interfere with their equivalent of small town politics. He settled for Naples, the thriving, utterly corrupt big seaport where all branches of the police would be easy to handle and where several ships a week would make communications with the United States fast and regular. In and around Naples were several dozen Italo-American gangsters who had been convicted of serious crimes in the United States and eventually, like Charlie Lucky, deported as "undesirable aliens." Most of them were of Sicilian origin, reliable mafiosi, and were an efficient pretorian guard for the Boss. Don Salvatore transferred his headquarters to the excellent Hotel Turistico in Naples, where an admiring and eagerly subservient staff soon became his personal retinue.

It was a secure fortress, as policemen and newspapermen were to discover.

Don Salvatore was again in business. None of his old executive ability or efficiency had been impaired. He had plenty of capital, in hard American cash. Money reached him regularly by courier from his "administrators"—he let the phrase slip once during a police interrogation—in the United States. It is a strict rule of the brotherhood that a mafioso in prison or exile gets dividends from the projects which he organized or helped to organize. The Guardia di Finanza, the Italian treasury police, have only once been able to prove this link. A courier was traced and it was found that Don Salvatore had received almost $50,000 in one batch. He was fined $4,000, which he paid cheerfully, and let off with a warning.

The Italian underworld soon began to feel the impact of Don Salvatore's superior imagination and organizational genius. The "American Colony," as the Italian police calls our deportees, jumped into action. A skillful generalissimo, Charlie Lucky soon had them posted in strategic places. In Rome, Milan, Palermo and other centers, his carefully selected deputies—formerly of New York, Chicago, Detroit—became local powers. In Genoa, for example, a former Brooklyn gangster took over the highly profitable smuggling operations in that port. He organized a flotilla of fishing boats which met the coasters that crossed the Mediterranean from the free port of Tangiers loaded with American cigarettes and other black market staples. Many Italians had acquired a taste for American cigarettes from our GI's during the war, but the duty imposed by the Italian government made them prohibitively expensive in the legal market. Don Salvatore's excellent Genoa organization and others which he established subsequently began to supply a large selection of our brands to dealers all over Italy at a price that the Italians were willing to pay. The don took a comfortable but not exorbitant cut. This lesson he had learned.

The strange, sullen capo mafioso with the mentality of a

Sicilian and the organizational ability of an American had reached a new phase of his career and so had, with him, the whole brotherhood. For the first time the Mafia had an international organizer of the first order. Don Salvatore's frequent tours of Italy were underworld affairs of state. He was finally barred from Rome as a "crime threat," but he made regular trips to Milan for the horse races, to Capri and Palermo to take the sun. Whenever the don arrived at his fashionable hotel in Milan or the famous Quisissana on Capri—flanked by Igea Lissoni and an impressive group of bodyguards—his local representatives would gather to pay their respects. As at the Waldorf and later, in prison, he would grant audiences, listen to his henchmen's problems, pronounce judgment and dismiss them with the air of the emperor that he was. At the races, of which he is a fanatic follower, he was always surrounded by a group of subordinates who murmured dutifully at his bets, which were never less than $100 a horse. Once, after a losing streak that cost him several thousand dollars, Charlie Lucky characteristically decided to make a fix. He bribed various jockeys. They took his money but failed to throw the races that he was gambling on. He thereupon sent some of his boys to extract the bribe money plus damages from the brash riders who apparently did not realize with whom they were dealing. They paid up. "Damned lousy dishonest wops" is an expression that Charlie Lucky often uses.

Don Salvatore soon had his fingers in various businesses of the usual kind. A Mr. Kenneth Rogers of New York, for example, had started a laundromat business in Austria. It was successful and he wanted to expand it into Italy. He had barely begun his applications for the necessary franchises and licenses in Rome when he was approached one evening at his hotel by two svelte but hard-eyed gentlemen with Brooklyn accents. They were very polite. They simply wanted to bring to Mr. Rogers' attention the fact that any laundromat operation south of Rome would have to have Mr. Lucania's approval. There might be difficulties otherwise. Mr. Lucania would, of course, expect to share in the profits of the venture in exchange for his services and protection. Mr. Rogers decided to give up the whole scheme.

But all business ventures were very small in comparison to the tremendous possibilities which Don Salvatore found in the field of narcotics. It was all made to order for him. The manufacture of heroin for medicinal purposes by pharmaceutical concerns was perfectly legal in Italy and its licensing carelessly administered. (Some Italian medical authorities still claim that properly administered heroin can be beneficial for various ailments; it has long been banned from the American pharmacopoeia as of no value and simply dangerous as the worst of the habit-forming drugs.) The combination of this safe and simple source in Italy with his connections in New York promised the capo mafioso with his lines of communication and expert couriers an important business. Don Salvatore went about the elaborate setup of his organization of it with great care. He did not intend to have his fingers burned again. The reliable Giuseppe Pici, formerly known in the American underworld as Joe Peachy, also a deportee, was made chief of staff for Sicily. Ralph Liguori, an exile as well, became his opposite number in Naples. The don himself from there on never handled so much as a grain of narcotics himself and had no direct connection with anyone who did. It was, and still is, quite an operation. A courier from one of the brotherhood's New York groups went to Palermo—always to see relatives. He, in the course of his visit, discussed price and delivery date of so many kilos of heroin with the executive on duty, usually a relative. If the price was right and delivery could be made, the courier went on to Naples to get final permission from the capo. If Don Salvatore, in a few moments of apparently chance meeting on the beach or in a well guarded café, gave consent, the messenger proceeded to Milan or elsewhere to contact the name which he had been given. There were no telephone calls; nothing was ever written down. As a rule, the job of the emissary would be finished when he reached Milan. He would pay an advance, and then a whole new system of controls would go into action. Another courier would take the heroin from the factory in Milan to Naples or Genoa and give it to one of the seamen-smugglers which Don Salvatore's group had carefully organized. After the narcotics had been delivered in New York, still another messenger—coming over with another order—would bring the cash agreed upon. No formal contracts were required; Don Salvatore's power in the United States was still such that any welching would have quickly brought severe punishment to the offender.

From the beginning in Italy, Charlie Lucky paid careful attention to his relations with the press. This was a lesson, as he has said himself, that he learned from his New York disaster. He is invariably affable—and he can be charming when he chooses to—with newspapermen and has taken many into camp. For a time he retained a former U.S. Army public relations officer to organize a campaign to make him respectable, as he put it quite frankly. At his periodic press conferences, which were usually lavish affairs, he had a regular routine. He explained that he no longer had any connections with the United States, that he had long since paid in full for his crimes, that he was being persecuted by U.S. federal authorities without justification and that all he wanted was retirement and a peaceful old age. "Anytime anything happens," he has said, "they blame it on me. Particularly that Asslinger. [He always refers to Commissioner Anslinger as "Ass-slinger" and has been known to spit after mentioning the name.] Somebody shoves some junk from Italy—I'm supposed to be responsible. Some racket guy gets killed—I'm supposed to be behind it." In a recent interview, when he was questioned concerning the meeting of the grand council at Joe Barbara's home, he revealed the contempt and lack of comprehension of law and order that is typical of the mafioso. "Until I read all that trash in the papers, I never even heard of Apalachin," said Charlie Lucky. "I still don't know where it is—and don't care. I'm clean. I even pay my income tax. They got nothing on me and never will have." He said he was making an honest living selling for an Italian pharmaceutical house. "All this publicity is hurting my business," he told the press. Most Italian newspapermen were inclined to believe the fifty-year-old, graying, apparently kindly man with the spectacles and low voice and to give him sympathetic treatment.

Commissioner Anslinger had no such illusions.

CHAPTER EIGHT

The Battle of the Mediterranean

The U.S. Treasury Department goes abroad.

By 1948 all of Commissioner Anslinger's fears and predictions had come true. Narcotics from Europe were pouring into the United States in unprecedented volume. Addiction was rising steadily and so was the inevitable crime rate that goes with it. The drug traffic was fast becoming one of our most serious social problems. The public, Congress, local legislatures and law enforcement agencies were lethargic, but the mafiosi here and abroad were in high gear. Don Salvatore and his assistants in Naples were encountering no resistance. In the don's inimitable diplomatic fashion, he had even arranged a working agreement with the Corsican criminal brotherhood in France. This nameless organization is smaller but very similar in philosophy and methods to the Mafia, and maintains invaluable channels to Marseilles, Cherbourg and Le Havre, their ships and sailors. Opium from the huge poppy fields of Turkey, Iran and Yugoslavia were flowing with little hindrance to the legitimate laboratories in Italy and the gang-controlled, clandestine kitchen cookeries in France. (The conversion of opium into morphine base and then heroin is a simple chemical process, unfortunately.) Behind a large part of the whole complicated business seemed to loom a droop-eyed, quiet man in Naples together with his fellow mafiosi.

In Washington, Commissioner Anslinger decided on a

drastic move; a supplementary police force of his own, right in the enemy's camp. A few years before, this would have been very difficult. Due, however, to the work of the United Nations and its Commission on Narcotic Drugs, on which Anslinger sits as the American delegate, new weapons had been put into his hands. First he sent abroad two of his most experienced agents, district supervisors Garland Williams and George White, to explore the unknown field. Williams, a dignified man whose practical police know-how is carefully concealed behind the demeanor of an under secretary of state, was not heartening. The French, Italian, Turkish and other police forces were sympathetic, but they could not understand the gravity of the American problem and would naturally resent any prodding from Washington. The commissioner decided to work on a different level and sent his second man, George White.

George White is a stocky man of 50 or thereabouts—well educated, articulate, charming, imaginative and very fast. The commissioner gave him the sort of directive that has become famous in the Bureau. "Go see whether you can get some of these fellows in Europe." That was all. What the commissioner meant, glowering from behind his desk in one of his typical ten-minute battle conferences which cover everything one really needs to know, was that White was to find out whether a narcotic agent could get after one of Don Salvatore's sources of supply successfully. White's most spectacular case, involving traffic between Turkey, Italy and the United States, was the forerunner of many others and is worth retelling.

It was late afternoon and the regular patrons were gathering at a small café not far from the U.S. consulate general building in Istanbul, Turkey. Vendors, beggars, people of every race and dress jostled each other along the street. No one paid attention to the workmen digging a ditch along the curb or noticed that their foreman kept glancing at a second-story window above the café. Suddenly a chair came flying out of that window. A dozen ditchdiggers dropped their tools, pulled out pistols, and boiled into the café and up the stairs. Whistles shrilled and several police cars drove up and stopped at the door. In a few moments four cursing men were escorted out of the café by the erstwhile laborers. Before a crowd could gather, all hands had been whisked off in the police cars.

Within the hour Commissioner Anslinger had a cable from White: "Able today to buy quantity of pure heroin from biggest ring of dealers here and arrest same. Received full and brilliant support from Turkish police who have seized refining plant, source of large shipments to the U.S."

Some months before Agent White's raid in Istanbul, district supervisors of the Bureau of Narcotics in the East and Midwest began reporting to Washington that large quantities of heroin were getting into the market through the usual Mafia channels but from apparently new sources. Underworld talk indicated that most of the new "junk" was coming from Turkey. Agents arrested several peddlers in New York and Chicago and sent samples to the Bureau's laboratory. Microscopic and chemical examination showed the heroin to be of Turkish origin.

Commissioner Anslinger telephoned the chief of the narcotics section of the Turkish police and then sent for George White. A few days later in Istanbul the Turkish police welcomed their American colleague. They briefed White on the figures of the Turkish underworld who might be involved, on their headquarters and habits, warning that undercover men had a way of being found in the Bosporus with their throats cut.

Soon White, in the role of an American merchant sailor, began frequenting certain waterfront bars. He dropped cautious hints that he had money to spend, had "connections" in New York and was open for business if the profits were right. The scouts of the dope syndicate reacted almost at once. For more than a week, White remembers, he was put through a grueling inquisition. Questioned and cross-questioned in curtained café booths and smoky back rooms by Turks who seemed to know a great deal about mafiosi in Italy and New York, he was constantly aware that one slip would mean a quick bullet or a knife in the back. White's answers, based on an encyclopedic knowledge of all of our criminal elements, passed muster, but he had some nasty moments. He was finally taken to the café where, in a heavily guarded room with lowered blinds, he met the four prime movers. After more hours of harrowing investigation, they agreed to let him have $6,000 worth of heroin the next day. It had been destined for Italy and transshipment, but they would make more money this way.

All arrived at the appointed hour. White was to signal the ditchdigging police squad outside by raising the window shade when the deal was consummated. After endless delays and arguments the precious carton containing the drugs was produced. White said that he wanted to examine his purchase in better light. And then—the shade stuck. White fought with it—too violently. The others reached for their guns. But the agent managed to get his out first. It was stalemate; gang lieutenants were waiting outside the door. The room was deathly still while he tried to decide what to do. There was a chair near him. He is a powerful man and, in a second, he picked it up with one hand and hurled it through the window. White says the pounding feet of the police on the stairs was the most welcome sound that he has ever heard. Simultaneously other raiding squads converged on other meeting places and plants of the gang which police shadows had discovered by trailing various gang operatives who had been contacting White. It was a clean sweep. One of Don Salvatore's sources had been mortally hurt.

Anslinger realized that he was on the right track. He also knew that the building of what would have to be practically an American police force in Europe and the Middle East would face staggering problems in Washington and abroad.

The State Department, much as it wanted to help the commissioner, did not like the idea of policemen being attached to our embassies. Our "legal attachés"—some actually special agents of the Federal Bureau of Investigation—and our "commercial attachés"—some of them from the Bureau of Customs—were frequently embarrassing enough without the addition of any of Anslinger's men. Professional policemen the world over are intense individualists and strongly nationalistic. They regard each other, essentially, as members of a family, but the privilege of interference in their own affairs is strictly limited. Real cooperation from such diversified organizations as the Guardia di Finanza and the Italian Questura, the French Sûreté Nationale and the Paris Prefecture, and the various Middle Eastern police headquarters was going to be hard to obtain.

The commissioner needed a versatile policeman who was also an unusually capable diplomat. He had several, but he picked Agent Charles Siragusa of the New York office of the Bureau for various reasons. Siragusa is a friendly, outgoing, enormously restless and energetic man of Sicilian extraction who has a fluent command of Italian and its various dialects. He had often demonstrated his ability to talk a narcotics merchant into selling him a quantity of dope which resulted in an ironclad prosecution and conviction, at the same time remaining on the best of terms with difficult local police agencies. Agent Siragusa was summoned to Washington and given one of the commissioner's ten-minute briefings. "The State Department will go along with us," growled Anslinger. "Go to Rome and see what you can do." That was all.

"Charlie," as he is now known to police chiefs around the world, went to Rome. The American Embassy regarded him with a jaundiced eye. He was sure to make trouble. On the contrary, within a few months he had such powerful friends in the Italian capital that the Embassy began to give his reports very close attention. The chiefs of the Guardia di Finanza, Italy's federal treasury and customs police; the

Carabinieri, the federal constabulary; and the local questura liked the enthusiastic little American who spoke their language so well and understood their problems so clearly and sympathetically. With their help, he recruited a small but effective corps of eager Italian officers and reliable informers whose channels of information went deep into the underworld. He knew where they would lead—to the Mafia and to Don Salvatore Lucania.

Italian police and newspapermen are always surprised that we know so little about the brotherhood and regard it as so much of a phenomenon. The police do not like to use the word Mafia publicly. They regard it as a national disgrace. Nevertheless, they frequently use it and mafiosi in their official reports. The press uses both constantly—as naturally as American newspapers would mention a common social institution such as café society or a gang of teen-age delinquents.

Late in 1950 Agent Siragusa got word through his extending network that one Matteo Carpinetti in Trieste was selling heroin in bulk to couriers from the United States. The business of arranging a contact with such a source is always difficult. But through several of his men, who had excellent underworld credentials, Siragusa managed it. He went to Trieste and, one of the smoothest undercover operators in the Bureau, it did not take him long to convince Carpinetti that he was talking to a big man from New York with a powerful gang behind him.

Siragusa, like many narcotics agents, is a gifted actor, but completely unlike the Hollywood conception of an undercover crimebuster. Underworld business is much more commonplace and direct than usually depicted. Siragusa knew it exactly and a deal was made. Five small bags of heroin and $15,000 in cash changed hands in his hotel room with no excitement, until Italian police emerged from closet and corridor.

The arrest was routine enough, but an astonishing discovery went with it. The neatly packaged bags of narcotics were stamped with the name of one of Italy's largest pharmaceutical manufacturers—Schiaparelli of Turin. Siragusa's investigation during the next months turned up leads to a conspiracy of a size that startled even Commissioner Anslinger. It became clear that the mafiosi in New York, Chicago, Miami and Kansas City were receiving much of their heroin from the supplies of reputable Italian pharmaceutical distributors. The Italian Commissariat for Hygiene and Public Health, under the law, was required to limit the manufacture and distribution of the drug to medicinal needs by a strict system of licensing, but made little effort to enforce its rules. The Italo-American gangsters could buy all they wanted and no one cared.

To prove this was another matter. The big Italian chemical industry has formidable political connections in Rome, and Siragusa had to walk carefully. And then the East 107th Street gang—the biggest in New York—unwittingly came to his aid. One of its principal members, Francesco Callace, came to Italy on one of his periodic buying trips. From the moment he arrived in Sicily to visit his family near Palermo he was being watched by Siragusa and his men. From Palermo Callace went to Milan to meet Joe Pici, now Don Salvatore Lucania's top henchman. The don already controlled a large part of the entire Italian traffic and his permission for a deal was necessary. Permission was granted from Naples and Pici produced three kilograms of heroin which Callace stowed into the false bottom of a suitcase. Callace was arrested a few days later en route to the United States with the suitcase, not knowing that Siragusa and his Italian associates had been behind him day and night watching the whole transaction, finding Pici's supplier—a wholesale pharmaceutical dealer in Milan with connections in the Schiaparelli Company—tracing Don Salvatore's chain of command and laying the groundwork for Siragusa's next move.

Next to Don Salvatore in importance in the Italian underworld, and a growing rival, was another deported American racketeer and brother mafioso—Francesco Coppola. While Don Salvatore, the old master, never handled narcotics himself and issued his orders in such a way as to make proof of conspiracy impossible, Coppola was noisy and brash. The brotherhood's arrangements between Italy and the United States, Siragusa and his friends calculated, could be more easily torpedoed through Coppola. Accordingly, for many weary months, agents of the Guardia di Finanza trailed various of Coppola's men until they had traced his long, devious and well protected trade route from a drug supply house in Milan to a depot near Rome and thence to his citadel and place of business in the hills behind Palermo, the Mafa's birthplace and historic stronghold.

Eventually Siragusa received word from Commissioner Anslinger's Detroit and New York offices of the impending arrival of a big buyer from a Detroit gang that did business with Coppola. When he arrived in Sicily, Siragusa was ready. The tedious negotiations between the buyer and Coppola were watched. When one of Coppola's men was dispatched to the Rome depot to fetch six kilograms of heroin, unobtrusive Guardia agents were with him all the way to see that he and his steel trunk with secret compartments came safely back to Palermo, and into the hands of the police. All of the gang except Coppola were arrested. (The gang chief himself managed to escape but was caught in hiding later when Don Salvatore, who hated his rival so bitterly that he broke the sacrosanct code for once, permitted information to trickle to Siragusa.) Records found in the gang's possession incriminated 23 more prominent underworld figures including four big Detroit racketeers and a respected pharmaceutical dealer in Milan.

Siragusa and the Guardia were now ready to attack the basic suppliers themselves. Gradually and carefully—from the Carpinetti, Callace, Coppola and many other smaller cases—they had pieced together evidence proving that Carlo Migliardi, an executive of the Schiaparelli Company, had diverted no less than 350 kilograms (worth more than $2,000,000 on the underworld wholesale market in New York) to a group of legitimate and supposedly reputable distributors who in turn sold it to the Italo-American mafiosi. Migliardi was arrested in 1952 and subsequently sentenced to 11 years in prison, and because he was socially prominent and well connected the affair caused a commotion in Italy.

Anslinger was not so interested in Migliardi as he was in putting a stop to the lax conditions that permitted the illicit traffic in narcotics. In New York, he went before the United Nations and suggested that the Italian government might repay some of our postwar generosity by putting an end to this kind of thing. This took effect. All manufacture of heroin in Italy was suspended, relatively severe legislation against illicit narcotics traders was enacted and a central police narcotic squad set up in Rome. To underline their determination to cooperate the authorities ordered Don Salvatore Lucania confined to the city limits of Naples, to obey an 11 P.M. curfew and to avoid association with anyone of police record.

Neither Commissioner Anslinger nor Agent Siragusa, however, had any illusions about the future. They both knew the Mafia, its resilience, and that their war against it had just begun. Siragusa with the commissioner's encouragement went right ahead with the building of his unique system. Lieutenant Mario Oliva, head of the tiny narcotic unit of the Guardia di Finanza, became his close friend. There was an immediate meeting of minds. Oliva was young, forthright, as energetic as his American colleague and as incorruptible. Another friend was Questore Giuseppe Dosi, one of Europe's greatest and most colorful veteran detectives. The chief inspector looked much like Mussolini—who feared him and had him put into a concentration camp for a long time—and had some of the Duce's dictatorial manner. He was in his way as unconventional as Siragusa in his. He believed, to the horror of many of his colleagues, in a maximum use of undercover agents, even in disguises and other supposedly antedeluvian police ruses and tactics which he used most effectively. All three—the American and the two Italians—hated the Mafia and its works. On occasion, Siragusa has explained his personal reason for this hatred. "Look," he says, as the bright eyes flash from behind his horn-rimmed glasses. "My father and mother came over from Sicily. Wonderful, kind, honest people. My father made picture frames in a little shop on the Lower East Side. But he managed to help me and my brothers through college. There are so many other Sicilians who have worked hard and raised decent families. Then there is this small group of mafiosi who make us all look like jerks. I just wish that more Sicilian-Americans would do more about getting rid of them instead of attacking the people who are trying to."

In Europe Siragusa found another powerful ally against the brotherhood. It was Interpol—then, officially, the International Criminal Police Commission, now the International Criminal Police Organization. There has been and still is a great deal of public misconception about it. Many sensational stories have been written about its mysterious operations and agents. Actually, there is no mystery about Interpol at all, and it has no agents.

Interpol was founded in 1924 by Dr. Karl Schober, then police president of Vienna and later chancellor of the Austrian Republic. Its purpose was to set up a central file of international criminals to which police agencies all over the world would contribute and which they could use. World War II smashed the growing organization; its invaluable records were moved by the Nazis from Vienna to Berlin, where they were destroyed by Russian troops during the occupation. Immediately after the war, however, four policemen, Inspector General F. E. Louwage of the Belgian Ministry of Justice, Prefect Louis Duclaux of France's Sûreté Nationale, Ronald Howe of Scotland Yard and Dr. Harry Sodermann of Sweden's famous Criminological Institute brought 19 countries together to start over again.

Interpol today has 65 national police forces as members.

Its General Secretariat, which ties them all together with a highly efficient communications network, is located in a large, old-fashioned house on a quiet side street in the heart of Paris—Number 37b, Rue Paul Valéry. It is probably the most unusual police station in the world. Its staff of 40 specialists under Interpol's Secretary General Marcel Sicot of the Sûreté speak many languages and includes experts on every type of crime and criminal. "We are a peculiar kind of policemen here," laughs Monsieur Sicot. "We do all the work from our desks." Number 37b has no agents of its own in the field. All investigations and arrests are made by the member police forces themselves, each of which, however, maintains a so-called Central National Bureau in its own headquarters for liaison with Paris.

In 37b's labyrinth of underground rooms is the nerve center of Interpol, the unique files which have been organized over the last ten years and now contain the records, fingerprints and pictures of more than 100,000 international evildoers. Their real names and origins, their aliases, methods and areas of operation, and personal descriptions are so cross-indexed that just a few clues to a criminal's appearance and habits are often enough for the Identification Section to quickly turn up his whole dossier. Immensely complicated by the number of nationalities and languages involved, the differences in the spelling of names and in the methods of description used by the various police forces, 37b's experts have nevertheless been able to design a master file—a 20-foot-long rotary card index—which is almost an electronic brain. This and the supplementary files to which it leads are staffed by a number of men with remarkable memories. "Machines and indexes are essential," says Chief Inspector Jean Nepote of the Sûreté Nationale and Interpol's energetic young deputy secretary general. "But good identification officers have to have unusual minds to operate them effectively." Number 37b has acquired a reputation among the member police forces for its extraordinary accuracy as a result.

Number 37b has a special index which lists the outstandingly active international criminals. It shows an interesting pattern as far as the Sicilian brotherhood is concerned. The Sicilian representation on the list is large—but almost always in organized skulduggery of some kind: smuggling, counterfeiting, narcotics, white slavery, extortion, and rarely in individual acts of violence, robbery, swindling. "How anyone can doubt the existence of the Mafia, I cannot understand," a high Interpol official said not long ago. "See for yourself. The interrelationship, cohesion, habits and mentality of these people are so clear." The files graphically showed something else. The activities of the brotherhood seemed to be limited to a geographical belt stretching from the Middle East through the Mediterranean and Italy to the United States. We asked why there were evidently so few mafiosi operating in Europe itself, outside of Italy. "There are several reasons," the inspector said. "First of all, the money and conditions they want are in America. So are their family ties. Very few have migrated to European countries. Then—in Europe we know them too well and we do not tolerate their operations. We have in France, unfortunately, a certain amount of organized crime. Our Corsicans, also of the Mediterranean and much akin to the Mafia in background and spirit, form the controlling element of our underworld as the mafiosi do in America. But they have no remotely comparable power or opportunities. The British, the Germans, the Low Countries, the Scandinavians would wipe out such organized crime as the Mafia represents even more speedily."

Commissioner Anslinger realized from the start of his European operation that Interpol was essential to his Bureau in its war against the Mafia. The brotherhood's intricate lines of communication and delivery of narcotics change continually. It was necessary for Siragusa to have more than the usual international cooperation of a dozen or more chiefs of various national police forces of different races, creeds and standards. Interpol made this possible. Once a year the chiefs of the criminal divisions of Interpol's members meet in one of the European capitals—Vienna, Istanbul, Rome, Lisbon, London have been the most recent hosts—to work out more efficient systems of liaison, faster methods of extradition, to analyze and act on the newest in both international crime and law enforcement. Just as important are the personal relationships which have grown up between these highly individualistic, usually nationalistic and always very opinionated men, all professionals of the first order. "Sharlee," as Siragusa came to be known with affection and respect among dozens of policemen from around the world, was able to accomplish amazing things as a result.

By 1954, Siragusa—to whom Commissioner Anslinger had given the title of district supervisor for Europe and the Middle East—had set up a unique office in Rome. Originally it was a very small room in the main Embassy building with barely enough space for a secretary or files. Siragusa, in characteristic fashion, didn't mind. He wrote his meticulous reports on a battered old portable, kept his invaluable records in shoeboxes, and caused one important arrest after another with the seizure of enormous quantities of narcotics before they reached the American market. Gradually the State Department began to realize the importance of the work he was doing. More than 200 leading Italian and American criminals was the score. The rise of the price of heroin in the United States plus reliable underworld intelligence indicated that the traffic from Europe had been cut by roughly 40 per cent. Siragusa was given the secretaries and the office space he needed, along with an electrically controlled wire mesh door, combination lock files and the rest of the trappings of a highly secret government operation. This didn't change him a bit. He stuck strictly with a command which Commissioner Anslinger had characteristically given him in the beginning. "Don't try to wear spats," the Old Man, as he is known to his people, had said. Siragusa never wore spats. But he accomplished some of the major feats in police history.

In 1954, Siragusa discovered from his sensitive network of informants that large quantities of opium and morphine base being converted into heroin in Italy and shipped to the United States were coming from Beirut. Beirut, Aleppo, Istanbul may seem very remote from New York's 107th Street and the Loop in Chicago, from Big John Ormento, Don Salvatore Lucania. Actually, they are quite close as far as Mafia business is concerned. Not knowing the brotherhood's adeptness at smuggling, one would be inclined to ask why the Italian police could not prevent the importation of the raw material into Italy, or U.S. Customs the bringing of the finished product into this country. The truth of the matter is that no country's border controls can be so tight in any but an absolute police state. The Guardia di Finanza can no more search every sailor, airman and passenger who lands in Naples or Palermo than the U.S. Customs can in New York or Baltimore. Sherman Willse, a narcotics detective with the New York City police for 18 years, has pointed out the close coordination possible through criminal control of segments of the import-export business, trucking, and waterfront labor. "When we realize," Willse testified before the McClellan Committee, "that sometimes a ship docks and stays in port for five days, and for about 8 hours a day there is a continual line of trucks going on and off the pier, and in conjunction with the longshoremen . . . it is practically impossible to stop this stuff from coming in." To Anslinger and Siragusa, striking at the source was more important and feasible than an eventual arrest in Palermo or New York.

Siragusa dispatched two young American narcotic agents from the Rome office. One was to play the part of a shady American businessman—a Mr. Johnson, according to his papers—looking for new ventures. His job was to penetrate the upper crust of the Lebanese gangsters. The other agent was to be a seaman, interested in smuggling possibilities, to work among the lower strata. To find a toehold in the highly organized and relatively small criminal fraternity of the Lebanese capital, where everyone knew everyone, was extremely difficult. Within a few hours after they began their first discreet inquiries, Siragusa's men knew that they were under the surveillance of an elaborate and ubiquitous anti-police security system of taxi drivers, café waiters and hotel employees and up against the most suspicious and circumspect crooks in their experience. Fortunately, they had as their guide and mentor a most unusual man—a so-called special employee of the Bureau, himself a former narcotics smuggler in the Near East who knew every trick of the trade and most of the people in it. The Italian and American mafiosi find it hard to understand—as has come out during interrogations—how Siragusa and his assistants gather these people. "Sharlee," when asked, just smiles. To us he once remarked, "Look, I have a lot of Sicilian in me. I feel things and I can talk to people." Through the special employee, the agents gradually met an extraordinary assortment of villains, from the polished European type who communicated with Palermo and Naples to burnoosed Arabs with daggers in their belts. It took two months of countless café conferences and endless cross-examinations before these cautious brethren were willing to accept the Americans as reliable and sell them small samples of narcotics. But their dollars looked good, they paid promptly and well, no trouble resulted, one underworld door after another opened to them and they began to get a clear picture of the huge traffic.

The head man in Beirut was a shrewd, elderly veteran smuggler and cutthroat named Abou Sayia. His organization extended over four countries—Lebanon, Turkey, Syria and Greece. His principal associate was another veteran, Ahmet Azsayer—a Turk with headquarters at Adana who bought crude opium from the Turkish poppy growers, converted it to morphine base and smuggled the latter to Abou Sayia's depots in Beirut and Aleppo from where it was shipped westward.

It seemed an almost impossible case. Four police forces, of countries whose relations with each other were none too good and whose attitude toward narcotic trading had never been too stern, had to cooperate if Abou Sayia and his formidable band were to be caught. But Siragusa had made personal friends of their various chiefs and was able by talking to each one to set up a powerful international task force. Emir Farid Shehab, director of Lebanon's Sûreté, Ethem Yetkiner of Turkey and Terksin el Kawas of Syria not only cooperated but each took personal charge of his part of the scheme which Siragusa had worked out. The chief of the Greek National Police, Gerasimos Liaromatis, even insisted on joining Siragusa as an undercover agent.

Siragusa, when he tells the story today, makes an important point. "The Mafia, goodness knows, is very clever. But I think we proved that we could do better."

The joint undercover operation took four months. Siragusa deployed his forces with care. He and his distinguished Greek assistant—in the guises of a crooked American army officer and a Greek heroin manufacturer respectively—went to Adana in Turkey and with the help of Turkish police operatives met Ahmet Azsayer and became his good friends. In Aleppo, one of the narcotic agents who had worked in Beirut—the "sailor"—became a member of the staff of Haji Mehmet Deniz, who managed Abou Sayia's Syrian organization. In Beirut itself, businessman "Mr. Johnson" was joined by another narcotic agent—"Lieutenant Marcus," ostensibly an American army pilot.

The trapping of Abou Sayia and the closing of an important channel through the Mediterranean to New York is one of the Bureau's classic stories. "Mr. Johnson" had come to know the old smuggler quite well and now revealed an ambitious plan to him. Several pilots in the U.S. Army Air Transport Service, he said, would be willing to carry narcotics in their planes to Europe. A fast, foolproof courier system could be organized; "Mr. Johnson" had worked out all the details with professional skill. Abou Sayia was impressed. "Mr. Johnson" produced his good old friend, "Lieutenant Marcus," whom the Arab liked immediately for some reason, and a deal was made.

In Turkey, Siragusa was also ready. Ahmet Azsayer was prepared to sell his new friend and customer—the Greek chief of police, alias heroin manufacturer—500 pounds of the finest opium. Siragusa's operation entered its final and most difficult phase. Azsayer in Adana and Abou Sayia in Beirut had to be made to deliver their narcotics, accept payment and be arrested within the same hour if both they and their men were to be caught. If news of the arrest of one reached the other before he himself was apprehended, at least half of the organization would vanish into thin air. As it happened, all went well. Siragusa and "Lieutenant Marcus," communicating through a tightly guarded police circuit, were able to set the day and hour. In Beirut, "Lieutenant Marcus" led the Lebanese detectives to Abou Sayia's cache. In Turkey Ahmet Azsayer walked into Siragusa's own trap on schedule. To an air strip near Adana he and his men had obligingly trucked a huge load of 250 kilograms of fine opium for delivery to the fake American army officer and his Greek friend who were to fly it to the West. They were met by Turkish police. In Aleppo the Syrian police simultaneously raided the warehouse of Haji Mehmet Deniz—with complete success. A dozen top Near Eastern traffickers were behind bars and that area had been dealt a crippling blow, for the time being. Commissioner Anslinger and Supervisor Siragusa knew that the victory was only temporary. This is and must be the thinking of the Bureau. But with every such victory, the international mafiosi's allies and the mafiosi themselves find it harder to do their business.

District Supervisor Siragusa's records and communications with Washington, Interpol, and many European and Near Eastern police forces now fill rows of cabinets in the Rome office of the Bureau. Out of them has come much of the data which has begun to convince Congress of the existence of the brotherhood with the factual explanation of its structure. These files contain enough material for a dozen books on the Mafia. The trouble which besets the occasional reporter who is permitted to see some of them is their immense complexity. Conspiracy follows conspiracy. Sometimes they are interlocked, sometimes not. Some names like those of Luciano, Doto, Pici run like threads through many of them, but the casts change continually. We once asked Siragusa how he and other narcotic agents ever kept even a part of this in their heads. "I don't know," was his answer. "I guess we just have peculiar minds." The International List of the Bureau of Narcotics, which is revised periodically in Washington, contains the names, descriptions and many pictures and fingerprints of more than 300 convicted, known and suspected dealers and smugglers. It is, literally, the Bureau's handbook of the international traffic. Four by nine inches in size and two inches thick, it is the carefully guarded bible of agents from Beirut to San Francisco. It is also a Social Register of the Mafia. It presents a very intricate pattern.

The complexity of this pattern is demonstrated by the dossier in the Rome files, (with copies in Washington and New York) of one Eugenio Giannini.

CHAPTER NINE

The Case of Eugenio Giannini

A mafioso who went wrong.

The late Eugenio Giannini was an unusual kind of mafioso. He enjoyed travel, for one thing. Most of the upper echelon of the brotherhood do not. They are uncertain of themselves in surroundings in which they have no friends and which they do not understand. Their own districts in the United States, their wintering places in Florida and on the West Coast, their family places of origin in Sicily and Italy are secure; but they are uncomfortable elsewhere. Gino, as he was known to his associates (FBI #154471, NYCPD #B-69813), was as much at home in Paris, on the French Riviera or anywhere else as he was in the Bronx where he lived with an obedient, patient and understanding wife in the traditional fashion. He had formidable family connections. Brothers-in-law, cousins and other relatives included the confidential secretary of a New York State Supreme Court justice, a Tammany Hall sachem and an assortment of major racketeers. But, as a Calabrian—he was born in Bari, Italy, in 1910, emigrated to the United States as a boy and grew up in the Greenwich Village section of New York—he always remained a brother of only middle rank. It was perhaps this that made him a disloyal one.

The stocky, ugly, lecherous little man with the perpetual scowling sneer first came to the attention of the New York City police in 1928 when he was arrested for armed robbery, convicted and sentenced to a five-to-ten-year term. In 1934 he was arrested again and charged with robbery and first degree murder when he undoubtedly shot and killed a New York police officer during a holdup. A fellow prisoner, without animus or chance of any advantage, reported to the police that Giannini had told him, indignantly, that he and not his partner as reported in the newspapers had shot the officer. As usual, however, the fellow prisoner decided against repeating his story in court. "This charge"—we are quoting from the official police report—"was subsequently dismissed although the defendant had boasted that he actually did kill this policeman." Giannini was released for lack of evidence. By the late 1930's he had become one of Charlie Lucky Luciano's principal henchmen. Expert bruiser and gunman, he acted as executive officer to Antonio Strollo, who ran Don Salvatore's national narcotics distribution. The don liked him and thought he showed promise. Gino, or Gene, as he was generally known in the fraternity, began branching out under this powerful protection into the typical enterprises. He bought into a restaurant supply business, then into a garbage collection concern with the wonderful name of the Eagle Waste Company. The restaurants on his imposing list purchased their food from him and had their refuse removed by his trucks—or else. Then as now New York restaurateurs had to pay substantial sums for these services to avoid stink bombs in the dining room and spoiled meat in the kitchen. It was a lucrative racket, but not enough for Giannini. From his comfortable office in East 74th Street he was making book on horses and numbers as well as arranging for the import and distribution of narcotics. In 1942, he was arrested by federal narcotic agents and served fifteen months for dope peddling. This affected him not at all. Arrest, trial, jail—grim experiences for even the most hardened of individual criminals—seem to leave the mafioso less moved than the average habitual lawbreaker.

Fully re-established by 1950 and back at the old stand with

narcotics, bookmaking and assorted rackets, Giannini suddenly had an urge to visit Europe and look up some of his old friends—including Don Salvatore Lucania. He had plenty of money, and he could have easily satisfied his understandable nostalgia honestly and peacefully with a normal vacation. But that is not the way a mafioso thinks. He has to be busy. Consultations followed with his old friend and associate Salvatore Shillitani (FBI #233625, NYCPD #B62385—sentenced once for robbery, then for first-degree manslaughter, recently for narcotics), and quite a few others prominent in the fraternity. One of these, for example, was Don Giacomo Reina. Here is a quotation from his well documented police record. "[His] family has a long record in organized crime in metropolitan New York. His father, Tomasio Reina, a Mafia power in New York, was shot down on an East Harlem street corner many years ago in a dispute over control of the ice distribution racket. Giacomo Reina inherited his father's title as a 'Don' in the Mafia and since 1940 has been used by Giannini for the backing and good will of the Mafia... in his activities." Giannini, Shillitani, the don and the others thought up a series of typically complicated and ramified projects for the traveler. They had heard from friends and relatives in Italy that drugs such as sulfa compounds, penicillin and vitamins of various kinds were in great demand. The Italian chemical industry had not yet begun to produce them and import duties made them prohibitively expensive. This was something to be exploited by promptly arranging a smuggling network to provide Italian needs at relatively reasonable prices to the Italians but with big profits to the organizers. Giannini had also heard from European sources that good counterfeit American currency was commanding high prices in France and Italy and could be easily and safely disposed of. This was also arranged by two brethren particularly interested in counterfeiting. The overall plan was to use the money brought in by these two operations to buy heroin for shipment to the United States.

It was a typical Mafia scheme, broad in scope, worked out in countless meetings over pasta and wine in the favorite restaurants where waiters hear nothing and will say less, on street corners usually in the garment district where small congregations of gossipers are common, during golf games, and on fishing expeditions. Most of the brotherhood, as policemen who have had them under surveillance on occasion have noticed, are very poor golfers and impatient fishermen—but no microphones can possibly be brought to bear on them.

In due course Giannini, the inevitable Cadillac, his wife and two children sailed for Europe. The record of the energetic mafioso during the next two years in the Bureau of Narcotics and other police agencies covers hundreds of pages of close typescript. It, like most records of the same kind, is so tortuous, so intricate and involves so many names and places that even the incisive legal minds of the best U.S. attorneys quailed when it was presented for the trial in 1955 of Pasquale (Paddy Mush) Moccio—a close associate of Giannini's—and had to be condensed into court-worthy evidence. For our purposes it can be put down much more simply.

In the course of a slow, stately and undisturbed progress from Le Havre through Paris south to Rome and finally Palermo, Giannini was very successful. He sold all of the American medicines, which he had in concealed compartments of his automobile, for a handsome profit, disposed of some $15,000 worth of counterfeit U.S. banknotes and made a number of valuable new connections. In Naples he was received in royal style by Don Salvatore Lucania and his henchmen, all old friends. Reunions of this kind, as we have had occasion to observe, at one of Charlie Lucky's favorite Neapolitan restaurants are quiet but impressive affairs. Later, in Palermo, Giannini was given a similar welcome by Giuseppe Pici, Francesco Callace and the other American deportees who are restricted to Sicily by the Italian government.

The longer Giannini looked at the situation the more firmly

a grand design for himself shaped up in his mind. He had excellent contacts in the Italian and the subsidiary French underworld organizations. All the important brethren knew and trusted him because he represented—and this they had checked and double-checked—important and wealthy American interests. What the brethren did not know, of course, was that the swarthy little man whose word was considered his bond informed regularly to the Bureau of Narcotics.

To understand Giannini and his relationship to the Bureau, an important instrument of police intelligence which is seldom brought to the attention of the public must be understood. Every detective worth his salt "develops," to use the police term, informers who are submerged in the underworld and have access to information which the police cannot possibly obtain on their own. There is frequently a cat-and-mouse element in this kind of informal arrangement. The informer is first of all a criminal and only secondarily a teller of tales, and he must try to make sure that his own questionable activities do not come to the attention of the police either through carelessness on his own part or through the whisperings of another informer. The law enforcement officer, on the other hand, must on occasion shut his eyes to an offense committed by his underworld contact in order to retain his pipeline of information to far more serious criminal activities. This is a fundamental practice of the FBI, the other federal agencies, almost every police department in the country, Scotland Yard, the Sûreté Nationale. It is standard police operational procedure and has been for centuries.

With his unusual connections, Giannini decided he could become the indispensable link between the Italian and French underworld combines and New York, keep the U.S. Treasury quiet with occasional tidbits of information and continue to shuttle back and forth across the Atlantic—trips which he enjoyed—all at the same time. For a while he did very nicely at it. During his visits to Paris he stayed at the pleasant Hotel California with an attractive Parisian named

Jeannine Diament. (Giannini never took his wife along to Europe again.) Madame Diament, former wife of a minor gangster, was a typical mafioso's mistress. An occasional prostitute, she was small, striking, with lush black hair, full lips and brilliant brown eyes. She was also both savvy and obedient, an efficient courier and a good companion as well. Reporters of the *Paris Herald,* the Paris edition of the New York *Herald Tribune*—whose offices are just across the street on the Rue de Berri and who gather in the popular California bar—used to wonder who she and her obviously sinister companion were. There certainly would have been a story in it.

In Italy, Signor Giannini had an equally comfortable arrangement. He established his headquarters in Milan, in the venerable Duomo Hotel on the piazza in front of the city's magnificent cathedral. The wealthy and generous American always stayed in the hotel's best suite, which he shared with one of Milan's spectacular ladies, "Countess" Matilda Farinelli. Gino was building up a pleasant and lucrative operation.

For Giannini, evenings in Paris were parallels of evenings in New York. The habits of this type of gangster are similar around the world. In secure little bars in Montmartre and Montparnasse, where any sort of policeman would be spotted immediately by the *patron* and reported to his habitual customers of doubtful reputation, the respected American with the important connections would meet with such top echelon French racketeers as Marius Ansaldi, Dominique Baldini, Josef Orsini and others of the Corsican fraternity. These men controlled narcotics and counterfeiting in the capital and in Marseilles, and had many associates in Le Havre, Cherbourg and other French ports. Such conferences are quite unlike the popular versions produced by script writers, who have gangsters huddle together and mutter tersely out of the corners of their mouths. Policemen who have been able to listen in on these gatherings know that in reality they are endless and boring. Women, horses and friends—the latter always guardedly—are discussed by the hour. Serious business, such as the sale of $20,000 worth of counterfeit money or a few kilos of heroin, is disposed of in a few minutes. These abrupt, informal but binding transactions come without warning, and the agent who has the group under surveillance must be alert to every scrap of conversation.

On one occasion District Supervisor Siragusa, who was slowly accumulating a file on Giannini, heard that the gangster was in Milan and paid him a visit. The imposing chief *portier* (an essential fixture in every European hotel of stature), seated at the front desk and wearing his long gray Prince Albert with the crossed golden keys on the lapels, doubted whether Signor Giannini would care to be disturbed before noon. Siragusa persisted. Eventually, after a muffled telephone call, he was taken upstairs and permitted to knock on the door of the great man's suite. "Come in, Charlie," shouted Giannini. In a huge four-poster in the bedroom lay Gino and an attractive woman. An array of bottles stood on a convenient side table. Siragusa will never forget the scene. "Charlie," beamed Gino, "you meet the Countess Farinelli." The countess smilingly acknowledged Siragusa's bow. "Now you sit down and we talk," said Gino. Siragusa sat down. Giannini gazed appraisingly at the federal officer for several moments. "Look, Charlie," he said finally, raising himself on his elbow, chin in hand. "You're foolish. Look what I got, A beautiful broad, swell rooms, good everything and plenty of dough." He waved a hand. "Why don't you quit this gumshoe job and get into a real business. I like you. I could get you started. You'd be much happier that way."

Siragusa laughed. "At least they don't put me in jail and I don't wind up dead in a gutter with a lot of holes in me, Gino." Then Gino laughed. "That sort of thing doesn't happen to me," he said easily.

Siragusa was playing one of the Bureau's grim games. He knew approximately what Giannini was up to, although not from Gino himself, of course. After months of patient, tedious investigation he had constructed an accurate picture of Gino's arrangements in Paris, in Milan and in Naples. Siragusa knew that it would be almost impossible to prove the existence of this intricate conspiracy in a federal court in New York. There he would have to present his case before a jury which would not have the faintest conception of what a man like Giannini does or how he lives, and would find fantastic the everyday activities that to Giannini seem perfectly normal. The district supervisor would have to offer incontrovertible witnesses and evidence, and the whole problem would be enormously complicated by distance and national boundary lines. As it turned out, Giannini's fate was settled by an agency of the Italian government, the Guardia di Finanza.

After one of his luxurious vacations on the French Riviera —he had come over from the United States just before— Giannini set off from Cannes for his usual business tour of Italy. He had gone through the San Remo border post dozens of times. Handling a very heavy flow of automobile traffic along the popular coast, the French and Italian police and customs men on both sides of the barrier are usually quite cursory, or rather they seem so. The officer who stamps one's passpost appears to be casual, even careless about it. Actually, just under the counter at which he stands are a number of small black books which he can consult quickly and unobtrusively while apparently fussing with papers and fumbling with his rubber stamp. One is the Interpol list of most wanted criminals, another that of the national Italian police agencies. Near the officer's foot is a button. This time it was pressed.

Mr. Eugene Giannini of New York was incensed when a uniformed Guardia di Finanza appeared behind him and with apologies took him firmly by the arm. Gino threatened immediate action by the American Embassy and terrible punishments for all. This did not produce any reaction. A few hours later, before a stern examining magistrate in the police headquarters in Ventimiglia, he demanded a lawyer, bail and his constitutional rights. But things don't work that way in Italy. The magistrate was unimpressed and shortly thereafter Gino found himself in the Poggio Reale Prison of Naples, where he was to await trial on a charge of complicity in distributing counterfeit money. One of his associates in the fake dollar deal of two years before had been caught and had named Giannini as his supplier. The Italian authorities are very strict about counterfeiting; real dollars are one of the most valuable components of the tourist trade and their security is essential. Italians are perhaps, complacent about such people as Luciano, Pici and the rest who do not harm the national economy; but Giannini was different. He, like all mafiosi operating in this fashion, was to be discouraged. Far away from his mistresses, silk shirts and good food, he had to spend ten months in Poggio Reale.

But Gino was a resourceful man. Although incarcerated in one of the worst prisons in Italy—and none of them are run according to our principles of penology—he managed to stay closely in touch with his various enterprises and make plans for future moves. His attitude toward the Bureau of Narcotics was equivocal. He complained that it was all the fault of the Bureau that he was in Poggio Reale, and at the same time he smuggled out information in the hope that the Bureau would arrange his release. His communications are astonishing. They are outstanding even in a file which is filled with masterpieces written by gangsters.

On one occasion he stated that he was in jail simply because he had done his duty by the U.S. government. "I've given you a lot of information," he wrote. "I gathered all this information the same way that got me into the jail that I am in now—by just mingling with people who are doing these things. I cannot get anything by hanging around or mingling with monks or people who work for a living. I thought I had the protection for this. But it seems that I was mistaken. Looks like someone had no faith in me," he concluded plaintively.

He was incensed to discover from a fellow prisoner—one of the "American colony," as deported racketeers are known—that he, Gino, had been under investigation by the American authorities. "I was being investigated for being mixed up with junk, I found out here," he wrote indignantly. "Well, you can look until doomsday. All you will find is talk, talk—what I spread around to make friends—but actual facts you will never find because there aren't any." This was while he was arranging through his brother-in-law, an American deportee who came to visit him frequently at Poggio Reale, for the purchase and caching of no less than ten kilograms of heroin against the time of his release.

One letter contained details of life in prison. "Please excuse my handwriting because I had to write this on the floor while a guy lit matches over me and if I sound sarcastic, I don't mean anything because my nerves are shot. For three months I am living in a cell without windows, and a solid door. No air or light. The heat and the flies eat me up. We have to eat, sleep and go to the toilet all in the same spot and smell it all day and night. Three of us in the same room cannot sleep at the same time. One has to stay up to stand guard for the rats for they too are hungry and big enough to take a bite out of us. The bedbugs are as big as cockroaches. I have to pay for water and a bunch of hay to sleep on. Put all this together and figure out why I'm not out of my mind yet or cut my throat. It's costing me $50 to sneak this letter out and for the paper and ink."

He became so desperate that he committed the final indiscretion. He not only offended against the code regularly, but now he put the worst of his offenses on paper. "I once gave you information," he wrote to the Bureau, "on Charlie Lucky [Luciano] and his connection man Joe Pici, of which in April from this lead they made an arrest here. Frank Callace and nephew got away. I know who gave them the stuff they had and where it was made. I know also Charlie Lucky's other connection man and where the stuff comes from. Some time ago I told you about a load of money that was being sent to Lucky for junk. Well, the police here found that money on Charlie Lucky. I have now the information that can link Lucky to all these affairs. I gathered all this information the same way that got me in the jail that I am in now—by just mingling with people that are doing these things. Please be careful with this letter," he pleaded in conclusion. "Destroy it after reading it. Should it get in the wrong hands, I may as well buy me a slot in some cemetery." Gino was not a stupid man but he had some blind spots in his understanding of the methods of law enforcement agencies.

From his office in the U.S. Embassy in Rome, Charles Siragusa was closely watching Giannini as he simultaneously complained and plotted his operations. Siragusa and the experts on international crime at District Two, the New York office of the Bureau, together with Commissioner Anslinger and his overall staff in Washington, were beginning to piece together the details of a big Mafia-led operation between Europe and the United States in which Eugenio Giannini was playing a major role.

The difficulties of untangling such an intricate web, the time and labor required, is never explained to the public on movie and television screens, and is seldom treated in articles or books. Gradually, very gradually, the details of the relationships and dealings between these peculiar people had to be dug out. An arrested smuggler who knew a little would talk in order to reduce his sentence. Peddlers here and there would add small bits. The dissatisfied mistress of a gangster occasionally contributed details. But all these leads, often conflicting, have to be checked and cross checked, and woven together into a case for a U.S. attorney. More than a dozen highly skilled narcotic agents had to work periodically for more than two years to map this ramified conspiracy and then collect the necessary evidence.

The broad outlines of the organization to which Giannini belonged were beginning to take shape. It was a typical Mafia syndicate. Beside Giannini, the principal names were Moccio, Pagano, Valachi, Quartiero and Reina; all with countless aliases. They had imagination, businesslike methods and skillful techniques. One of their agreements, for example, called for a permanent fund of at least $300,000 to be maintained at all times for sudden advantageous purchases of heroin and emergency expenses for couriers and lawyers. This reserve went as high as $500,000 and more on occasions when big buying was expected. The group functioned partly through France with the help of Corsican racketeers in New York, Paris and Marseilles; through Italy via strictly Mafia channels from Palermo, Naples and Milan.

The dispatch of a courier from New York was handled with care. He or she had no police record. At times, even, the courier was entirely innocent. A none too intelligent, and innocuous, relative of one of the syndicate would be given a car by his uncle, the necessary money and told to take a vacation abroad with his wife to visit relatives in Italy. One grateful and happy nephew, for example, was told to visit a friend of his uncle's in Marseilles before he went on to Naples to see other people to whom he had introductions. Nephew sailed joyfully from New York with an absolutely clear conscience, blessing his unexpectedly generous relative. In Marseilles he and his family stayed with the very friendly and hospitable friend number one, who happened to be a garage owner. Nephew's car was of course whisked away for thorough servicing free of charge. The servicing consisted of building concealed compartments into the body of the automobile. In Naples nephew was again royally entertained while bags of heroin were put into the hidden receptacles. Nephew completed his pleasant tour and eventually returned to the United States.

U.S. customs inspectors are a very efficient lot, all in all, but they have far more to do than they can handle thoroughly. The complete searching of a car takes a lot of time, and when a transatlantic liner comes in with a hundred of them, it's a tough job. A good inspector develops an instinct. Even the most practiced smuggler seems to emanate involuntarily a nervousness, no matter how unconcerned he seems to be, of a kind which an experienced, alert officer seems to detect. Some very large seizures of contraband have been made in this way. Most, of course, are made as a result of information obtained by the customs agents, the intelligence unit of the Bureau of Customs which is similar to and works closely with the Bureau of Narcotics and the other Treasury enforcement agencies. But nephew emanated nothing. The car was quickly searched—and passed. A week or so later, uncle borrowed it from nephew—because his own car was being repaired, he said—and shortly thereafter quite a few kilograms of heroin were on the market.

This may seem to be an overly elaborate and expensive procedure. But it was not. High purity heroin could be bought in France and Italy for between one and two thousand dollars a kilogram (approximately two pounds) and sold in New York to the large-scale dealers for between ten and fifteen thousand. Here, incidentally, is another example of the international power of the mafiosi. The European price has been held down to this day to permit the American section of the brotherhood to make the really big profits. This sort of price fixing seems to be one of the functions of Don Salvatore Lucania, for which he is handsomely paid from New York. In any case, by subsequent estimates the syndicate to which Giannini belonged was smuggling an average of 12 kilograms a month into the United States and doing a gross annual business of well over a million dollars.

There are, constantly, incidents in such an elaborate investigation which do not fit into a script writer's book at all. They are too confusing. But policemen have to face them all the time. District Two of the Bureau had pretty well put together the picture of the relationship of Giannini, Moccio and the other New York mafiosi with the New York and Paris Corsicans. It was a question of finding out who the prime movers in Paris and Marseilles were and getting evidence against them. For weeks at 90 Church Street, District Supervisor James Ryan mulled over the problem with agents John Cusack, Joe Amato, Benedict Pocoroba, Anthony Zirilli, Armando Muglia and others. Through a series of bewilderingly intricate maneuvers Agent Cusack, through a "special employee" (the Bureau's official euphemism for a regularly paid informer) who worked with the main New York gang, was actually able to arrange an introduction for himself to the Paris operation as a courier. The usual letter of introduction, which would seem entirely innocuous to anyone outside the brotherhood, was dispatched from New York with a picture of the new courier enclosed. Cusack followed it a few days later by plane. In Paris he was duly contacted and then had to go through the interminable business of being questioned and inspected by minor gangsters in countless bistros, on street corners and in hotel lobbies to test his underworld knowledge and integrity before being introduced to the higher ups. This is always a grueling and nerve-racking experience. One slip may mean a quick bullet or a knife in the back; not when one is discovered to be a police officer, but when one is suspected of belonging to a rival gang. "You say you know Shillitani," a grim Corsican flanked by a couple of equally menacing mafiosi would ask. "Well. When did you see him last? And how is he?" The agent, of course, never knows how much his interrogator knows. "I hear that Alfredo is in jail," comes the query. The agent must know who Alfredo is and that he is not in prison—or else. No one is ever in a hurry in well run rackets; the successful racketeer knows that haste is extremely dangerous. Cusack did very well and got to the top man quickly—to one Marius Ansaldi, who dealt in $50,000 lots of heroin and whose skillfully concealed factory and depot just outside Paris accounted for most of the supplies reaching New York. Cusack could hardly believe his good luck when Ansaldi suddenly agreed to negotiate the sale of 50 kilos, a huge amount. Cusack knew that in the course of the elaborate negotiations which precede such a big transaction, he would be able to trace many of the connections between Paris, Italy and New York. Such a deal is never consummated in an evening or even a few. The haggling over price, dates and places of delivery is long-drawn-out. Again, carelessness or haste is very dangerous for the trader. The next meeting was set for the next week in a café on the other side of Paris. It never materialized. Suddenly Cusack's original contact man, the others with connections to Italy and America and Ansaldi himself vanished like so many puffs of smoke. An American gangster who happened to see him had, it was later discovered, recognized the new "courier" as none other than Narcotic Agent Cusack. The great opportunity, the kind of which every agent dreams, had vanished also. But Cusack and Inspector Baileul of the Sûreté Nationale's narcotics division who worked with him had managed to find out a great deal. Ansaldi and his big plant were subsequently found as a result and put out of business for the time being. New York's principal supply of heroin was temporarily closed.

In the meanwhile Eugenio Giannini had been released from prison. He had been tried on the counterfeiting charge and acquitted for lack of evidence. The associate who had denounced him suddenly lost his memory under pressure from the brotherhood and recanted. There is also strong evidence that a New York lawyer who acts for many of the higher brethren went to Italy specially to see Giannini in jail and made certain arrangements with one of the top prosecuting attorneys in Naples.

Even the dreadful Poggia Reale had changed Gino not a bit. He had big plans. He knew that the elimination of Ansaldi would make heroin scarce in the United States for a while and was all set to take advantage of the abrupt rise in its price. The trouble was that he was now under indictment in New York on a former narcotics trading charge and would be arrested immediately if he went home. He decided to stay in Italy and even become an Italian citizen. Supervisor

Siragusa had other plans, however, and the cooperation of the Italian government. Giannini's application for citizenship was refused, he was ordered expelled and duly flown back to the United States. An ingenious system, incidentally, has been developed through Interpol which makes the shipment of such a prisoner without a guard possible. He is simply put aboard a plane at the starting point and all airport police in countries where the aircraft is to touch down en route are notified. At Paris, Shannon and Gander Gino was not out of sight of the police for a moment, and anywhere else on the way to New York he didn't want to get out, as he remarked ruefully.

Giannini was duly arrested at Idlewild by federal agents, arraigned and released in $15,000 bail. His release and bail were made easy for a reason. As expected, he was back at work very soon. Before leaving Italy he had made all the necessary arrangements with various brethren to keep handy the ten kilograms of heroin which he, his partner Giacomo Reina and a few lesser investors had bought and paid for in Italy prior to his prison term in Poggio Reale. The heroin was now in the keeping of Giannini's brother-in-law, Giuseppe Pelligrino —a stupid, small time but trustworthy gangster deported from the United States—in Salerno, south of Rome. It had almost doubled in value since the time when it had been bought; in New York it would bring well over $100,000. District Two in New York and Siragusa in Rome, through "special employees," were watching every move.

Gino, it turned out, was formulating a plot to cheat his partners—Reina, Moccio and the rest—out of the larger part of the ten kilos. This sort of thing happens rarely within the brotherhood. One may shoot a rival, or have him shot, under sufficient provocation; one may not swindle a partner. But Giannini was not an orthodox mafioso. He was looking for a courier entirely unknown to his syndicate to go to his brother-in-law in Salerno and collect six of the ten kilos and bring them into the United States for his own, lone, $80,000 benefit.

This news had reached the Bureau through a "special employee" who was close to Giannini. The Bureau reacted immediately with one of its counterplots. The "special employee" was prevailed upon to introduce Narcotic Agent Anthony Zirilli, in the role of a small-time but ambitious racketeer, to Giannini as a reliable messenger. Zirilli can be very convincing—as most narcotic agents are—in his schooled, dead pan, apparently casual manner. Gino liked him on sight and a deal was made. He was to travel with an unattractive but veteran and trusted operative of Giannini's, Yetta Ricciardi. Couriers are often dispatched in pairs—so that they can watch each other.

Reading the lines and between the lines of a treasury agent's formal report, despite the carefully stilted and precise language, gives a much clearer commentary on actual law enforcement than most screen or printed presentations. It is not necessarily thrilling fare; there is generally little drama, violence or glamorous sex in it. But it is real. Here is part of Agent Zirilli's report (the comments in parentheses are editorial):

On August 12, 1952 at approximately 7:00 P.M., this agent left Idlewild Airport in New York with Yetta Ricciardi aboard TWA flight 984, destination Rome, Italy.

On August 13, 1952 at 11:30 P.M., this agent arrived at the Rome Airport with Yetta Ricciardi.

This agent (secretly) had a conference with District Supervisor Charles Siragusa of the Bureau of Narcotics and Captain Zuchetti of the Italian Guardia di Finanza.

This agent made arrangements that evening that he, the previously mentioned officers (Siragusa and Zuchetti had been introduced to Yetta as friends of Zirilli's) and Mrs. Ricciardi were to proceed the following morning to Amalfi.

Upon arrival at the Hotel Luna in that city, Mrs. Ricciardi and this agent approached the desk clerk and learned that there were no rooms available.

They looked for hotel rooms elsewhere but there were none to be found, as this was the eve of *Ferro Gasto,* the biggest holiday of the Italian summer. (Such events sometimes interfere with the most carefully laid plans.)

This agent and his companion returned to the Hotel Luna.

This time this agent told the desk clerk that he must have two rooms and that a friend of his whose name he did not know, had already reserved rooms for him and his companion. (This strange statement of having a friend without name made perfect sense to the hotel man.)

At this point the clerk asked this agent his name and this agent gave it to him.

The clerk then asked this agent to wait and disappeared into another part of the hotel. He returned in a few minutes together with a man whom he introduced to this agent.

This man stated that he was Joseph (Giuseppe) Pelligrino and that he was Giannini's friend. (He was, of course, actually Gino's brother-in-law.)

Pelligrino took this agent and Mrs. Ricciardi to the street level of the hotel where he introduced them to one Genaro Rizzo.

Pelligrino said that he would find hotel rooms for them.

After making inquiries in a few hotels in Amalfi, he told them they would have to go to Salerno, a town nearby where he lived.

This agent, Pelligrino, Rizzo and Mrs. Ricciardi then drove to Salerno in an automobile hired by Pelligrino and Rizzo.

During the drive, Pelligrino told Rizzo that this agent was the person who was going to carry the heroin to the United States. (Pelligrino was convinced that Zirilli was Giannini's bona fide courier; a picture of him had been sent from New York and half of a one-dollar bill, to which Zirilli had produced the other half.)

At Salerno, Pelligrino was unsuccessful in finding hotel rooms. This agent and companions then had supper at a restaurant, Piazza Vittorio Veneto, 25.

Rizzo left and came back shortly. He had found two rooms upstairs in the same building as the restaurant.

Rizzo said that these rooms were in an apartment owned by a relative.

Rizzo and Pelligrino then took Mrs. Ricciardi and me to this apartment.

While Rizzo was in the kitchen, Pelligrino spoke to me in my bedroom and said that he would give me the heroin any time I wanted it.

I told him that this was not agreeable to me since I did not want to keep the heroin in my possession until my departure from Rome on August 26. (A plan for the final coup was taking shape in Zirilli's mind. In his excitement, he had switched from the formal "this agent" to the first person singular.)

Pelligrino suggested that I remain in Salerno but I told him that was out of the question, since the town was too dirty and unattractive and it was impossible to find hotel rooms.

I suggested to Pelligrino that perhaps he should deliver the heroin to me in Rome. Pelligrino said we would discuss the matter later.

The morning of August 15, 1952, I telephoned District Supervisor Siragusa at the Hotel Cappuccini at Amalfi (Siragusa and his Italian colleague were hovering nervously nearby) to inform him of the developments to date.

Later that morning, Pelligrino came to Piazza Vittorio Veneto, 25, to pick up Mrs. Ricciardi and me.

We went to the Brazil Bar which is located in the center of Salerno about 10 streets from the above address.

Pelligrino said that it would be impossible for him to deliver the heroin to me in Rome. (This is standard operational procedure in the brotherhood. The seller never does exactly what the buyer wants.)

He instructed me to return to Rome that morning and come back to Salerno on the evening of the 24th.

Pelligrino said that prior to leaving Rome I should write him a letter addressed to Joe America, Brazil Bar, Salerno.

Pelligrino said that everyone knows him by that nickname in Salerno. And this letter is to confirm my arrival of August 24.

Mrs. Ricciardi and I were to go to the Hotel Diana where Pelligrino would be waiting for us.

Pelligrino said that in the meanwhile he would try to reserve rooms for us in that hotel.

Pelligrino asked me whether Giannini had given me four plastic bags and whether I knew how to pack the heroin which he would eventually give me.

I assured him that everything would go as planned.

Pelligrino then accompanied Mrs. Ricciardi and me to the Salerno railroad station where he bade us farewell. We returned to Rome.

I discussed the events that had transpired to date with Supervisor Siragusa and we thought it best not to follow Pelligrino's instructions to return to Salerno on the evening of August 24. (It would not have been according to the brotherhood's pattern of behavior for the courier to stick to the schedule agreed upon either. To have done so would have made Pelligrino suspicious at once.)

Accordingly, I sent the following letter to Joseph Pelligrino at the Brazil Bar on August 20, 1952:

Dear Joe,

I thought it best not to come to Salerno Sunday night since it would be hard to find hotel rooms. Yetta got sick when we were there. Yetta and me will arrive at Salerno on Monday, August 25 on the Rapido. Have the package ready to give us the same afternoon so Yetta and me can return to Rome that same day. This way we don't have to sleep over that night in Salerno.

Regards,
Tony Zirilli

(Agent Zirilli's grammar is ordinarily good. In communicating with Pelligrino, however, correct syntax would have been a mistake.)

On August 25, 1952, at 4 P.M. I arrived at the Salerno railroad station on the Rapido train from Rome with Yetta Ricciardi.

We walked into the waiting room where I left Mrs. Ricciardi. I went to the sidewalk and saw Joe Pelligrino who was walking away. (The tactical arrangement of the actual delivery of the contraband is always very complicated. This is a dangerous moment for both the buyer and the seller, who never really trust each other.)

I called to Pelligrino and told him that Mrs. Ricciardi had been upset by the trip and was in the waiting room. (Supervisor Siragusa and two agents of the Guardia di Finanza were sitting near her, convincingly relaxed behind newspapers.)

Pelligrino, however, insisted that I get Mrs. Ricciardi.

I got her and then crossed the square in front of the railroad station and entered a restaurant on the corner.

Inside this restaurant, I told Pelligrino that we would like the heroin delivered inside the railroad station. (Agent Zirilli was worried that the Italian policemen might be recognized by someone in the café.)

Pelligrino was unwilling to do this. However, he agreed that after he delivered the heroin to me inside the restaurant, he would accompany me and Mrs. Ricciardi to the railroad station. (Siragusa had decided what to do. These are the touch and go moments of an important arrest and mistakes are not excused. The supervisor and his two Italian colleagues sauntered out of the station toward the restaurant. There is an art in a policeman's sauntering, if he is skillful. A policeman has for some reason a way of walking and looking as he walks which immediately identifies him to an experienced lookout. Siragusa and colleagues took position around the restaurant without incident.)

Pelligrino left the restaurant; in a few minutes he returned. (One of the Guardia detectives followed him to a marble cutter's establishment not far away and back. The marble cutting yard belonged to Genaro Rizzo, friend of Pelligrino, who had the heroin in his safe.)

He told me that the heroin was ready and I gave him a small overnight bag instructing him to insert the heroin therein.

Pelligrino left the restaurant again now carrying the leather bag. (The other Guardia detective was behind him this time.)

As Pelligrino was about to re-enter the restaurant, I saw him arrested by Supervisor Siragusa, and an Italian policeman who entered the restaurant behind Pelligrino and another policeman who came in through another door simultaneously. (As Siragusa gripped Pelligrino's arm, the former New York gangster wheeled purposefully. The supervisor, who rarely carries a gun but was armed this time, went for his revolver but never drew it. An incredulous look was chased across the big racketeer's face by a wry but huge grin. "I'll be a son of a bitch," he exploded, recognizing the man who had once arrested him before in New York. "Siragusa!" There was no violence.)

Pelligrino, when he saw the officers, dropped the bag and it was seized by the police. (There were six kilos of heroin in it.)

So ends Agent Zirilli's report. Neither he nor Siragusa knew that the supervisor's hand on Pelligrino's arm signed a death warrant to be executed four thousand miles away. News travels over the underworld grapevine very quickly. American papers did not publish an account of Pelligrino's arrest, but the Italian press did. Within a few days Reina, Moccio and the rest of the syndicate in New York had the picture. Gino had obviously tried to bring in six kilos which belonged to them all without telling them. That could mean only one thing. An investigation by the syndicate followed. The mafiosi are never careless about establishing guilt. The results were positive.

Just a month after Pelligrino's arrest in Salerno—at 5 A.M. on September 21, 1952—people on Second Avenue between 111th and 112th streets in New York were awakened by the wicked noise of gunfire. Most probably thought it the backfire of a truck. But someone who recognized the unmistakable bark of a heavy revolver called the East 126th Street police station. A squad car of detectives came quickly. All they found was an elderly Italian, Thomas Steo, tidying the sidewalk in front of the Jefferson Major Athletic Club. Yes, he had heard noise "like backfiring." It had awakened him. So he thought he might get up and do some chores. One of the detectives suddenly bent down over a red mark on the sidewalk, sniffing. "This is blood," he said. Mr. Steo's eyebrows rose. "Blood? Blood? Where should blood come from?" The detectives went away. Shortly after 6 A.M. the owner of a little delicatessen in East 107th Street came to open his shop for the day. Somewhat nearsighted, he thought at first that it was a bundle of rags put near the garbage cans in front of 221 East. Then he looked closer. It was a bloodied body, face up, in the gutter. The merchant nervously ran to his shop, shakily unlocked its door and went for the phone. Roaring sirens from the East 104th Street and East 126th Street stations converged. The detectives of both stations had sensed that the blood on the sidewalk on Second Avenue meant something big. They recognized the corpse at once. It was Eugenio Giannini in a light tan sports jacket, brown slacks and shoes, an expensive Swiss watch on his left wrist, $140 in his pocket and two .38 caliber bullets in his brain. The killers who shot him down in front of the athletic club on Second Avenue and dumped his body on 107th Street—a typically symbolic gesture since Gino had long belonged to the 107th Street gang—were never caught. Reina, Moccio and several others were brought in for questioning. They, of course, knew nothing. Gino had been their friend and they were very sad. They could not understand, they said, how anybody could do such a thing. Gino had always been such a nice, kind man. They could not understand. . . Their alibis were airtight.

The Bureau regarded the passing of Gino with mixed emotions. It represented no great loss to society. He had, however, been extremely helpful to the Bureau both voluntarily and involuntarily in one of the biggest cases ever prosecuted against a syndicate of the brotherhood. Ironically enough, it was not for this—as conclusive subsequent evidence proved —that he was shot. He had been so shrewd and the Bureau so secure that the brethren never suspected for a moment that he had given information against the rivals that he wanted to eliminate. He was executed for the swindle, and nothing else.

In May, 1955, District Supervisor James C. Ryan submitted to the United States attorney for the Southern District of New York a two hundred page information on the case of Pasquale "Paddy Mush" Moccio, Pasquale Pagano, Giacomo Reina, et al. An information is the prosecutor's basis for seeking an indictment by a grand jury and his work sheet in preparing the case. The indictment was handed down.

Case NY:S 9400 involved the testimony of no less than 34 witnesses. Fifteen were federal narcotic agents who had operated from New York to Salerno. Two were U.S. customs agents. One was the *portier* of the Hotel Principe di Savoia in Milan, another Commissaire Michel Hugues of the Sûreté Nationale. The *portier* and the French policeman were flown over to New York at government expense. They each testified for only a few minutes; but their testimony was essential to prove meetings between various of the conspirators and Giannini in Paris and Milan at certain crucial times. It took U.S. Attorney Patterson two full weeks to lead the jury and Judge Alexander Bicks thought the intricate maze of the last years of Gino's life and their connection with the men being tried under 18 United States Code 371, "conspiracy to import illegal narcotics into the United States." The jurors had a hard time. What seemed perfectly clear to narcotic agents like Cusack, Pocoroba, Giuliani, Zirilli, Muglia, and a matter of course, was often confusingly amazing to the solid citizens in the box. They goggled openly as Jeannine Diament, attractive and convincing, testified quite frankly about her former lover, Giannini, their trips through Europe together and the people they met.

Against the wall of the somber courtroom sat seven men in a row, the defendants, flanked by officers. By the hour they were bolt upright in their chairs. "There," said Agent John Cusack to this writer, "sits the Mafia." And there, indeed, sat the Mafia. One was primarily a dock racketeer who had become involved in NY:S 9400 because his longshoremen had brought narcotics in from the ships they were servicing. He had a reputation for being able to break a man's leg with one kick. The criminal records of the rest ranged from homicide, robbery and extortion over almost every category of lawbreaking on the lists. Different as the seven faces were in their individual features, there was an identical denominator in each one. It was not the feral quality that one finds in so many habitual criminals. It was something quite dignified in a strange way; brutal, vicious, evil, but dignified just the same. All were tense but no one was frightened. Even their heads rarely moved. Only their eyes blazed occasionally at prosecutor, judge or compromising witness as the incontrovertible case was gradually built up. When Jeannine Diament took the stand to deliver her crucial testimony, she met seven stares so malevolent that they had almost physical impact. For a moment, the pert little Parisian cringed. Then she began to stare back. "That girl's got guts," a federal agent whispered. "If those bastards had looked at me that way when I was testifying, I'd be worried."

The jury found all defendants guilty. There was no noticeable reaction from any one of the seven. They filed out of the courtroom stiff-backed. Some weeks later they stood in a line before Judge Alexander Bicks in the same courtroom for sentencing. Five years penitentiary was the maximum sentence that the judge could impose for first offenders in drug trading under the law which was then in force. He gave them the maximum, with weariness and a trace of frustration in his voice. He knew that after all the tremendous effort of the Bureau and its agents, the work and expense, these sneering social parasites would serve approximately three years (the brotherhood always behaves well in prison and receives the customary time off for good conduct) and then be back in business. After the sentence had been pronounced each bowed gravely to the court, as he would have in Palermo, and followed the guards into the detention room.

Not long after the trial of Moccio, Reina, et al., we spent an evening with another experienced judge who has tried many such cases. We had told him our observations of the trial. "I can't begin to tell you," he said heavily, "how we feel sometimes when we're up there on the bench. There I am, in my robes and everything, surrounded by policemen, all of the panoply. I feel, and I think rightly so, that I am supposed to represent not only the laws but also the basic decency and integrity of the American way of life. That's what we're there for. And most of us do our best. And then we're faced with these insolent villains, these peculiar villains, and their shrewd lawyers who make a mockery of the law. They're not bank robbers or swindlers, or even normal murderers." He laughed wryly. "We know what to do with those. These are something else. This is a breed for which we do not have adequate laws."

"You mean the mafiosi, primarily," we suggested.

"Of course I mean the mafiosi," he answered. "There are many others, naturally. But the core is the Mafia. It has been, for many years. The Mafia has been in my courtroom hundreds of times. I know when it's there. The faces, the attitudes, the bearing of the defendants are unmistakable. So are the tactics of their lawyers, these so-called attorneys-at-law who drag the traditions of the bar through the dirt for the money that the mafiosi pay." The judge mimicked a famous New York criminal lawyer, placing a hand under his double-breasted jacket. "Your Honor. May it please the court. My client is the father of three splendid children. He is an honorable husband. He deserves consideration." The judge dropped his pose and continued in a milder tone. "The man is, oddly enough, a good father. He is devoted to his children. He is not faithful to his wife but she is the first to get the mink stole or the Cadillac when he can afford it. At the same time, he has no compunction whatever about ordering the murder of a competitor, the beating of a rebellious truck driver, the selling of narcotics that he knows are going to cause untold misery." The judge paused. "And what can I do about it?" he asked aggressively. "With all my robes and my policemen, they sneer at me as they sneer at Senators in Washington. What can any of us do against this damnable brotherhood of evil that is eating at the whole nation?"

CHAPTER TEN

Senator Kefauver's Voyage of Discovery

How a soft-spoken man from Tennessee, a shrewd old lawyer from New Hampshire and other senators met the brotherhood for the first time.

The date was May 28, 1950; the place was Senator Estes Kefauver's suite in the Hotel Columbus in Miami, Florida. It had been an exhausting day for the Senate Crime Committee of which he was chairman and which had begun its subsequently much publicized probing into the nation's rackets and racketeers. With a sigh the big Tennessee legislator stretched out his long frame on a couch in the living room. "You know," he said in his slow, deliberate way to Rudolph Halley, the chief counsel of the committee, "I'm not sure how far we're going to get with this. It's so tremendous and so outrageous a conspiracy that a lot of people simply aren't going to believe it." Halley, slouched in a deep chair, nodded gloomily. The young New York lawyer who had served on the Truman Committee and knew a lot about rackets was as depressed as the senator.

A series of startling witnesses had appeared under subpoena at Miami's Federal Court House, where the hearings were being held. The sheriff of Dade County, which includes Miami and Miami Beach, "Smiling Jimmy" Sullivan, had dodged, squirmed and then finally admitted that he had "saved" more than $70,000 during his five years in office. Members of a gambling combine known as the S & G syndicate admitted quite casually to their enormous incomes. It became apparent that a substantial proportion of campaign funds for certain high offices had been contributed by shady elements. "Well," said the senator, "goodness knows where this is going to take us or how long we'll be at it. But it's just got to be done, that's all."

The colossal job of charting the underworld of the United States took him a year, 52,000 miles across the whole country and cost approximately $250,000. But never has an awakening of the American public to its peril cost so little. The effects of the Kefauver Committee's investigations are only now really beginning to be felt. The records of the committee contain the testimony of more than 800 witnesses in Miami, Tampa, New Orleans, Kansas City, Cleveland, St. Louis, Detroit, Los Angeles, San Francisco, Las Vegas, Philadelphia, Washington, Chicago and New York. They are much too ponderous and intricate for the public and even for most lawmakers, and even a condensation of them is next to impossible, but they have served and continue to be the foundation for much work which has followed the tireless senator's labor.

Some critics of Senator Kefauver have called him naive—usually newspapermen with magnificent hindsight. The senator, at the beginning of his inquiry, was as naive about the details of organized crime as any other decent legislator, executive or average citizen without extensive police experience would have been. But he learned fast. He is anything but naive.

After the conclusion of his committee's work, Senator Kefauver wrote a book, *Crime in America.* For some reason it never received the attention it deserved. In it there are some forceful conclusions, extremely important to us today. Their validity has not decreased. They are a severe indictment.

[Through it all [wrote the Senator, in reference to the hearings], I listened with mounting indignation and revulsion to the shocking story of our national disgrace. When it was over we had established the following major conclusions:

1. A nationwide crime syndicate does exist in the United States of America, despite the protestations of a strangely assorted company of criminals, self-serving politicians, plain blind fools, and others who may be honestly misguided, that there is no such combine.

2. Behind the local mobs which make up the national crime syndicate is a shadowy international criminal organization known as the Mafia, so fantastic that most Americans find it hard to believe that it really exists.

3. Infiltration of legitimate business by hoodlums has progressed to an alarming extent in the United States. The committee uncovered several hundred instances where known hoodlums, many of them employing the "muscle" methods of their trade, had infiltrated more than seventy types of legitimate business.

Here was, in the unjournalistic words of a trained and careful lawyer, what Commissioner Anslinger and others without a national forum at their command had been trying for so long to point out. Senator Kefauver had not arrived at his words easily. When witnesses before the committee first began mentioning the Mafia, senators Kefauver, Charles W. Tobey and their colleagues were both puzzled and skeptical. Kefauver, from Tennessee, and Tobey, the spare newspaper editor from New Hampshire, who liked to wear a green copyreader traditional eyeshade, found it hard to believe what experienced narcotic agents and local police chiefs as well were trying to tell them. Even Rudolph Halley was inclined to be incredulous as narcotic agents White, Siragusa and Claude A. Follmer, inspectors Frank Ahern and Thomas Cahill of the San Francisco Police Department, Chief Edward Allen of Youngstown, Ohio, and other officers—local, federal and international—led the senators through the brotherhood's fantastic maze of conspiracies, relationships, philosophy, murders and skulduggeries. Well-trained policemen such as these are good witnesses in court but they are seldom eloquent. Nevertheless, the weight of their solemn testimony began to tell.

By the time the committee arrived in Kansas City, Missouri, they were ready to listen most carefully to a statement made by Agent Follmer. The narcotic agent was testifying under oath.

The case of Nani, Antinori, Lopiparo, et al—about which the agent was telling—had been routine to the Bureau. In 1942, Commissioner Anslinger's organization had discovered from informers that a powerful combine of the brotherhood had been set up to bring heroin from Marseilles via Cuba to Kansas City for distribution in the Midwest. One of the Bureau's long-range, carefully organized operations began. Finally, early in 1943, the case came to a head. Agents were able to get a microphone into the Kansas City hotel room occupied by Antonio Lopiparo and Giuseppe Antinori—one from St. Louis, the other from Tampa—who were temporarily running the organization of distribution for the local syndicate. Agent Follmer produced a transcription of one of their conversations for the committee.

Each, separately, had been picked up for questioning and then released. Each knew that the other had been interrogated. They met, finally, in their hotel room. No one knows what pacings and starings preceded their talk. But their talk is Bureau and Senate record. "If anybody has been talking," said Antonio Lopiparo—alias Lolip, often called Lollipop—"I sure would like to know who it is." Giuseppe Antinori answered quickly, "You know you don't have to worry about me. Whatever I know I'm going to keep to myself. It don't do you no good to talk and have to face two or three sons of bitches on the outside when you come out." Lopiparo was apparently still dissatisfied. "Somebody must have put the finger on me, and I have a hunch who it was."

And then came the part of Agent Follmer's transcription that rocked the senators. There had been a pause in the exchange between Antonio and Giuseppe. "They even asked me about the Mafia," said Antinori in a strained, quiet tone. "As if I'd say anything about *that.*" Again there were silence. Lopiparo, apparently, was thinking. "You just wait," he said finally, "until the time comes and we'll come out okay. You know these government charges are pretty tough, but there's ways of getting around them, too. Money talks. We'll stay to the finish and see who all snitched."

As the hearings went on the eyes, ears and minds of the senators, Halley and assistant counsel became more and more closely tuned to the unmistakable frequency of the brotherhood's wavelength. Their questions on the subject became increasingly penetrating. But only three members of the brotherhood made any mistakes; the rest would say nothing whatever. Every single one, however, the committee noticed after a while, tautened visibly and audibly when this line of questioning began. The regular interrogation about their individual backgrounds, associations, business and income were bad enough. Men who were usually entirely self-possessed and even insolent squirmed occasionally when Counsel Halley bore down on them in these matters. But the moment the Mafia was mentioned they froze in a peculiar way. The body stiffened, the eyes went blank, the voice became flat.

In Chicago, the chief counsel was able to spell the code of *omertà* out even more clearly. Philipo D'Andrea, summoned before the committee from Los Angeles, had been one of Al Capone's closest associates in Prohibition era Chicago and his favorite bodyguard. His criminal record was very long and he had just been released on parole from a sentence for extortion from a California prison. D'Andrea, a small nervous man in his fifties, was jittery. Defiance of the committee, he knew, might mean the revocation of his parole and several more years of jail. He was relatively expansive about various rackets in Chicago and on the West Coast. And then Associate Counsel George Robinson, who was asking the questions that day, came to the inevitable query. Had D'Andrea ever heard of the Mafia? Yes, having been born in Sicily, he had heard of it since he was a child. He was taut as a bowstring. Did he know anything about its present activities? Was it connected in any way with the Italo-American Union or the Unione Sicilione? No, definitely not. He knew nothing of its current activities whatever.

"Would you say," asked Robinson, "that it would be unusual for any man of your age who was born in Sicily to say that he knew nothing about the Mafia?" D'Andrea shrugged with clenched hands. "Yes, I would think so. If he was born in Sicily I would think so. Because as I say, years ago it was a byword in every family. People were scared to death of having a little home for fear someone would come over and blow it up, or for fear that they would receive a letter. That was the condition here about twenty years ago that I recall." (Twenty years ago D'Andrea had been in Chicago, not Sicily.)

D'Andrea's fright at his peculiar confession was suddenly obvious. His hands clenched more violently. George Robinson continued:

"What would you say were some of the other concepts or principles of the Mafia that you recall from your childhood, having heard talked about in the family?"

The clenched hands cramped again and the eyes narrowed to slits. "One of the concepts," said D'Andrea slowly and with emphasis, "was that it would be a good idea to keep your mouth closed."

Robinson had one more question. "Is the Mafia a subject that is discussed among Italian families?"

D'Andrea looked incredulous, puzzled, and then incensed. "Oh God, no, sir," he exploded. "No, sir! It is not discussed out of the home—ever."

In Kansas City Senator Kefauver had Antonio Gizzo in the witness chair during an "executive session" of the committee. An executive session of a congressional investigation group is held in private with only the legislators and their staffs present with the witnesses. Public and press are excluded and the testimony is not officially published. The purpose of this is to make it possible for witnesses to talk without fear of reprisal.

"Do you know Balestrere?" Halley asked Gizzo. (Giovanni Balestrere was recognized racket leader of Kansas City.) "Yes, sir," Gizzo answered. Halley's next question came in a bored, almost absent tone. "He is rather widely known as a prominent man in the Mafia, isn't he?" "That is what you hear," Gizzo answered easily. "What do *you* hear?" snapped Halley. Gizzo fumbled for a moment. The implications of his statement had not yet reached his rather slow brain. "The same thing that you just said there," he mumbled. Then, apparently, he realized what he had said. From then on, although he had nothing to fear from the committee, he resembled a trapped animal. Later on Halley asked him suddenly, "Do you now belong to the Mafia?" This time Gizzo was ready. "What is the Mafia?" he asked with a puzzled frown and a gesture of wonderment. "I don't even know what the Mafia is."

Senator Kefauver listened to all this and a lot more. His original frank disbelief changed to doubt and then conviction. "Everywhere it went," he wrote, "the committee found evidence to support the belief that the underworld cognoscenti found it healthier not to talk about the Mafia. We questioned a number of witnesses. . . . None of these vaunted tough boys wanted to admit any knowledge of the Mafia. But the Mafia is there all right."

But it was New York City that hit the senator and his colleagues in the midriff. Halley was at home in New York and he prepared his show with both skill and detailed knowledge. It was not easy. Kefauver, Tobey and the others, able legislators though they all were, had the almost involuntary awe for the vast city and its government which most non-New Yorkers have. In the early days of the Kefauver Committee Mayor William O'Dwyer, always a shrewd and far-sighted operator, realized that the senators would inevitably get to New York and tried to take certain precautions to protect some of his friends. Among other things, he dispatched a police inspector whom he trusted to Washington to "help" the committee. Kefauver was delighted. "You see," he said to the press at the time, "you must be overly concerned about conditions in New York. This is a very fine gesture of the mayor's, sending one of his best men from Centre Street to aid us. Why would he do that if he had anything to hide?" The press suspected that the inspector had been sent more as an observer than a helper, and talked to Rudolf Halley about it. "Don't worry about it," was his comment. "They'll see for themselves when we get to New York."

For eight days of public hearings in March, 1951, the top New York City racketeers and their political associates squirmed as Halley calmly and carefully dissected them before the fascinated gaze of the whole country through television. Kefauver's use of TV on this occasion—for the first time in this kind of procedure—drew criticism from many newspapermen as a "cheap extravaganza," a "political circus." Various crime reporters have remarks in articles and books on the naivete of the questions asked by the senators and their whole procedure. "Look," said Halley to the writer on one occasion. "You and I know what this thing looks like. So do a lot of well-informed reporters, policemen and other officials. But the public does not. They've got to be *shown*. They can read all the stories in the newspapers and magazines. They still won't have a notion of what makes these gangsters tick until they *see* them and have been explained in a way that they will understand." That was the real purpose of the spectacular New York hearings. In them Kefauver, Tobey, Halley and the rest performed a very valuable service, with lasting results. It showed people, among other things, a very clear picture of how the brotherhood operates.

Governmental corruption and political skulduggery in New York City is nothing new. No one was much surprised when ex-Mayor O'Dwyer, who had in the meanwhile, incredibly enough, been made United States ambassador to Mexico, was invited to appear before the committee. O'Dwyer arrived in New York dapper, cocky and obviously convinced that his prestige would carry him through a short interrogation without difficulty. Halley had planned the proceedings somewhat differently. Little by little, O'Dwyer's habit of exchanging favors at his command for political support and "campaign funds" evolved. John P. Crane, then president of the city's Uniformed Firemen's Association, testified under oath that he had given the mayor $10,000 cash in one envelope and his first deputy fire commissioner and unofficial general political officer, James J. Moran, $55,000 in instalments for pushing an increase of firemen's pay through the Board of Estimate. This sort of thing had been standard procedure with many mayors since the foundation of Tammany Hall. Few New Yorkers were very shocked. The ambassador and ex-mayor himself did not seem particularly worried over these charges.

Halley next began to question O'Dwyer about the years when he was district attorney, and was investigating Albert Anastasia and the organization known as Murder, Incorporated. For the first time, O'Dwyer became irritable and openly nervous.

Murder, Inc.—as the newspapers came to call it—was unquestionably the invention of three dons: Anastasia, Joe Adonis and Frank Costello. Actually, it was not an invention at all. It was simply the transposition to the United States of an ancient Sicilian system. The three New York capi mafiosi had realized that the whole business of corporal punishment and eventual execution was being administered in a sloppy and dangerous manner. They must have, as one had in Sicily, a pool of trained, experienced and reliable bravos who would maim or kill on order for a reasonable stipend. This seemed to them not only reasonable but imperative. After careful screening of many candidates, they picked Abe (Kid Twist) Reles, a vicious and utterly ruthless sharpshooter of the Brooklyn rackets as well as a competent executive, as leader of their unique squad. Abe Reles was no mafioso. The brotherhood rarely makes an appointment of this kind, but Kid Twist was unusually able. Immediately under him was a solid phalanx of mafiosi: Carmine Scaffo, Harry Maione, Louis Capone (a very distant relative of the great Alphonse), Tony Romeo, Vito Gurino, Dandy Jack Parisi. Below these were other non-mafiosi. The employment of Reles at the top and other non-mafiosi at the bottom was to prove a very serious mistake. In less than a decade Murder, Inc., at the behest of its masters, disposed of approximately 130 rivals and recalcitrants with gun, icepick, cleaver and rope.

Finally, over the years, the police had been able to accumulate enough information from subordinates to construct a strong case against Reles. Kid Twist was arrested. To the amazement of the district attorney's office he broke down almost immediately. In exchange for a promise of leniency for his own crimes, he began to talk. Even the district attorney's office of New York County had never, nor have they since, heard such a recitation of almost incredible, cold-blooded savagery. Reles was not only willing to talk, he was also willing to testify in court. District Attorney William O'Dwyer's brilliant assistant Burton B. Turkus was in charge of the case and prosecuted it vigorously. Eight murderers went to the electric chair and 47 of their assistants to prison for long terms. The district attorney's office was getting ready to arrest and prosecute Albert Anastasia, whom Kid Twist had denounced with others as corroborative witnesses, when one of the most fantastic incidents in the often fantastic history of the New York City Police Department occurred. Reles, who had made a sworn statement that Anastasia was the executive head of Murder, Inc. and had directly given him orders for several assassinations, was in protective custody awaiting Anastasia's indictment and the trial at which he was to testify. Six detectives of the district attorney's staff, under the command of Captain Frank C. Bals—a favorite of

O'Dwyer's whom he later made a deputy police commissioner—guarded the vicious, chunky gunman in a suite of the Half Moon Hotel in Coney Island. Any jail in or around New York would have been unsafe for the crucial witness, no matter what precautions were taken. "Anastasia could have reached right in throught the bars," as Turkus put it. Anastasia reached right into the Half Moon Hotel anyway. Six supposedly picked policemen were apparently asleep when Kid Twist plunged to his death five stories below from the window of his bedroom. The real story of his death will probably never be told. What evidence there is, however, indicates murder.

In any case, the law stopped abruptly in front of the door of Don Umberto. All charges against Anastasia were dropped. His "Wanted Fugitive" card in the Police Department's active file was withdrawn at the behest of James Moran—the same Moran who later became O'Dwyer's executive when he was mayor—who was then chief clerk of the Brooklyn district attorney's office. His appointment had been arranged by O'Dwyer.

As all this began coming out with Counsel Halley's probing, Senator Tobey sensed the possibility of bringing the whole "tawdry mess," as he called it, into sharp focus before the television cameras. First Tobey, with a definite pattern of procedure forming in his mind, went for Frank Bals, the ex-detective and ex-deputy police commissioner. Bals finally had to admit that Kid Twist would not possibly have been trying to escape from the hotel—his life would have been in far greater danger outside—and that suicide, by virtue of Reles' very nature, was out of the question. Then Bals, as Tobey had hoped he would under the goading, came up with a foolish story. The body of Reles had been found spread-eagled on a ground floor roof of the hotel with two knotted bedsheets near him. Bals suggested that the gangster must have improvised the bedsheet rope, intending to climb into a window on the floor below, come back up through the hotel and surprise his guards—all for fun. The bedsheets had parted and Reles had fallen. The "peekaboo theory," as Tobey immediately named it, was so ridiculous that everyone at the hearing began to laugh. Kid Twist, despite his aptitude for murder, was actually a cowardly man and no athlete; he also could not have known, particularly at night, whether the window below his, which was as far as the bedsheets reached, would be open. The absurdity of Bals' statement made Tobey's point more than clear. Kid Twist had obviously been pushed or thrown from his window by one of the policemen supposedly guarding him, or by someone whom they admitted. It was also equally clear by the time Tobey was through that neither Bals nor his chief, the district attorney, had done very much about finding out who the executioner might have been.

If Ambassador O'Dwyer was uncomfortable then, he was to become even more so. Kefauver, Tobey and Halley put other pieces together slowly and methodically. Anastasia himself had testified in an executive session of the committee, and his testimony was never made public. It was far from cooperative, but it furnished many leads indicating his close contacts with his equally exalted brethren, Joe Adonis and Frank Costello, and through them with Tammany Hall and finally the mayor. Joe Adonis testified openly. Without his seeming to realize it, the capo mafioso shocked even Halley. His police record was very long and included arrests for extortion, kidnaping, grand larceny and felonious assault. Halley asked him why on the occasion of various arrests he had used different names, DeMio, Arrosa and a dozen others. "I've used all kinds of names in those minor conflicts," was the astonishing, gravel-voiced reply. With relatively little pleading of the Fifth Amendment, Don Giuseppe took the senators through his extraordinary career from the time that he was proprietor of Joe's Italian Kitchen at the corner of Fourth Avenue and Carrol Street in Brooklyn, to the present. After his pistol carrying days of the Prohibition era were over and he had made a substantial fortune (like so many of the mafiosi), he became a combination restaurateur, political fixer and financier. He was good at all three avocations. He was an excellent host and his food was superb. He was also very shrewd politically. The small politicians that the prematurely gray-haired, always polite and softly spoken Sicilian picked as his favorites almost invariably became big politicians. The list of the regular guests in his restaurant became increasingly impressive. There were an assistant attorney general of the state, the minority leader of the State Assembly, the Democratic leader of Brooklyn, judges ranging in rank from city magistrates to State Supreme Court justices, borough presidents, Tammany sachems and district leaders both Democratic and Republican. Don Giuseppe didn't care about party affiliation. In their early days he had given many on both sides "personal loans" and turned out his highly efficient corps of vote riggers to boost them at the polls. He never had to demand favors in return; he simply got them, almost without asking. One of Don Giuseppe's most regular patrons was William O'Dwyer—as district attorney of New York County and later as the city's mayor. Others were Don Umberto Anastasia and Don Francesco Castiglia, two of Don Giuseppe's closest friends.

"We further learned," Senator Kefauver wrote after all the information was in, "that Adonis had sizable investments in a number of fields of legitimate enterprise.... There was no doubt in the minds of the committee members that this gangster had achieved pre-eminence in all three fields that have become an unholy trinity in areas of the United States—crime, politics and business."

Then came Frank Costello. The committee's investigators had dug up every available detail of his career, his connections and his extraordinary power. Don Francesco was quite relaxed when he first appeared in the brightly lit chamber in the Federal Court House and faced the senators and the television cameras. "A damn moom pitcher set," he commented without rancor. He was prepared to enjoy himself. Publicity, dangerous as it is, has an almost hypnotic sort of fascination for even the shrewdest of the racketeers; it makes them great, up to a point, in the eyes of the brethren. But within a few hours Don Francesco was insisting that his face should not be photographed, and there followed the famous incident when the camera focused on his restless, nervous hands.

Halley and the senators began to explore Costello's personal, business and particularly political relations. Anastasia and Adonis had obviously been very close to him for many years. So had Tammany Hall. It was shown beyond doubt that the Hall's most prominent sachems presented themselves most respectfully at Don Francesco's cocktail and dinner parties. Several newspaper reports which had been branded officially as political rumor mongering were established as fact. One was the amazing story of Thomas A. Aurelio's nomination and subsequent election by Tammany Hall forces as a justice of the State Supreme Court. Don Francesco's legally tapped telephone line, in 1943, had yielded a memorable conversation with the late Michael Kennedy, at that time a powerful Tammany leader. Costello suggested Aurelio's nomination. Kennedy demurred. Aurelio was only a city magistrate with little political following. His election might cause political trouble. "Are you a man or a mouse?" growled Don Francesco. Kennedy complied and Aurelio was duly elected. Actually, any aid contributed by the brotherhood toward the justice's election turned out to be a mistake on their part. His record is immaculate.

Halley suddenly asked Don Francesco whether he had supported any candidate for judicial office recently. Costello was caught completely off guard. "Oh no, Mr. Halley," he said earnestly. "With the Aurelio case I burned my fingers once and I never participated in any candidates since." Don Francesco may or may not have given up tampering with the judiciary, but the committee accumulated enough evidence to write into their report to Congress the following official lines: "There can be no question that Frank Costello has exercised a major influence upon the New York County Democratic organization, Tammany Hall, because of his personal friendships and working relationships with its officers, and with Democratic district leaders even today in ten of the sixteen Manhattan districts. Costello also had relationships with some Republican political leaders."

Here, in Part 7 of the minutes of the Kefauver Committee, are the unmistakable mafiosi—Costello, Anastasia, Adonis, Profaci—their equally unmistakable attorneys and assistants. Here also is a former district attorney and mayor of our largest city. Other witnesses range from narcotics addicts to Tammany Hall leaders and the superintendent of the New York State Police. And all of their testimony, willing and unwilling, fits together into one of the most shocking indictments of an American city and its government ever put on paper. No clearer picture of a modern operation of the brotherhood could be drawn, either.

The Ambassador to Mexico was being questioned along these lines by Senator Tobey:

Tobey: This question comes to my mind. In Murder, Inc., who was the president or the chairman of the board of directors?

O'Dwyer: I can only answer that on the basis of the evidence that was given me by Reles. He said that the term for the organization was "the combination" and that as far as he knew there was no chief man in charge. It was a combination, an alliance. But there was a mutual understanding....

Although he did mention the Mafia . . . I never felt that Reles knew too much about the Mafia as such. [But] he knew it was there.

Tobey: Who, in your opinion, was the paymaster for Murder, Inc.?

O'Dwyer: There never was payment for a given crime. The troops, as they called them, were generally little fellows, and they were given by the combination such jurisdiction—whether it was pinballs or whether it was houses of prostitution, or things of that kind—and I didn't find much of

> that, I must admit . . . but there were certain unlawful activities whereby in neighborhoods they could collect money to keep them going.
>
> The work, the services that they were to render for that purpose were that whenever they were called upon to steal a car or drive a car to a murder or to commit the actual murder, that they had to stand by; and when—in this neighborhood—when Anastasia gave the order to selected men, they were supposed to do it.

The casual mention of Anastasia's name was not lost upon Senator Herbert R. O'Conor, who questioned O'Dwyer a few moments later.

O'Conor: It is very evident then that, in your opinion, Anastasia was one of the highest in command of this notorious outfit?

O'Dwyer: He was entrusted with all the murders, official murders of theirs, committed by the Brooklyn group, no matter where they were committed.

O'Conor: And over what period of time were you in office after his indictment was returned?

Suddenly the ambassador seemed to realize the implications of what he had said under oath and to anticipate what was coming as a result. He plucked at the lapels of his immaculate jacket, smoothed his trousers while he thought. There was no sound in the hearing room. The silence had almost physical impact. Kefauver, Tobey, O'Conor and Halley gazed steadily at the ex-mayor. Finally, O'Dwyer said: "He was never indicted, sir."

Fifty-four closely printed pages of the record report O'Dwyer's attempt to explain why Anastasia was not prosecuted. In his efforts to extricate himself, the ambassador only spelled out even more clearly the details of a careless, badly run operation of law enforcement hedged in by traditional politics, major and minor corruption and an utter lack of fundamental integrity. Important documents were wrongly routed or lost entirely. Police officials as close to one another as are Brooklyn, Manhattan, and Jersey across the river, a matter of a few miles, failed to communicate with each other about the most crucial situations. "It was out of our jurisdiction," O'Dwyer kept saying. The matter of jurisdiction, as every policeman knows, can be easily overcome by a short telephone call. Subsequently, for another 89 pages, New York's former chief executive explained to the senators as though they were school children how impossible it was to stop dock racketeering, to discipline the Police Department, to curb gambling effectively, and all in all to run a decent government in the city. The senators sat there and looked alternately exasperated and nonplussed as the curious answers followed the committee's questions.

Tobey: In 1939 was the Department of Investigation of the City of New York investigating the murder of one Panto and widespread rackets on the Brooklyn water front, involving six Camarda locals?

O'Dwyer: Yes, sir.

Tobey: Were these locals under the control of Albert Anastasia, Emilio Camarda, Jack Parisi, and Anthony Romeo?

O'Dwyer: My information, as I recall it, at that time was that Camarda—there were several heads of the unions, but the information we had was that Albert Anastasia ran the waterfront.

Tobey: He was the tops.

O'Dwyer: Yes, sir.

Tobey: In the examination of the more than 100 witnesses in this case, was it disclosed that Anastasia and Romeo and other gangsters had been stealing hundreds of thousands of dollars from the unions and had destroyed their original books and records?

O'Dwyer: You couldn't arrive at any other conclusion.

Senator Tobey slowly took off his green eyeshade. "I beg your pardon," he said. O'Dwyer tried to meet the blazing glance of the old gentleman. "You couldn't arrive at any other conclusion," he repeated nervously.

Tobey: Now, did Chief Assistant District Attorney Joseph J. Hanley swear that three days after the start of the investigation you, as District Attorney, ordered him off the case and stopped him from continuing with it?

O'Dwyer: I don't know how long it was, but I know we had enough information as we needed at that time regarding extortion, but we were working feverishly on murder.

And so it went, hour after hour and page after page. After hearing all of the often staggering testimony of the New York group—of O'Dwyer, Costello, Adonis, the Anastasias, and the rest—the Committee, with great labor and without any sort of political animus, put together their final presentment to Congress:

Neither he [O'Dwyer] nor his appointees took any effective action against the top echelons of the gambling, narcotics, waterfront, murder, or bookmaking rackets. In fact, his actions impeded promising investigation of such rackets. His defense of public officials who were derelict in their duty, and his actions in investigations of corruption, and his failure to follow up concrete evidence of organized crime, particularly in the case of Murder, Inc., and the waterfront, have contributed to the growth of organized crime, racketeering, and gangsterism in New York City.

The principal witness before the committee concerning the brotherhood's ties between the United States and abroad was Charles Siragusa. The narcotics agent—he was then not yet a district supervisor—outlined the web that binds organized crime in New York and the United States and also across the Atlantic. Senator Alexander Wiley and Chief Counsel Richard Moser, who had replaced Rudolph Halley, had become fascinated by the documentation in a previous executive session of the role of Don Salvatore Lucania. A lengthy discussion of Charlie Lucky took place. (The comments in parentheses are editorial.)

Moser: Just tell us generally—well, tell us first about the Callace story and then point out how you think it is a typical Mafia situation.

Siragusa: Well, you have this Frank Callace, this 28-year-old man from 107th Street who goes to Italy.

Mr. Moser: He is a member of what is called the 107th Street mob; is that correct?
Siragusa: Yes, sir. He went to Italy in April of 1951.
Mr. Moser: And where did he go first?
Siragusa: He made a beeline right for Palermo, where he met his uncle who has exactly the same name.

In detail, Siragusa took the senators and counsel along with him in their minds' eyes as Frank Callace and his uncle Frank Callace—a fugitive from the United States and the FBI, incidentally—traveled to Milan to see Joe Pici, Luciano's lieutenant in charge of narcotics negotiations, then to Naples to get final approval from Don Salvatore himself, then back to Palermo to await the final and always complicated closing of the deal. Eventually, the Callaces were summoned by a cryptic telephone call back to Milan where they paid for and received from Pici three kilograms of heroin.

Mr. Moser: How do you know all that?
Siragusa: We have admissions by the Callaces.
Senator Wiley: Have you got the heroin?
Siragusa: Yes, sir; we have the heroin in Italy.
Mr. Moser: Didn't you receive some kind of tip after they had received this heroin?
Siragusa (almost obviously impatient): Yes, sir. Here is where we stepped into the picture. They (the Callaces) left Milan by airplane en route for Palermo, which is about seven hundred miles. The police at Rome received an anonymous telephone tip (actually from one of Siragusa's undercover agents) that on this particular airplane would be a certain Callace with a quantity of drugs. The Italian police met that plane (when it touched down at Rome) and arrested the nephew Frank Callace.
Mr. Moser: That is the young man from the 107th Street mob?
Siragusa: Yes, sir.
Mr. Moser: They arrested him at Rome?
Siragusa: At the Rome airport.
Mr. Moser: What did they find?
Siragusa: They found three kilos of heroin in a suitcase.
Mr. Moser: In his possession?
Siragusa: In his possession. He was carrying the suitcase. The

Italian police did not know at that time that there were two Frank Callaces on the airplane. They just arrested the young Callace.

Mr. Moser: And the uncle got away.

Siragusa: He got away temporarily but not for long.

It all sounded so simple, as Siragusa told it, but the senators were beginning to grasp what was involved.

Mr. Moser: You told me one time that you are sometimes able to identify leaders in the Mafia by some title they have; is that correct?

Siragusa: The big shots of the Mafia, the older men, the men that sit in on these grand councils, the policy meetings have the title of *don* . . . It is the title of respect given to members of the higher echelon.

Mr. Moser: Did you find that any of these associates of Callace that you checked up on, including Luciano's associates, were called don in that manner?

Siragusa: Yes. Lucky himself and Nichola Gentile (who also came from America).

Senator Wiley: You are of Italian descent, and we want to make it clear, because I think all over America some of our best citizens are Italians. You think only relatively few of the Italian people are mixed up in this Mafia business?

Siragusa: Yes, sir.

Senator Wiley: Have you any basis whatever to give us an estimate of the extent of the Mafia in this country?

Siragusa: I would say that in all principal cities there are segments of the Mafia, and I would say that New York probably has the big bosses.

Senator Wiley: You have given us a pretty clear-cut factual statement showing Luciano's connections in Italy with the trade in this country. Have you any information to tell us whether or not Luciano has the power to enforce his connections here through threatening or coercion or through gunmen or any other methods? If he is the kingpin, we want to know how far his domain extends.

Siragusa: From what I have seen, and I have spoken to some members of his gang there in an undercover capacity (the narcotic agent at the time was passing himself off very successfully as a big buyer of heroin from New York), I would say, if he is not the kingpin, he is one of the royal family. The fact that he receives large sums of money from American gangsters indicates to me that he has definite word in policy matters and that he is still deriving an income from American rackets.

Senator Wiley: You state that he is one of the royal family. Does that mean he has this power that he can enforce through gunmen and coercion and threats his mandate here in this country?

Siragusa: Yes, sir. ("Yes, *sir*" was the way the agent said it.)

There followed a discussion of the ways and means of combatting the brotherhood. Agent Siragusa pointed out to Senator Wiley that in fascist countries, such as Italy under Mussolini, strongarm methods were employed that could not be used in America. Senator Wiley replied:

Senator Wiley: I wouldn't suggest anything of that character, naturally. But I will not admit that we are unable to cope with this problem once we center our attention to it. I think it must be met. Otherwise it will lay a pattern for other organizations to think they are bigger than the state.

This last remark of Senator Wiley's, as Siragusa finished his testimony, like so many others from Kefauver, Tobey and Halley in the course of the whole inquiry, is lost in the sheer mass of the accumulated evidence in many thousands of pages of the record. Nevertheless, the committee had succeeded in turning the spotlight on organized crime.

The total accomplishment of the Kefauver Committee has never really been totted up for the public to see. Its effects were scattered and diverse, but impressive as a whole. Private crime commissions have been set up by dedicated citizens in hundreds of large and small communities. Inefficient and corrupt policemen are afraid of them, honest law officers who want to do a job welcome them. Grand juries all over the country have been affected by a grasp of the pattern of organized crime which they have never had before. In almost every state in the union, legislatures began taking a much closer look at the destructive effects of gambling, narcotics, labor racketeering and the people behind them. Many new laws and sensibly increased police powers have been created as a result on the federal, state and municipal levels.

"But there is so much left to be done," a senator said to us recently. "We've only begun to work, really. And we haven't begun, yet, to control the situation. It's not a very pretty commentary on the state of the nation. But it happens to be true."

The committee in its final report included a somber, disagreeable warning:

It is apparent that public interest in law enforcement will continue only so long as a spotlight is directed at the problem. ... There is serious danger that public complacency and indifference will take the place of the present state of vigilance. Obviously, local governments cannot be expected to turn the spotlight on themselves; the pressure must come from an outside force that is not subject to improper local influences.

The brotherhood of evil has always thrived on public complacency and indifference. Despite the work of Kefauver and his associates, the mafiosi had little reason to believe that the situation was changing as far as they were concerned. It was, very gradually, but they didn't know it.

CHAPTER ELEVEN

Three Mafiosi

Three very recent incidents in the history of the brotherhood demonstrate how faithfully the old precepts and connections have been maintained. One don is assassinated, one escapes a decreed execution by a hair's breadth, one is arrested by federal agents.

I. *"Dear Don Ciccio"*

New York City had begun to swelter under the summer noonday sun of June 17, 1957, as Don Francesco Scalici walked unhurriedly along Arthur Avenue in the Bronx. The street, lined with little Italo-American shops, was crowded as usual with busy men, baby carriages and gossiping women. People nodded respectfully to the dapper figure in yellow slacks and matching sport shirt, immaculate as always despite the heat. Gravely, the don acknowledged every salute with a princely wave of the hand.

Don Ciccio, as he was known to many of Italian birth and extraction, was a very important man in the Bronx—a booming borough with a population of more than a million and a half. In three prominent banks, senior executives hastened to shake his hand when he came to do business. He liked to say that he was "just a little contractor." But no one, for example, could profitably run a plastering business in his section of the borough without his consent. Officially he was only a vice-president of the relatively modest Mario &

DeBono Plastering Company of Corona. But his grip on the whole building industry of the Bronx was tight. When Mr. Scalise, as he preferred to be called, visited a new construction job, supervisors and laborers alike of all trades stood at almost military attention when he spoke to them. There was never anything even remotely menacing in Mr. Scalise's voice or manner. The trio of assistants who usually accompanied him looked like certified public accountants. He was an apparently mild man of 55, almost bald, with a thin mustache, a big nose, deep laugh wrinkles, a throaty but pleasant way of speaking, a sense of humor and a persuasive smile. "But ya hadda watch his eyes," as one of his former associates put it. "They was kinda *hooded,* ya follow me. They could be friendly as hell, when he wanted. Then, maybe, he'd get sore all of a sudden. He'd never say nothing. But them lids would come down over them eyes. Then ya'd better watch your step, ya follow me. I seen him, many times, start or stop a strike without hardly so much as a word. All he done is give them a few of them looks." The picture of a typical capo mafioso could not have been more clearly drawn.

No important underworld racket could function in the Bronx, either, without Don Ciccio's permission. The numbers and other gambling interests paid regular tribute. The distribution of narcotics in the borough was under his thumb. So was most of the underworld's peculiar finance in the area. If a bookmaker or a numbers shark was embarrassed by heavy losses which endangered his ability to pay off, and therefore his life, he could apply only to Don Ciccio—who, if satisfied with the applicant's credit, would advance money at a monthly interest of 25 per cent or more. No one questioned his authority. Among his most intimate friends, of many years' standing, were such powers as Don Giuseppe Profaci of Brooklyn, Don Umberto Anastasia and Don Francesco Costello of Manhattan, Don Vitone Genovese of New Jersey. When he made one of his frequent trips to Italy, he invariably visited Don Salvatore Lucania in Naples and Don Giuseppe Doto in Rome.

It was just half past one when the don paused in front of Mazarro's fruit and vegetable store at 2380 Arthur Avenue. The typically Italian sidewalk stands were attractive and tempting. Enrico Mazarro, a fat, genial little man, bowed and beamed as the *padrone* entered the store. Knowing that Don Ciccio did not like anyone to hover over him while he selected what he wanted to buy, the little Sicilian did not follow him into the shop. Instead, he polished his spectacles, began rearranging some trays of grapes outside and anticipated with pleasure the short but thrilling conversation which he would have—as on almost every day for years—with the great man before he left. Signor Mazarro hardly noticed the two young men with rolled up sleeves who suddenly brushed by him, their hands in their pockets.

The expert assassination was over in a few seconds. The don in his careful fashion was counting the change from a five-dollar bill for his ninety-cent purchase, which had been given him by one of Mazarro's obsequious helpers. He probably did not see the two young men as they took practiced positions on the balls of their feet directly in front of him; his eyes were focused on the money in his hands. Two .38 caliber revolvers roared five times in quick succession. Two bullets drove holes through his throat, one slashed open his left cheek, and one caught him in the right shoulder spinning him sideways as he fell. Don Ciccio was already dead, blood gushing from his blasted carotid arteries, as the young men pocketed their guns, again pushed past the staring, stunned Signor Mazarro, climbed calmly into an old black sedan which was double parked in front of the door and drove away. Signor Mazarro stumbled to his telephone.

It was only a few minutes before the first police car arrived, its siren droning to a stop. A patrolman bent over the torn face on the floor, stared and dashed for his radio transmitter. "Frank Scalise," he barked. "He's been dumped." Squad cars loaded with detectives and uniformed officers came quickly. A number of plain-clothes men, according to standard police operational procedure, mingled unobtrusively with the crowd which had gathered to listen for remarks from possible witnesses. Others began talking to Signor Mazarro. Staring incredulously at the body at his feet, the little shopkeeper alternately wiped his hands on a grubby apron and raised them in supplication. "I ain't seen nuthin'," he wailed repeatedly. "These two guys brush by me, see. I hear some shots and I turn around. They brush by me again. They get into an old black sedan and go up Arthur Avenue. That's all I know. The whole thing goes so fast, I can't describe them, the car, or nuthin'." The detectives on the sidewalk were having an equally difficult time. No one, it seemed, had seen anything. Everyone had apparently arrived only after the shooting. All questioned had that sudden vacant look in their eyes that New York police officers know so well.

There was an explosive, very Latin, interruption. One of Don Ciccio's three brothers, Giacomino (New York City Police Department record #B86502), who owns a candy store a few blocks away and with whom the don had lunched just before his death, came on the run, screaming and with tears running down his cheeks. He was joined by brother Giuseppe (New York City Police Department record #B95249), and both had to be restrained by patrolmen from falling to their knees and hugging the gory corpse in their sobbing frenzy. "Death to the murderers," shouted brother Giacomino. "We will find them," shrieked brother Giuseppe.

A few hours later in the office of Assistant District Attorney Albert Blinder of the Bronx, however, the brothers had themselves well in hand. "What enemies?" said one blandly. "Frank didn't have no enemies. Everybody loved him. This was some kind of a mistake." Neither they nor any of the other potential witnesses whom the police had brought in chose to know anything about Mr. Scalise's affairs. All they knew, they said, of such people as Luciano, Strollo, Costello,

Lansky was what they read in the papers. Mr. Scalise couldn't possibly have had anything to do with such people. He was much too nice a man. Wearily, Mr. Blinder finally received the press. "It has all the elements of a gang killing," he said, and left the story at that.

The shooting of Mr. Scalise was no mere gang killing, however. It was a highly important and significant Mafia execution—decreed, planned and carried out strictly according to traditions and rules now 200 years old. Almost everyone who was on the street in front of Mazarro's store when Don Ciccio died knew or sensed that. They knew that the assassination of a capo mafioso was a very grave affair, which might set off a series of other sudden deaths by gunfire. They also knew, from the stories of their parents and grandparents, and from their own experience—sometimes—how dangerous it is to interfere in the Mafia's intimate business or to express any opinions about it. One hears, sees, knows and above all says, absolutely nothing.

Some months before, Don Ciccio had taken one of his periodic flyers in high underworld finance. Heroin was in great demand at the moment. The New York City police and federal narcotic agents had discovered and arrested a number of principal sources of the drug. Judge John A. Mullen, the angry and brilliant senior justice of New York's Court of General Sessions, who has known the Mafia and its methods for years, had sentenced Antonio Velucci and his partner, Nathan Berman, to an unprecedented term in the penitentiary for the possession of over a million dollars' worth of the insidious poison. Recent federal legislation had also greatly strengthened the powers of the Federal Bureau of Narcotics and stiffened the punishments which U.S. judges could impose on the dope peddlers. Almost all of the big traders were nervous. Don Ciccio was not. He summoned a meeting of associates. Everyone would put up a substantial sum of money, Lucky Luciano would be contacted in Naples and 20 kilograms of heroin would be in New York in a matter of weeks to be sold at huge profit. The wholesale price was then $12,000 a kilo. His fellow mafiosi apparently nodded approval. Business such as this in the brotherhood is done simply by the shake of a hand; nothing is ever put on paper. But that handshake is far more binding than any contract in a court of law; its violation means a trial far quicker than those before our legally constituted tribunals, and a much more violent sentence.

In due course, 20 kilograms of heroin were in a carefully concealed locker on the SS *Excambion* of the American Export Line which plied between Naples, Barcelona, Marseilles and New York—through the devious but rapid arrangements, methods, and routes which was explained in an earlier chapter. But from the beginning, contrary to Don Ciccio's confident expectations, he and his syndicate were in trouble. The Bureaus of Narcotics and Customs had information that American ships were being used for considerable smuggling, and federal agents swarmed over every incoming U.S. vessel. The seamen who were to act as couriers did not dare to bring their valuable cargo ashore. Three times the *Excambion* made her complete circuit without delivering the goods. Don Ciccio, desperate, decided on a radical move; the narcotics must be transferred to a French or British ship not under suspicion. Messages went from New York to the proper people to that effect.

The *Excambion,* in the harbor of Marseilles, had just cast off her lines when her captain, leaning over the rail of the bridge, saw a sack fly out of one of the ship's open ports and thud onto the concrete of the pier below. He had a hunch, ordered the engines stopped, eased back to the quay and sent one of his officers on the double to have the bundle picked up and brought back aboard. It was obviously ship's property, he had every right to do what he did and neither French police nor customs men objected. A little later, out at sea, he discovered that the sack contained 20 kilograms of a white powder neatly packaged in small containers. On arrival at

Barcelona, his next port of call, customs men quickly confirmed his suspicions; it was heroin. The captain hastily handed the embarrassing property over to the Spanish authorities and washed his hands of the whole matter.

It was not long before word of the catastrophe reached New York—and the Bronx. It was Don Ciccio this time who was summoned to a meeting. He must have faced a circle of stern faces. It is a cardinal rule of the Mafia that a man who organizes such a venture is financially responsible if it fails. The rule is rigidly enforced and no excuses are acceptable. Don Ciccio evidently promised full restitution. But he waited to produce it. It was a lot of money. And, in the Mafia, one's creditors sometimes die suddenly and leave no list of outstanding financial transactions.

Don Ciccio, however, waited too long. The wheels of Mafia enforcement began turning. This is never a careless procedure; it is particularly deliberate in the case of a capo mafioso. A formal gathering of the offended mafiosi generally takes place before one or more disinterested and ranking members of the brotherhood. If a sentence of death is agreed upon, a small committee is designated to implement the decision. One of these writes to a cousin or uncle perhaps in Chicago, Detroit or elsewhere in the almost indecipherable Sicilian-Italian dialect for "two good men" to do "some heavy work." No such letter, even if found, would ever prove anything in court. Before long the two "good men" arrive, for example, in New York. Their preparation for the task is always meticulous, which is the reason that Mafia killers are so seldom caught. For days, sometimes for weeks, they study the habits and schedule of the condemned.

There is a peculiar, almost ritualistic phase of the preparations for a Mafia execution. It is an ancient rule that a mafioso, no matter how serious the offense which he has committed against the fraternity, must be killed suddenly and unexpectedly. If the condemned is unsuspecting, his executioners are introduced to him by a third individual, get to know him and on the day set for his extinction give him a sumptuous dinner with as much wine as he can drink before he is taken for his last ride in an automobile. If possible, also in deference to tradition, a shotgun is used. In Sicily to this day the mafiosi load their shells with handmade lead pellets approximately the size of buckshot filed into pyramid shape known as *lupara.* When the Mafia in Sicily asassinates someone, the killing is described this way by the natives: A *pezzinovanta* (leader who intimidates others) has ordered two *boia* (executioners) to "give the *lupara* sickness" to that someone. It is not very different in New York City. Lighter and more convenient ordnance has replaced *lupara,* which is too troublesome to make, and the shotgun, which is difficult to conceal in most cases. It was found that bullets of heavy caliber from a handgun properly used accomplished the essentials equally as well as the *lupara,* which literally cuts a victim to pieces. American Mafia killers, as with Don Ciccio and many others, aim for the head and neck. Whether or not the wounds are instantaneously fatal, which they generally are, the victim can rarely articulate the name or description of his assailant before he dies; which is the point of the procedure.

Don Ciccio had undoubtedly been trailed for days. Apprehensive of almost all of his usual associates, he was unapproachable for what the Mafia considers a decent execution. This made it difficult. The two killers had to discover a place and time at which he could be shot with a minimum of possible witnesses and a maximum of ensuing confusion. Professional Mafia *boia* think such strategy out with great care; both their personal safety and their reputations depend on perfect performance. Don Ciccio's house in City Island had too many close by and interested neighbors who might react quickly and effectively to a blast of fire by reporting license numbers and descriptions of the assassins. When Don Ciccio drove from home to business in his blue Cadillac, he drove fast and skillfully. Finally they discovered his habit of lunching with his brother, and afterward a walk up Arthur Avenue, and the *boia* picked Mazarro's store. The don was as good as dead.

Immediately after the murder, detectives of the 45th Precinct headed for Don Ciccio's house in City Island with a search warrant. Detective Lieutenant John Gannon and his chief, Inspector Walsh, both experts of long experience in the ways and personalities of the Mafia, did not really expect that anything of value to them would be found. A mafioso does not, by tradition, keep records or letters which might possibly provide the police with any sort of ammunition. But Don Ciccio was an exception. In his desk the officers found what turned out eventually to be a treasure of information. In an obvious desk drawer were, amazingly, photographs, letters and address books containing approximately 400 names, addresses and phone numbers which formed the most complete recent picture of a single mafioso's operation in the United States and abroad that has been discovered. The address books, which will undoubtedly furnish heavy ammunition for future congressional and local investigations of organized crime, listed the top known racketeers of the nation in New York, Chicago, Boston, Las Vegas, Los Angeles, Kansas City, Detroit and a dozen other American cities. Havana and Mexico City were represented as well as Paris, Marseilles, Milan, Rome, Naples and various Sicilian towns. An impressive number of important officials and political figures in many of these places also were apparently available to Don Ciccio by correspondence or telephone. There was also pictorial evidence of both the don's underworld and legitimate connections. Among the photographs was one, taken only a few years ago, of Don Ciccio with Don Salvatore Lucania and his mistress of long standing, Igea Lissoni, on the terrace of the Hotel Excelsior of Naples. The beaming Don Ciccio is standing arm in arm with his fellow capo mafioso who, for the dour, rarely smiling Luciano, wears an unusually pleasant expression.

But, as far as the mentality of the mafiosi, their personal relationships and the tight connection today between the Italian and the American Mafia are concerned, the letters between Palermo and the Bronx were the most revelatory finds of all. The communications, which were recent, were written in the provincial Sicilian dialect. The translations made little sense to Lieutenant Gannon, who had a hunch that there was more in them than the bland family chit-chat which appeared on the surface. He sent them to the New York office of the Bureau of Narcotics. Agent John Amato, a veteran of the Bureau and himself of Sicilian extraction, with a perfect command of Italian and of the Sicilian dialect, had the same feeling as the lieutenant. There were phrases in the letters which he did not understand and which, he sensed, had double meanings. Amato had a relative in New York who was born in Sicily and reared in a Mafia-controlled area of the island. Although the old gentleman had lived in America as a naturalized citizen for many years he was still frightened about handling the material; the phraseology of it was familiar and clear to him. And the danger of prying into the affairs of a mafioso is very real to anyone who has been brought up in a bailiwick of the brotherhood. This was a prying, moreover, that went deeply not only into the business of an individual mafioso but into the very existence and spirit of the Mafia as well.

Characteristic are two letters from the correspondence between Don Ciccio and Nino Torres, an important mafioso and racketeer of Palermo well known to the Italian police and the U.S. Bureau of Narcotics.

One was written by Don Ciccio on September 10, 1956. Strangely enough, he kept a copy:

Dear Nino:

Perhaps in the near future I will have the pleasure of meeting you in person to express my *fraternal* respect which attracts me to you.

I am enclosing a letter, the original of which was sent to a friend—Signor Nicoletti, chief of the factory of Palavicino. I do not know what the relationship is between you and the above-mentioned, but I am obligated because of our relationship to tell you of anything that occurs here in order that you and my *fraternal* friend can form your opinions.

I hope that you will excuse me for troubling you.

I assure you of my availability for anything you may need.

Regards and embraces from the friends and relatives here.

In clear language without the mafioso's typical circumlocutions, the letter, as much recent information reveals, might have been written this way:

Dear Nino:

We have some serious Mafia business to do. I would much rather discuss all this with you in person, but at the moment it would be dangerous, because of the attention being paid me by the Federal Bureau of Narcotics, for me to come to Palermo or for you to come here.

I am enclosing a copy of a letter which I have written to Signor Nicoletti, concerning the shipments of heroin which I require. I know that he is the chief of the Mafia unit of Palavicino and therefore must be treated with respect, but I consider him not quite trustworthy and would like you to keep your eye on him.

Since the selling price of heroin is fluctuating so violently at the moment, I cannot give you a fixed offer at the moment. But as soon as I come to an understanding with my associates, I will let you and the capo mafioso of Palavicino know. You will then bring the amount needed from Signor Nicoletti's stocks to Naples and, with Don Salvatore Lucania's permission, get it aboard a vessel to New York.

You will give the arrangement for the secure transportation of the narcotics from Palermo to Naples your closest personal supervision.

You may call upon me for whatever financial assistance you require in the meanwhile.

My associates and I rely upon you for the usual fraternal cooperation and devotion which will make this venture a success.

Nino Torres' acknowledgement of this directive was delayed for several months due to circumstances beyond his control. The Sicilian questura, under severe pressure from

Rome, had begun one of the periodic attacks against the Mafia which makes the international conspirators and smugglers in Palermo and vicinity discreetly lie low for a while.

Nino Torres' reply to Don Ciccio on February 10th, 1957, told the story quite clearly—in Mafia language:

Dear Don Ciccio:

In replying to your kind letter, please excuse me for not having answered sooner. In regard to the copy of the letter (to Signor Nicoletti) which I received, I understand what it is all about. But since Signor Nicoletti is at present at odds with *Uncle Angelo,* we have been unable to talk to him personally. I have however sent him the letter so that he knows that I have been informed by you to take care of the matter.

Nino Massiglia, chief of the factory of Palermo, is at present on *Ustica.*

Even I have been dispersed as have almost all the rest of the chiefs of factories. Therefore I beg that you wait a little while longer until we can get together to discuss what you have written me.

For the present, *Uncle Angelo* is making even more trouble than he did in 1925. Hoping that this letter finds you in the best of health, as I assure you I am in, I extend affectionate embraces to you, my other friends and relatives.

Your Fraternal Friend,
Nino Torres
Piazza Principe 92
Camporeale, Palermo, Sicily

This may be read as follows:

Dear Don Ciccio (The proper, respectful mode of address from "Dear Nino" to his superior):

Please forgive me for not having confirmed and acted upon your orders more promptly. But much has happened here recently.

I understand that I am to watch and expedite your negotiations with Signor Nicoletti for the delivery of the heroin which you require. I agree with you that he is not too reliable.

Unfortunately, Signor Nicoletti has been for some time a fugitive from the police (*Uncle Angelo* is the Mafia expression for law enforcement officers), and I have been unable to talk to him personally. I have, however, sent your letter to him at his hiding place so that he knows that I have authority from you to carry on with the necessary arrangements myself. He is a very dangerous man and I do not wish to have difficulties with him later which might involve my contracting the Lupara Sickness.

The situation here at the moment is extremely serious. Nino Massiglia, for example (a formerly prominent New York City racketeer), although capo mafioso of Palermo and as you know one of our most important brothers, has been arrested and sent to Ustica. (Ustica, some 50 miles off the northwestern coast of Sicily from Palermo, is an island penal colony.) Even I, despite my influence, have been compelled to suspend my operations in smuggling, as have almost all the other capi mafiosi. Both the local police and the Guardia di Finanza are making more trouble than they did even in 1925 when Prefect Mori tried to eradicate the Mafia here. We will undoubtedly be able, however, to ride out this storm successfully as well.

I beg you therefore to wait a little longer until we can meet at some secure place to discuss our business.

I am in no danger of arrest or any other trouble and you need not worry about me or the future of our operation.

Signor Torres was right. The pressure of *Uncle Angelo* gradually relaxed, Signor Nicoletti was back in business, and the heroin which Don Ciccio wanted in the Bronx found its way to the *Excambion*. The ensuing disaster was not, in the eyes of the Mafia, Nino Torres' fault. He had obeyed orders and kept Don Ciccio completely informed—all in all a straightforward and honorably conducted operation. He is alive and well today. The entire blame rested on Don Ciccio.

The New York City Police Department has no idea, as of this writing, who the young men with rolled up sleeves on Arthur Avenue were. Centre Street and the Bureau of Narcotics hazarded guesses about who belonged to the syndicate that financed Don Ciccio's fatal deal. But the district attorney could prove nothing in court. The assassination of Francesco Scalici, like so many Mafia executions, was a perfect job. After all, two centuries of history, policy and know-how lay behind it.

II. *A Don Is Arrested*

On a June evening in 1958 Don Ettore Renallo* left his shop in Manhattan's garment district, where so many members of the brotherhood have offices for their trucking, garment and labor activities. Don Ettore took the usual precautions. He had been caught at the Apalachin meeting, been summoned before the Watchdog Committee to which he had given only his name and address—and nothing had happened. But there were all sorts of rumors around. The don was jumpy. He talked briefly to the drivers of some of his trucks parked on the street outside, his eyes scanning both sidewalks for loungers who might mean trouble. The mafioso has an uncanny instinct for the presence of gangmen as well as police of any kind. Then he walked rapidly to a garage down the street where his black Chrysler Imperial was waiting just inside the door. Watching traffic and lights with an experienced eye, he executed an intricate maneuver which had long become habit for him. He shot out of the garage, turned abruptly right onto Eighth Avenue, right again at the next crosstown street, and then stopped to watch for any flurry of pursuit. He repeated the maneuver around several more blocks before he set off complacently and at the slow pace at which he usually drives on his usual errands and visits.

The don could have spared himself the elaborate tactics. The three men from the Federal Bureau of Narcotics who were waiting in a nondescript car around the corner were only making sure that he was functioning normally. They had a warrant for his arrest, but they were in no hurry. They had been watching his habits for weeks. They also had a warrant to search his house in Brooklyn. They wanted to serve him, personally, in his home; a thorough, legally airtight search would only be possible if he was taken on the

*The events described in this section are true. The names of the principals involved have been changed.

premises. Over a dozen men and women in various parts of the metropolitan area were to be arrested as simultaneously as possible.

The organization of simultaneous raids over such a relatively small area is extremely intricate. Complications, accidents and near misses are inevitable. Unless the raids are timed very closely, a warning can get out on the underworld network with amazing speed, and the whole operation may evaporate. The people most wanted just don't go home. Invariably, there are mishaps; a car breaks down, a radio fails, a suspect picks just that day to alter his usual habits. On TV the agents who were after Renallo would have been right behind him every moment. In New York traffic this was quite impossible. It was also unnecessary, although attempted as a matter of routine. "Well," said one of the agents, "I guess we have lost him. But he's doing the usual. He ought to be home about eleven." The three men drove to Brooklyn and had supper. Then they parked their car about a block from Renallo's house.

At 10:50, precisely, the black Chrysler came down the boulevard in that section of Brooklyn and turned into the driveway of Number 481. "Let's wait about ten minutes before we hit it," said one of the men. "He'll have time to take off his coat and shirt." At 11:05 one of the agents rang the doorbell. Another agent covered the rear of the small middle-class house.

This part of such an arrest is always a somewhat nervous moment for a policeman in plain-clothes. A mafioso, surprised at home at night—particularly when he is as jittery as Renallo was—may think that the officer is an executioner, and start shooting. If he sees a badge quickly enough, a man of the don's caliber and intelligence will surrender quietly. But you never can tell.

The next two or three minutes dragged. The three men had their badges out and the flaps of the little leather cases in which they are carried—always attached, by regulation, to one's belt with a chain—were open. Federal agents rarely draw guns at this point. Then a latch clicked and in the doorway stood a chunky, heavy jowled, ugly man. For a moment he stared intently. His eyes became slits as he paled. He had seen the shields glittering under the fanlight. "An arrest?" His voice was hoarse. "Yes," came the answer. "You are under arrest. We are federal officers. We have a warrant for you; also a warrant to search your house. May we come in, please?" As Renallo backed away from the door, he waved his hands. "Now you donta get excited," he suddenly shouted at the agents. "Donta you get excited. You notta marcha all over my house." This was the only time during the next hours that he ever raised his voice; the iron self-control of a mafioso had him in hand almost immediately. "*We're* not a bit excited," said the agent. Suddenly Don Ettore smiled. "Please come in and sit down," he said with all the graciousness of a welcoming host. "Sit down please. We notta get excited."

The attack materialized from an entirely different direction. Behind Renallo, staring at the intruders, stood his father and mother, with whom he lives. The old man, with the finely chiseled face of a Sicilian peasant-aristocrat, folded his arms and watched silently. But his eyes were murderous with hatred. The elderly woman, still quite handsome, put the ancient hatred into words. Her expressive hands became fists, then claws. "De poliss," she breathed, "de *poliss*!" Her voice was low, throaty, controlled. All at once it rose to a scream. "My son. You arresta my son!" The hands went to the hips; she stood with her legs apart, her eyes blazing at the agents. "Youa filth," she spat. "Youa dirty cops. Youa sonnasabeeches. *Sonnasabeeches!*" Two spread fingers, the evil eye, were pointed at the agents. "You gerrouta here." Her voice was low and menacing again. "You gerrouta here an go wherea you belong," she shrieked. "An youa know where!" Then, suddenly, she sank into a chair, sobbing and muttering with her hands pressed to her face. Her son bent over her. "Look, Mama," he murmured in the dialect. "You must be calm. Everything will be all right. I will not be harmed." She looked at him for a moment, she nodded, and her eyes turned back to the agents. Fingers spread once more, she began a slow chant. It went something like this: "I make this curse. It will last 200 years. Your wives will deceive you. Your sons will be cuckolds as well. The sons of your sons will be cuckolds. The sons of your sons' sons will be cuckolds." (A brief pause for sobs and groans.) "Your legs will drop off. Your arms will drop off. All your other things will drop off. The legs of your sons . . ." and so forth.

"My God," said one of the agents, himself of Sicilian extraction. "Are we in Brooklyn or Palermo?" Even the most experienced and hardened officer is naturally disturbed by such an expression of agony. He is also doubly watchful. The mafiosi's women have grown instinctively skillful over the generations. Part of their almost inevitable emotional outbursts in such situations is sincere. But the sudden hysterical throwing of china, fainting spells, heart attacks and other kinds of convulsions may also be diversionary tactics to permit an escape or the concealment of something in the ensuing confusion. When Mama Renallo fainted for the first time and slumped to the floor, the agents were solicitously helpful but also very careful. One was behind Papa Renallo, one behind Don Ettore every second while the third helped lift Mama back into her chair. She was not unconscious for long. A few minutes later a fresh tirade and another stream of amazingly complicated curses began. They were all to die extremely unpleasant deaths. Her son had never done anything dishonest in his life. Various saints were invoked to cause the policemen's eyes to fall from their sockets. Her son was an upright man. The agents, in hell, would be put to horrible tortures. She would pray to that effect. For the hour during which the house was being searched the incantations continued, punctuated by unnerving moans and gasps. Papa Renallo stood by, his face stony. Don Ettore was polite and helpful. He had no secrets, he said. This was all a dreadful mistake. "Look. The kind of house I live in. Itsa clear. I'm a poor man, a business failure. Itsa crazy mistake." Over the furious anger which was boiling in him as the agents carefully went through room after room, took various documents, sealed them in envelopes and had him sign them, was the rather impressive clamp of the code. The cords in his neck and the veins in his forehead would stand out, but his voice was merely sad; he was suffering a great injustice.

The search had been completed and Don Ettore, elegantly dressed, was ready to go, when further complications developed. Mama fainted once more. This time the collapse looked real. Renallo insisted that she was seriously ill. Could he telephone his sister, who lived nearby, to come and take care of her? She would know what doctor to call and what to do. For the agents this was very tricky business. The mafiosi have ingenious codes and fast methods of communication which they use in emergencies. Don Ettore might with a single word to his sister sound an alarm that would be all over New York in a few minutes and frustrate other raids that were just beginning. On the other hand, if the signora was really sick and medical help were impeded, there would be hell to pay. "I'll dial the number," said an agent. "Then you just tell your sister, 'Mama isn't feeling well and would like you to come over.' And that's all you say or I hang up." Don Ettore obeyed.

A few minutes later the back door of the house opened and a broad-shouldered woman in her forties came in hurriedly. First she saw her mother slumped in the chair. She looked at her brother and the men standing around him. She had barely opened her mouth to say something when the situation was clear. *"Police,"* she screamed instantly, "dirty police. You arrest my brother?" No one had said a word. "Sons of bitches. I spit on you. I kill you." She advanced threateningly toward one of the agents, who hurriedly backed away. "I kill you." Don Ettore stepped in front of her, raising his ham of a fist. "You shar*rup*," he thundered. "You shar*rup*.

You don't no say one more word, or I bust you right in the nose. You unnerstand. No more words. No nuthin. You take care of Mama." She stopped, her bosom heaving, glared at each of the agents in turn and subsided.

One of the Narcotics men called 90 Church Street. The operation was going well, and on schedule; the other arrests had either been made or were set; it was safe to leave and let Renallo's sister do whatever she wanted with the telephone. "All right," said one of the agents. "Let's go." Don Ettore went to the front door and opened it. "After you, gentlemen," he said courteously. From back in the kitchen came Mama's strident voice once more—she was evidently recovering. The officers filed out, but one stayed close to the door until Renallo crossed the threshold himself. Dignified arrests have their protocol, but also their precautions. There was no hand on the don's arm. Holding or handcuffs would have been entirely unnecessary. He walked jauntily to the car as though he hadn't a care. "Itsa crazy mistake," he laughed. "Nothing like this ever happen to me before. Itsa crazy." Amazingly enough, his laugh was easy. One of the agents grinned and shrugged his shoulders.

The don was relaxed all the way to the Federal Court House in Manhattan, where he was to be examined by the U.S. Attorney that night, locked up and arraigned before a federal commissioner in the morning. Sitting on the back seat of the car between two officers, he chattered incessantly. They might have been old friends. "They're gonna take my picture?" he inquired suddenly. "Yes," replied one of the agents. "They'll take your picture." Renallo slapped his knee. "Fine," he said. "Ain't had my picture taken in years." There was a brief pause, and then, "You see, I'ma justa like Jesus Christ." There was a stunned silence. "Yes," the don continued solemnly. "I'ma justa like Jesus Christ. All my life I bear a cross—many crosses. My mother; she is sick. My sister; she is sick. I suffer with them for years. I suffer very much." A long and detailed explanation of the operations which his sister had undergone followed. There was no comment. His voice grew plaintive. "And now you make everything worse. You imagine. Tomorrow they read about this in the papers. They get sicker. It willa be your fault." A lengthy dissertation on the value of religion followed. The officers listened, fascinated, all the way to Foley Square. As they pulled up in front of the Federal Court House, the don squirmly slightly. "Why we can'ta go in the back door? I don't like to go in the front door." He was told that he had to go in through the main entrance. "But then people see me," he complained as he walked up the steps.

"What did I tell you," said one of the agents when it was all over. "That's the way they always are—the scenes at home; everything. By his standards he really believes that he hasn't done anything seriously wrong. He's poor, he's miserable, he hasn't a friend in the world and he's being persecuted. But no matter how high his bail is set tomorrow, it'll be furnished within an hour and he'll go right back to his business. He'll be making crooked deals until the day he goes to trial."

Later that morning Don Ettore was taken before a federal commissioner. His lawyer pleaded eloquently, and the don was released in $35,000 bail which was produced at once. On his way out of the hearing room to temporary freedom he was still muttering, "It's alla crazy. Itsa crazy mistake." And he looked as though he really thought so.

III. *A Don Obeys the Code*

Just before 11 o'clock on the evening of May 2, 1957, Mr. Frank Costello—gambler extraordinary, financier and politician—got out of a cab in front of the large and decorous apartment house where he lives at 115 Central Park West in Manhattan. He said good night to his friend and factotum, Philip Kennedy, who had brought him home, was respectfully greeted by the doorman—an elderly Scot named Keith

—entered the building and walked across the tastefully decorated lobby toward an elevator. He had not noticed the big figure that had slid out of a car parked nearby and waddled after him. "This is for you, Frank," barked the fat man with a gun in his hand. Costello, still very quick in his late sixties, turned in a flash and saved his life. The .38 roared and a bullet tore through the gambler's hat plowing a shallow furrow through the right side of his head. Costello staggered, felt the blood streaming down his cheek and sank into a chair. The fat man, apparently satisfied that he had done his job, quickly waddled out again with his gun trained on the dazed, terrified doorman, got into his car and drove away. A revolver of that caliber makes a characteristic and unmistakable noise. Philip Kennedy, stopped in his taxi by a red light at the next intersection, heard it and sensed what had happened. He raced back. A few minutes later Costello was in Roosevelt Hospital not far away and police headquarters on Centre Street had been notified.

Mr. Costello had not been bady hurt. Centre Street, nevertheless, went into action. Ordinarily, the attempted killing of a racketeer does not rate very high priority at headquarters. As in most big cities, the chief inspectors and their staffs regard such an assault as no great offense against society. Don Francesco Castiglia, to call him by his real name, is no ordinary gangster, however. Police Commissioner Kennedy realized that this was a very complicated case and possibly an explosive one. He assigned some of his best men to it, and the Police Department's intricate network of experts and informers who specialize in the underworld's upper brackets was put in high gear. This system can discover most anything if Centre Street is really interested. When all the rumors, whispers, and other information had been gathered, the most likely suspect seemed to be a hulking former prizefighter named Vincent Gigante, 30 years old, an apartment house superintendent in Greenwich Village who did odd jobs for Antonio Strollo—alias Tony Bender—a well-known narcotics, extortion and gambling racketeer. The grapevine also reported that a violent feud which had developed between Don Antonio and Don Francesco was responsible for the shooting. But immediately after the attempted murder "The Chin," as Gigante is known in underworld circles, disappeared from his home and usual haunts. It was three months before he finally surrendered, with the time-honored excuse that he hadn't known he was wanted. The police suspected that he had gone into hiding on orders from his gang to lose weight and generally alter his appearance. Nevertheless, when he was paraded with a number of other suspects at a special headquarters lineup, doorman Keith said at once that he recognized the pasty faced, thick lipped gunman. New York's District Attorney Hogan thought that he had sufficient evidence, Gigante was indicted for attempted murder and in May 1958 the trial of the case of The People vs Vincent L. Gigante began before John A. Mullen, senior judge of the Court of General Sessions.

Judge Mullen, in his late sixties, is one of the country's most experienced criminal court justices, and a remarkable man. He is highly respected by the bar and the various police agencies; he is respected, feared and hated all at once by the underworld generally—and particularly by the brotherhood. The judge understands the Mafia and knows a great deal about its background, mentality and methods of operation. He can smell a mafioso at once, and as he says occasionally, "I don't like the smell." His patience was to be severely tried during the next days. The mafioso involved in the case gave a characteristic performance.

Mr. Frank Costello, from the minute the first detective questioned him after the shooting, had stuck to the code as he, Don Francesco Castiglia, was bound to do. He had not seen his assailant, who had shot him from behind, he insisted, and had not the faintest idea of who might have wanted to kill him. He had been shown pictures from the police Rogues'

Gallery of suspects, including Gigante's; he recognized no one. Nevertheless, he was subpoenaed for The Chin's trial. Assistant District Attorney Alexander Herman had a plan.

Within a short time after the proceedings began, Herman had established two facts beyond reasonable doubt. When Costello heard the shout, "This is for you, Frank," he had turned, and been shot from the front. He *must* have seen his would-be assassin. A ballistics expert from police headquarters testified in detail that his examination of the hat the gambler had been wearing showed without any question that the bullet had gone through it from front to back. The doctor from Roosevelt Hospital who had examined and treated Costello immediately after the attack was just as definite. It was perfectly clear from the way the skin had been ripped, he said emphatically, that the shot had come from the front. It couldn't possibly have happened any other way.

The assistant D.A. had hoped that this almost incontrovertible evidence would shake or provoke Don Francesco into giving honest testimony. He had miscalculated. Elegant, pomaded, immaculate as always, the don took the stand with a slightly bored expression. He explained to Herman what he had done on the evening of May 2 and how he had come home. Outrage and anger were permitted to break through only a few times.

Q: Now, will you tell us as exactly as you can remember what happened from that moment on?

A: I entered the foyer and I heard shots which sounded like a firecracker to me at the time. I hesitated; didn't pay much attention to it for the moment, until I felt something wet on the side of my face; and it was blood; and I knew I was shot.

Q: Now, which way were you facing when you say you heard the sound of a firecracker and then felt something wet, and you indicated the right side of your face or head?

Costello repeated that he had been walking into the building, his back to the entrance.

Q: Now, Mr. Costello, there has been testimony offered in this court . . . by a certain Doctor Priebe . . . that you suffered a wound of entrance in the front part of your head on the right side. In view of that testimony do you still say, Mr. Costello, that you were proceeding forward, as you call it, with your back to Central Park West and the entrance doors when you were shot?

A: Yes, sir.

The assistant district attorney showed Costello a battered brown hat. It was his hat, yes. Did he have it on that night? Yes.

Q: Now, there has been testimony here . . . Ballistics Bureau . . . a bullet hole of entrance on the right side of your hat, which enters from the outside, through the silk ribbon around the hat . . . proceeds slightly backward and comes out inside the hat at the sweatband. . . . Do you still testify. . . ?

A: Yes, sir.

The don was not to be shaken. The assistant D.A. tried some swift psychological lunges, but none succeeded. Costello was instructed to put on the hat. He was obviously highly annoyed. A property clerk's tag dangled from it in front of his eyes, he tried angrily to brush it away and the courtroom tittered. Don Francesco is not accustomed to being laughed at. But his lips only tautened.

When the time came for the positive identification, or rather refusal of it, Costello and Gigante stared fixedly at each other for the first time during the trial. Oddly enough, they had barely looked at each other before that.

Q: Isn't it a fact, Mr. Costello, that you saw this man? Isn't that a fact?

A: No. I haven't seen no man.

And that was that. Defense Counsel Maurice Edelbaum, an attorney who specializes in this type of criminal law managed to discredit the testimony of the doorman, Norval Keith, now the only identifying witness, without too much trouble. Mr. Edelbaum brought out the fact that the elderly Scot was almost blind in one eye and was inclined to enjoy a dram or two, particularly at night. Counsel got Keith to admit that he had only seen a part of the shooting. The fat man with the gun had been directly between him and Costello when the shot was fired; Keith could not see which way the gambler was facing after the gunman had shouted, "This is for you, Frank." Keith testified further that as the fat man walked by him waving his gun, he had stumbled in his terror and almost fallen. Yes, his eyes had been more on the gun than on the fat man's face.

The state's case had obviously fallen to bits. Nevertheless, the blue ribbon jury deliberated for eight hours before they reluctantly returned a verdict of not guilty. When the foreman announced the verdict, Gigante's mother put away the beads she had been telling all through the trial, father Salvatore Gigante clapped and shouted and so did some 40 other relatives and friends. Judge Mullen banged his gavel, thanked the jury and left the bench as quickly as possible.

What was really significant about the trial was not much analyzed by the newspapers. Whether The Chin shot at Costello or not is relatively unimportant. The trial presented, however, an amazing picture of a capo mafioso, a non-touchable—in the person of Don Francesco Castiglia—his origin, career, a day in his life, and his attitude toward the law.

Two incidents particularly highlighted the last point. The tempers of both prosecutor and defense counsel during the questioning of Costello had risen to the boiling point. The arrogant witness, completely at his ease, was obviously obnoxious to both of them. Mr. Herman was trying to make him say that he had seen Gigante. Mr. Edelbaum was trying to make him say that he had seen *somebody* shoot at him, that he didn't know who it was and that it wasn't Gigante. The don, who has considerable knowledge of the law and was not laying himself open to a charge of perjury in the future—

besides not breaking the brotherhood's rules—stared at each in turn as though they were vermin. Both had been shouting at him. Counselor Edelbaum was asking him a question. Suddenly the don drew himself up in his chair. "Counselor, if you please," he rasped, his gravely tone carrying over the lawyer's, "don't you raise your voice to *me.*" Counsel, the court, the jury and the spectators tensed at the incredible impertinence of the man before New York City's superior tribunal. Judge Mullen leaned forward. His words were judicial and mild enough, but the tone of his voice commanded attention. *"I* give the directions in this court, Mr. Costello," he said. The don tried to brace himself against the blazing eyes and the pointed finger, but the judge's anger had a white-hot intensity and a meaning that penetrated even Costello. He sank back, dropped his eyes and quietly said, "Yes, your honor." And he meant it.

Later, Don Francesco showed his contempt and indignation in an even more dramatic performance. Counselor Edelbaum was questioning him about some of his former gambling enterprises. The reasons for this interrogation, which would seem to have little to do with Gigante's innocence or guilt, will become clearer later on. Mr. Costello had reluctantly admitted that he had owned several hundred slot machines in and around New York City in the early 30's, but had had to go into other business. "What happened in 1931?" asked Mr. Edelbaum. "Did you voluntarily give them up?" Mr. Costello began to snarl. "No. I was shut down." Counsel looked puzzled. "What?" Mr. Costello was getting angrier. "Who shut you down?" asked Edelbaum. "The administration," hissed the gambler. "You mean LaGuardia," said counsel. "That's right," answered Costello. "So when Mayor LaGuardia came into office he put you out of business, is that right?" counsel asked gently. "That's right," barked the don as the pitch of his voice rose and veins stood out on neck and forehead. "He violated an injunction that I had restraining him." There was a stunned silence in the courtroom. The idea of a gangster obtaining a court order against the beloved little mayor whose integrity raised the city out of a moral morass seemed fantastic. (As a matter of fact, Costello *had* been able, by sheer political pull, to obtain a State Supreme Court injunction restraining any interference with his slot machines.) Even Counselor Edelbaum could not believe his ears. "I didn't hear that," he said. Judge Mullen's shoulders under his black grown were shaking with silent laughter; this time it was so outrageous that it seemed funny. The jury began to grin, too. Trying hard to maintain his judicial composure, the judge repeated what Costello had said: "He violated an injunction that I had restraining him." The don nodded violently in agreement. And hotly, with sincerity and conviction in his voice, Costello shouted, *"He committed a crime."* Again there was silence. "I move to strike that out, your honor," said Edelbaum weakly, "about Mayor LaGuardia committing a crime." Judge Mullen had become very serious. His face set in grim, bitter lines. "That would be for the judge who signed the injunction to decide," he said heavily. The weight was on the words "the judge who signed the injunction."

Fascinating also were some of the other facets of Don Francesco's life which his testimony contributed in bits and pieces, probably without his realizing it.

Mr. Edelbaum was questioning the witness.

Q: Were you born Frank Costello?
A: What has that got to do with this issue?

Mr. Edelbaum asked Judge Mullen to direct an answer. His honor complied. "Answer the question," he said sharply.

A: Castiglia.
Q: What is your full right name?
A: Frank Castiglia.
Q: Did you change your name legally?
A: I have taken out my citizenship and changed my name to Costello.

Q: Did you ever have it changed legally to *Costello*?—By court order?
A: No.

The don looked surprised by the question. It had evidently never occurred to him that judicial consent was required to change one's name. His expression conveyed his outrage at the thought. Counselor Edelbaum continued.

Q: When did you come to the United States?
A: Oh, I don't know; it's so far back. I imagine 1895, 1896 or 1897.
Q: How old were you then?
A: A couple of years old.
Q: Did you go to school here?
A: Yes. . . . In 108th Street. . . . I believe it was Public School 81.
Q: How high did you go in school?
A: Oh, just about the eighth grade.

Don Francesco's face has a Latin mobility which he cannot control. His body was apparently relaxed, but the play of his facial muscles was automatic. Anger and apprehension chased each other. To a mafioso any inquiry into his history seems not only impertinent but dangerous. By the training and instinct of many generations, it is almost impossible for him to give a straight answer to even an innocuous question, in or out of court.

It was hard to understand why Don Francesco had not learned at least a few lessons from his experiences with the Kefauver Committee in 1950, when his obtuseness resulted in a jail sentence for contempt of the Senate. Ever since that time Costello has been in trouble. The Department of Internal Revenue is after him for tax evasion and the Immigration and Naturalization Service is preparing a new denaturalization case against him. As a result, he has been constantly in and out of the courts and occasionally in and out of jail.

Don Francesco was a badly harassed man when he was shot at on the night of May 2. It was suggested to him later that the charges against him might be scaled down or even dropped entirely if he would say who shot him, what the motive was, and give the federal authorities at least an idea of the gangland maneuvers behind the attempted assassination.

The don, it is reported on good authority, while denying that he knew anything, inferred that he might think it over. The conflict within him during the months before the trial of Gigante began must have been severe. He is a vain man and he likes the very best in food, clothes and surroundings. On the afternoon and evening of May 2, for example, he had made his usual regal progress around town. He had taken a Turkish bath and had a rubdown at the Biltmore Hotel, then gone to the pleasant bar at Chandler's—one of the quietly fashionable places where he has held court for years at regular hours. At seven, he and his close friend Kennedy, who calls him "Uncle Frank," strolled to L'Aiglon, one of the city's most expensive restaurants, where an excellent meal lasted until about nine. At the table were Mrs. Costello, a rather handsome, polished woman; Generoso Pope, a power in New York City politics; Mr. Albert Miniacci, who has slot machine interests; and a few others. At nine, the whole group walked over to the Monsignor, not far away, an equally opulent place. Proprietors bow, headwaiters hover and are magnificently tipped. This is the kind of an evening the don enjoys. A prison cell, prison clothes and food for a number of years in contrast are a very real concept to him. He has known the endless days, the routine, the excruciating boredom that being behind bars presents to a man of his mentality. Exile to Italy for the rest of his life would be as bad if not worse. He would be in the same class as Luciano and Adonis and be able to live extremely well, but Costello is a New Yorker to the core—of a peculiar kind but still a New Yorker. To be banished would be terrible punishment.

No one knew when Mr. Costello came into court and took the witness chair what he was going to do. In a few minutes, with his knowledge, he might have exploded a hydrogen bomb over the brotherhood. There were some tense faces among the audience all through his testimony, particularly as the elderly racketeer clearly began to tire toward the end of the long questioning. His voice had become reedy, his temper was on edge.

Prosecutor Herman was interrogating. From various police agencies he had received detailed information about the fellow racketeers with whom Costello has had most to do recently and who might have most motive to send a killer after him.

Q: Do you know of any reason why anybody in the wide world should want to kill you?
A: No, I don't know of any human being that had a motive.
Q: Do you know a man named Anthony Strollo, otherwise known as Tony Bender?
A: Yes.
Q: How long have you known him?
A: Oh, I don't know how long. I don't see the man. I mean, I wouldn't know. I know of him: see him once in a while.
Q: Are you friendly with him?
A: For years.
Q: Are you presently friendly with him?
A: I haven't seen him.
Q: My question to you is: are you presently friendly with him?
A: I have no reason not to be friendly with him.
Q: Do you know where he lives or did you ever know where he lived?
A: No. Never knew where he lived.
Q: Do you know what his business is?
A: No.
Q: When did you speak to him last?
A: I don't believe I seen the gentleman in years.
Q: I didn't ask you when you saw him. When did you *speak* to him last?
A: If it is years back, then I might have spoken to him years back and ran into him.
Q: You say you haven't *spoken* to him in years?
A: I haven't *seen* him in years.

The don was in a spot at this point. He didn't know whether a wiretap could prove in court that he had spoken with Anthony Strollo. If he denied speaking to him recently, he would lay himself open to a perjury charge. If the don admitted speaking with Strollo, he was breaking the brotherhood's rules. He chose the former course. After a few moments' hesitation he denied having spoken to Strollo in years.

Don Francesco had made up his mind and braced himself. His voice became stronger. He did not know Thomas Eboli, who controls the slot machines of lower Manhattan, at all. He knew Vito Genovese slightly but hadn't seen him in a long time. And so on through a list of others: Mauro, Miranda, the Anastasias, the Morettis. Yes; he had known most of them. No; he hadn't known what they did, where they lived or anything else about them. No; he had never done any business with any of them. No; he did not and never had had any business connections in gambling or anything else with Las Vegas or Havana. He was not to be shaken. Don Francesco stepped down from the stand tired, but with his shoulders back and his head erect. Both the assistant district attorney and defense counsel lashed out at him unmercifully later in their summations. He had forfeited any consideration that the federal government might have given him. But he had kept faith with the brotherhood.

After the trial a federal official who has had years of experience with the mafiosi tried to analyze the don's behavior. "Look," he said. "Any normal individual, criminal or not, would have been so mad about getting shot that he would have tried to crucify somebody. Costello didn't, although he knew perfectly well who shot him and why. Then he threw up every chance of getting out of the raps against him. Now why? you say. I'll tell you. Sure, Costello was afraid that he'd really get killed this time if he squealed. He can afford hiring a bodyguard, a battalion of them, and it would take a while to get him. He'd have to be afraid all the time. But it's much more than that. He couldn't—and I'm saying this very seriously—reconcile his giving any information with his conscience. He sees himself, from a capo mafioso's point of view, as a good soldier. He'd be committing treason—high treason—by going over to the enemy, which is the way he sees us. He might be executed at the end of a .38, but he would certainly be punished by something which to him seems even worse—ostracism and the contempt of the brothers, who are the only people that he really knows. You've just seen the Mafia's *omertà* working, my friend. It's more than a code or a pattern of faith. It's almost a religion—with teeth in it—in this world."

CHAPTER TWELVE

Twilight of the Villains?

The brotherhood still thumbs its nose at government. But legislators and public are beginning to understand its mentality and purpose. And something is being done.

The responsibility for the extent and menace of organized crime in the United States, the racketeering of which the Mafia is such an important element, rests on many shoulders. Most legislators, both state and federal, have been either ignorant of the facts or lethargic. Many of our law enforcement agencies, federal, state and local, have not cooperated sufficiently because of traditional jealousies and jurisdictional disputes. Many of our courts, particularly the federal judiciary, have too often put legalistic hair splitting above basic, realistic justice. The brotherhood has thrived as a result.

It is a shocking and outrageous fact, for example, that not one of the 20 top mafiosi of the country who have brazenly defied various congressional investigating committees, been cited for contempt and then voted in contempt by Congress, has been punished as of this writing. Accardo, Fischetti, Costello, Licavoli and the others who have over and over sneeringly pleaded the Fifth Amendment have continued to stay safely and smugly behind the shield of a decision of the United States Supreme Court in 1951 which established the doctrine that a witness must give only his name and address; he need answer no further questions whatever—birthplace, business, finances; nothing. Lower courts, bound by this decree, have dismissed one case after the other. The code of *omertà* could not have been more firmly supported than by this action of our highest court.

A formidable tide, however, has been gradually but steadily rising against the Mafia. At times during the last eight years it has seemed to recede, but its momentum has actually been gaining through four principal phases—the Kefauver hearings, the Daniel investigation, the consequences of the Apalachin meeting and now the McClellan inquiry. And for the brotherhood it is a dangerous tide indeed.

Senator Kefauver and his committee officially recognized the existence of the Mafia in 1951, explained much of its working and brought out its dominating position in the national and international underworlds with many hundreds of pages of indisputable testimony. The effects of the senators' findings were not immediately apparent, but they began to produce a cumulative result. Their findings explained the Apalachin meeting when it was exposed; they made Costello, Anastasia and the rest easier to understand. They did more—which has had little recognition. Kefauver, Tobey, O'Conor, Halley and their associates carefully put together 22 basic recommendations to Congress for measures against organized crime. They were designed to strike at every one of the brotherhood's most important operations. They were neither complicated, offensive to civil liberties nor expensive. It is astonishing that it has taken so long for even the most obviously needed to be implemented.

As the coordinators and spearhead of an overall offensive the committee suggested the creation of a special antirackets squad in the Department of Justice which would devote itself exclusively to obtaining and collating every available scrap of information about the country's criminal combines and devising new ways of smashing them. Amazingly enough, until very recently, there has been no such comprehensive organization. The Federal Bureau of Investigation has never been authorized to set one up and although the superb files of the FBI contain an enormous amount of information on racketeers of every kind, this invaluable intelligence had not been fitted together into either a picture or a program.

The committee urged a much expanded and more active antiracket section of the Internal Revenue Service which could hack at the brotherhood's vital financial blood vessels. The senators pointed out tartly that the organized gangsters not only commit countless crimes of violence and extortion, but also happen to defraud the government of several hundred million dollars in income tax revenue every year; and that very little seems to be done about it. In this connection, the committee underlined a number of irritating facts. While honest taxpayers, for example, keep troublesome books on income and expenses and are frequently harried by time consuming inspections by Internal Revenue agents, members of the brotherhood even in the obviously top income brackets get away usually with the skimpiest of obviously inaccurate records. When challenged, the latter will appear with a small sheet of scribbled writing. "This is all I can remember," is the invariable explanation. "I throw papers away. I'm no business man. I don't understand these things." Very few are prosecuted; and the underworld knows that. "The biggest farce and effrontery," Kefauver wrote, "is the fact that the present law permits gamblers to deduct wagering losses and overhead expenses. Such deductions often include the hidden bribes paid to law enforcement officials."

The concrete laws which the committee proposed would have hit the mafiosi hard if they had been passed. Trading in narcotics was to draw far stiffer penalties. Interstate gambling was to be blasted by a severe prohibition against the use of the mails and all other public communications for the making and paying of bets. Racketeering in the interstate, gangster infested trucking business, wholesale liquor traffic and other fields where federal permits are required was to be curbed by requiring the Interstate Commerce Commission and the Treasury's Alcohol Tax Unit to investigate their licensees with care. A very much stiffened immigration law was to be aimed at the Mafia itself, specifically and directly. Kefauver discovered that many of the mafiosi who had come to the United States, particularly those who had criminal records in Italy, had never bothered with either immigration formalities or naturalization. Quick and effective deportation procedures against criminals who were either noncitizens or had obtained citizenship without revealing their former police records were to supplant the cumbersome ones in existence, so full of legal loopholes that a wealthy racketeer with clever counsel, no matter how clear the case against him, could delay his expulsion order sometimes for years.

The Kefauver Committee's project was too ambitious to be realized quickly as a whole. Most of the suggested laws fell by the wayside. The many volumes of thick green books turned out by the Government Printing Office of the minutes of the committee's hearings—an encyclopedia of the underworld, or rather the foundations of one—went into legislators' back files, into wastebaskets and out of print. Nevertheless, Kefauver, without actually realizing the impact of his work himself, had started a trend of thought among his colleagues, in government and across the country, which was to eventually have profound effects.

When Senator Price Daniel and his Judiciary Subcommittee started their investigation in 1955 of the narcotics traffic, they already had a lot of information to go on, from the Kefauver Committee's files. Their own investigators added to it. And there was the same pattern again—the same names, the same methods, the same kind of murders, the same kind of organization. There, again, was the Mafia at the heart of the nation's big crime. But there was a new atmosphere in the Senate and House committees that were considering revision of legislation after the Daniel Committee report was in. Commissioner Anslinger and others expected from sad experience, as they testified, the usual indifference on the part of the legislators. For once, they were wrong.

Public Law 728 has long, sharp teeth that have already bitten deep into the brotherhood and its lucrative trade in poison. A convicted narcotics trader now gets a mandatory five to ten years for his first offense—without possibility of parole—ten to twenty for his second, twenty to forty for his third. And here Congress became really, and rightly, grim. Even in its stilted legal language, Section 107 has the ring of the anger that went into it:

> ... whoever, having attained the age of eighteen years, knowingly sells, gives away, furnishes, or dispenses ... any heroin ... brought into the United States, to any person who has not attained the age of eighteen years ... shall be imprisoned for life, or for not less than ten years, except that the offender shall suffer death if the jury at its discretion shall so direct.

The provision for a life sentence and even the death penalty under circumstances was not carelessly granted to the federal courts. The senators debated long and hard. Only murder, kidnaping and high treason draw similar punishment after all. But the legislators came to the conclusion that the trapping of minors into addiction—at which the capital clause is particularly aimed—is in effect murder in the first degree in very many cases, slow but sure.

The bill included other unprecedented measures. A narcotics smuggler and his co-conspirators—in other words the courier from Naples or Marseilles, as well as the members of the syndicate in New York or Chicago that financed him—if convicted, get five to twenty years for a first offense, ten to forty for a second. The reason for the spread in these sentences is to allow the trial judge to punish according to the amount and kind of business done.

Much red tape was cut away from the catching and prosecution of offenders in every bracket. It is now a crime, punishable by two to five years, to use the telephone, the mails, or any other kind of communication, public or private, for trading in illegal narcotics. The bill's definition is draconic: "... writings, signs, signals, pictures, and sounds of all kinds by mail, telephone, wire, radio, or other means of communication." This is invaluable help to the federal agent working against the brotherhood's age-old skill in secure communications.

A series of legal restrictions which often crippled investigations, arrests and prosecutions at crucial moments was removed. Search and arrest warrants are more easily obtained; the arrest and search of a suspect without warrant when necessary, formerly complicated and touchy for the officer, has been made much simpler and more sensible. And a whole welter of legalistic ifs and buts, which helped the gangster with a shrewd lawyer far more than it protected the innocent, was cleaned out.

The mafiosi almost immediately recognized the menace of the new legislation and, in characteristic fashion, quickly shifted position. At what meeting or series of meetings of the various members of the brotherhood primarily interested in narcotics, in 1956, the decisions were made is not definitely known. The small top echelon gathering of Barbara, Galente, di Palermo and Garofola in Binghamton was unquestionably one of them. The reports of undercover agents and informers leave no doubt that a complete shift of personnel and method was decreed by various capi mafiosi. When the fangs of the new law snapped shut on the next big national-international narcotics case in September 1957, the principal defendant was racketeer Harry Stromberg, a former gambling boss of Philadelphia. Known in the underworld as "Nig" Rosen and very wealthy, he had been financing a huge smuggling operation—or rather part of it—with investments of $100,000 every few months for single shipments of heroin. The other principals were John Baruche, Jean Aron, Saul Gelb and Nathan Behrman. Among all 46 indicted there was only one prominent mafioso—Antonio Velucci. The rest of the brethren who had been connected with the gang for years had bowed out in well-disciplined Mafia fashion just in time, leaving their less farsighted associates to take the punishment. All of the principals were convicted and sent to prison. The brotherhood congratulated itself on having withdrawn from the line of fire.

And then came the Apalachin catastrophe. The New York State watchdog committee irritated the brotherhood but did not disturb it too much, according to the grapevine. They thought that the excitement would die down as usual; Uncle Angelo would get tired. The mafiosi had no idea of what was in store for them. Many of Senator Kefauver's suggestions of six years before began coming to life again. Young, energetic William Rogers, the attorney general, turned his careful, precise and imaginative mind to devising a long range campaign against organized crime—one that would not and could not bog down. "I am not interested in the political kudos of so-called gangbusting," he said firmly to a meeting of the chiefs of all the federal law enforcement agencies. "What I want is a permanent, a permanently functioning organization that will knock out, and *continue to knock out,* the interstate gangster. We must lay plans not only against those now in existence but also against those who will take their places."

The attorney general had a very concrete program. It was not an easy one. The jurisdictions of the various federal agencies are very tightly defined by law and by tradition. A "T-man" or a "G-man" on television wanders happily through cases in a manner that would cause the immediate dismissal of a real Treasury agent or a special agent of the FBI. The jurisdiction of the FBI is strictly limited to crimes covered by federal law—but only some such as the flight of a murderer across a state line, interstate robbery, kidnaping and crimes involving national security. The intelligence unit of the Internal Revenue Service has the exclusive job of finding tax frauds. The Bureau of Narcotics is autonomous in its field. So is the Secret Service in finding and prosecuting counterfeiters of "the public monies." The inspectors of the Post Office

Department have their own, and very secretive, organization to track down misuse of the mails. The Customs Service has another system of agents who deal with smuggling, the Immigration and Naturalization Service still another to cope with the fraudulent assumption of American citizenship. All of these services and agencies have extremely able and therefore very individualistic chiefs. Hoover of FBI, Anslinger of Narcotics, Baughman of Secret Service, Swing of Immigration and Naturalization and the rest all have strong personalities and positive ideas in their almost fanatically dedicated fashion. It was a question of getting them all together for a common purpose. The attorney general, a skillful planner, has been remarkably successful with the fusing of the elements.

"It [is] obvious that the information obtained by separate investigating agencies must be fitted together by the prosecutors," the attorney general said recently, "more effectively than in the past if we are to meet today's crafty challenge of the organized criminal.

"We will give top priority to 100 of the top racketeers in the United States. That is not to say that we will ignore the others; for we plan to attack crime on as many fronts as we can. It does mean, however, that we will give immediate and concentrated effort to the 100 worst racketeeers in the country.

"The list of names will not be made public for two reasons. In the first place, it would tip our hand and make the investigative work more difficult. In the second place such publication of the names might be attacked as prejudicial in the event of trial. After there have been convictions or deportations we will announce the names and will replenish the list with others who are deserving.

"The members of these top level planning boards are also the key figures in organizations with headquarters in New York, Miami, Chicago and other cities in the United States. Here the multimillion-dollar businesses take shape. It is our purpose to concentrate on these overlords. We plan to find out everything we can about them—their sources of income, their present activities, how they invest their money and how they avoid paying their taxes. Without in any way denying them any of the rights which our citizens have under our system of justice we will attempt to find out what federal law they have violated and to obtain necessary evidence to prove it.

". . . what we are in the process of establishing is a unified prosecutive command, where all information on racketeers from all investigative agencies will be studied, correlated and acted upon.

"The program we have in mind is not intended to produce quick or sensational results. It will be a long range program built on policies which will be lasting and intended to meet a continuing and constantly changing problem. From my experience in law enforcement work I have noticed that efforts directed against organized crime are apt to be sporadic. This is going to be a *permanent* program."

As a result, when Senator John McClellan of Arkansas and his antirackets group—officially, the Select Committee on Improper Activities in the Labor or Management Field—began their investigations in 1958, they had a volume of accurate, sorted and collated information at their disposal far more comprehensive than any which had reached Congress before. The senators and Chief Counsel Robert Kennedy knew what they were doing. And the mafiosi sweated.

The early hearings of the McClellan Committee were hard enough on the brotherhood. In New York, for example, it became clear that John Dioguardi and Antonio (Tony Ducks) Corallo were so powerful in various labor unions that even the mighty James Hoffa, dictator of the teamsters, could not function in the key city without the support of these capi mafiosi. It is developed that one of their principal associates, Vincent Squillante—godson of the late Umberto

Anastasia—controlled the private garbage removal industry of the city.

But worst of all for the Mafia were the four black days of July last year in the big caucus room of the Senate Office Building in Washington. Senators McClellan, Ives, Kennedy, Church, Curtis, Ervin, Goldwater, and Mundt sat down to a careful, patient dissection of the very heart and an analysis of the soul of the brotherhood.

"We are going to call in," said McClellan, "some of the leading figures in the national crime hierarchy. These people are all involved in legitimate enterprises, management, and labor. As a starting point . . . we intend to focus on the criminal group which held a meeting at the home of Joseph Mario Barbara, Sr., in Apalachin. . . ."

This time the complete records of the Apalachin delegates as well as those of their principal associates were before the legislators. Both federal and state agencies had worked hard. Everyone was there, from Antonio Abate to Frank Zito. Their family relationships had been traced out in detail as well. Then the witnesses began. Sergeant Croswell repeated the story of the meeting. He was followed by Narcotic Agent Martin Pera, one of the Bureau's experts on the brotherhood. Senator Mundt seemed rather incredulous as Pera so casually explained it and its workings. "I would assume," he suddenly shot at the agent, "that in all these years that the Mafia has been operating we must have had some success . . ." Pera nodded. "Oh yes," he said quietly. "We have had people very close to the Mafia. We have had people that have been trusted among leaders of the Mafia. We have agents that have worked that close to the group under cover." It was the first time that the Bureau had ever seen fit to officially announce the fact. Commissioner Anslinger had purposely waited for an effective psychological moment. And this was it. When Agent Pera began to read and explain the Scalise letters, the senators sat forward in their chairs. "[But you mustn't] look at these people," said Pera, "solely from the point of view of their narcotics activities. The Bureau of Narcotics has maintained lengthy files for many years on various individuals and developed them, from an intelligence point of view . . . not only in the field of narcotics but from their activities as an organized entity. You have to consider their operation as a whole."

From there on the senators were led through a maze of Mafia names and activities. But this time, with the information they had before them, it all made sense. The ramifications of the brotherhood could actually be presented in chart form. The Apalachin delegates alone were shown to be in no less than 30 different kinds of rackets and semirackets with legitimate fronts. Police officers and crime commission officials from New York, Miami, Chicago, San Francisco, as well as the committee's own investigators, clarified many of the transcontinental connections. But worst of all for the brotherhood was the fact that the word Mafia had obviously become a definite concept in the Senators' minds—far more so than during the Kefauver hearings. The senators and police officers used the name of the brotherhood frequently and without vagueness.

All of the gangsters who had come to Washington at the committee's summons were obviously extremely nervous as they took the witness stand. There was none of the braggadocio that had been displayed before the Keafauver and Daniel committees. With monotonous regularity most of them pleaded the Fifth Amendment throughout, but with a marked difference of manner. They were frightened men. And they became increasingly frightened as they realized more and more clearly how accurately aimed the senators' shafts at them were.

Rosario Mancuso of Utica, New York, was on the witness stand. Senator McClellan and Chief Counsel Robert Kennedy were interrogating.

Q: Have you been president of the New Form Concrete Company of Utica?

A: I refuse to answer on the ground it may tend to incriminate me.
Q: . . . you became a union official in November of 1953?
A: I refuse to answer . . .
Q: . . . you became president of Local 186 of the International Hod Carriers and Common Laborers' Union of America?
A: I refuse to answer . . .
Q: . . . as supposedly a union official, you attempted to obtain a liquor license for a restaurant?
A: I refuse to answer . . .
Q: . . . we have information that in Utica there was a wide-open gambling game, with very large stakes, operating in 1957, and that you acted as doorman: is that right?
A: I refuse to answer . . .
Q: . . . this gambling operation was broken into and the money all picked up by another group of gangsters . . . came in, robbed this game . . . made everybody take their pants off and then took all of their money?
A: I refuse to answer . . .
Q: . . . wasn't one of the individuals that was supposed to be responsible for raiding that gambling game a man by the name of Hap Longo?
A: I decline to answer . . . (Mancuso had been nudged by his attorney, Anthony Fernicola, into the more respectful formula of refusal.)
Q: Do you know that Hap Longo has disappeared?
A: I decline to answer . . .
Q: According to the information we have, the last time Mr. Longo was seen was by Mrs. Longo when she saw him in your company?
A: I decline to answer . . .
Q: Did you kill him?
A: I decline to answer . . .
Senator Ives: I don't blame you. (The senator's face was grim, not sympathetic.)

Counsel Kennedy switched suddenly to a new approach. He was telling the story of the Falcone brothers, Giuseppe and Salvatore, who control the rackets of Utica and a sizeable section of upstate New York.

Here are the questions that told the story, with the monotous, identical answers deleted:

We understand that the Falcone brothers . . . were very close to Albert Anastasia?
Isn't it a fact that it was from Utica that Albert Anastasia registered and was inducted into the army? (Fantastic as it may seem, Don Umberto while being sought for the killings done by Murder, Inc.—which he headed—was securely anonymous as a private in the armed forces.)
Isn't it a fact that he gave as his address at that time a vacant lot in Utica?
Do you know how he was able to make that arrangement in Utica, to be taken into the army like he was?
I would like to ask this witness if he himself is in any way associated with the city administration in Utica.
You were backing fights?
Isn't it correct that the money used in that operation came from the Falcone brothers?
Could you tell the committee why just one or two companies in Utica are able to get all of the building contracts in that area?

Counsel Kennedy referred to an elaborate list compiled for the committee of telephone toll calls between known racketeers.

You have been calling Darling Ice Cream Company of Syracuse?
Do you know why other people with criminal records such as Manuel Sicari, Salvatore Falcone, Barbara, and Monachino would all be calling this company?
We have information . . . that you used Joe Foti in union business while he was a narcotics fugitive; is that correct?

To all of these and other questions Mancuso had answered with the same formula, "I decline to answer on the ground it may tend to incriminate me." Senator McClellan had pointed out to him several times, with sarcasm in his voice, that he could, after all, say "no" if he felt he could make an honest denial, without fear of punishment for perjury. Stubbornly, the witness had shaken his head.

The senator was ready for the windup.

"How long have you been a member of the Mafia?" asked McClellan in a casual tone. Mancuso jumped slightly in his chair, despite himself. "I decline to answer . . ." he growled. "Were you born into membership, or did you marry into membership?" Mancuso squirmed. This was getting much too close to the most private part of a mafioso's being and revealed far too much knowledge on the part of the enemy. "I decline to answer . . ."

There it all was—the complete picture of a mafioso of lesser importance, but characteristic. A union official, restaurateur, gambling organizer, boxing promoter and general handyman for his superiors in the brotherhood, the Falcone brothers—intimates of Anastasia. Louis Larasso from New Jersey, the next witness, followed exactly the same pattern; trustee of a big hod carriers local, construction labor foreman, gambling organizer, friend of the three dons—Profaci, Genovese and Anastasia.

As the questioning went on, the witnesses were of higher and higher caliber and their enterprises more and more impressive and complicated. But Robert Kennedy was determined that the growing, almost incredible picture should be kept clear as it developed. Interspersed between the testimony—or rather questioning without answer—of Profaci, Genovese, Miranda, Plumeri, Bufalino, Luchese, was the testimony of police officers and other experienced investigators from various parts of the country which kept pulling together the complicated strands of the brotherhood between New York, Chicago, Detroit, Los Angeles, Miami and their other centers. Finally, the picture was both clear and detailed.

Some had export-import firms as fronts, which gave them legitimate access to the docks where their "muscle squads" exacted tribute from both longshoremen and shipping companies. A recalcitrant stevedore finds himself without a job, a stubborn shipper keeps having "accidents" happen to his crates and bales, a cab company finds it must pay fifty cents a vehicle each week for protection against "accidents." Other hoodlums owned trucking companies so that their torpedos could more easily associate with other truckers and, when necessary more safely pour sugar syrup into the gas tanks of the vehicles of companies that would not pay "fees." (This method of sabotage is known as "syruping" and completely ruins the expensive engine of a big truck.) The largest number of mafiosi with legitimate fronts are in labor unions and labor-management relations setups of various kinds. No less than 22 of the Apalachin delegates were in this field with its literally limitless possibilities for lucrative skulduggery. The story of the "paper unions" of New York City, the "sweetheart contracts," the strike-making and strike-breaking techniques has been thoroughly told and does not warrant repetition. What the McClellan hearings brought out was the *extent* to which the Mafia has penetrated labor organizations, the garment industry, trucking, and the rest, across the entire country.

One Fifth Amendment plea followed another in the caucus room. Toward the end of the Washington hearings James Plumeri was on the stand. Known as "Jimmy Doyle" in the underworld, in good Mafia fashion, he was born in Sicily in 1903. His record included eight arrests for various degrees of extortion and felonious assault including homicide, and one five-year prison sentence. He owns two sizeable trucking corporations and two dress concerns. On every point of the record Mr. Plumeri pleaded the Fifth.

Q: According to police records, you were one of the five leading underworld figures in New York City, Mr. Plumeri.
A: I respectfully decline . . .
Q: Did you take part in keeping certain dress companies from signing a contract recently with the ILGWU?
A: I respectfully decline . . .
Q: Isn't it a fact that you flew up especially from Miami to give advice and counsel in those negotiations?
A: I respectfully decline . . .
Q: Are you a member of the Mafia?
A: I respectfully decline . . .

Mr. Russell Bufalino declined to admit that he was born in 1903 in Montedoro, Sicily—the "men of Montedoro," as they call themselves, are the staunchest and most orthodox of the mafiosi—and that his sister-in-law, who worked in the Record Office of Wilkes-Barre, Pa., had inserted faked documents into the file to prove that he was born in Pennsylvania. He respectfully declined to admit six arrests, all on serious charges. He declined knowledge of his brother-in-law, the notorious Angelo Sciandra, and of the dressmaking, trucking and construction companies in which he is interested with him, Plumeri, Barbara and others in both New York and Pennsylvania. He declined to admit that he knew James Hoffa, or that his cousin, William Bufalino, was head of the big Local 985 of the teamsters. He declined to say whether or not he was responsible for organizing—for his close friend and associate of many years, Don Giuseppe Barbara—the whole Apalachin meeting. (The committee had very reliable information that he did.) And finally he respectfully declined to say whether or not he was a member of the Mafia.

The last of the capi mafiosi had testified, the committee had conferred at length and the chairman was ready with their closing statement.

"The testimony we have heard," said Senator McClellan, "can leave no doubt that there has been a concerted effort by members of the American criminal syndicate to achieve legitimacy through association with and control of labor unions and business firms. The extent of this infiltration poses a serious threat to the very economy of our country.

"The criminal syndicate which we have identified here as the Mafia has revealed an arrogant challenge to the government and to the decent people of this country."

This challenge, as the investigating senators of the last three probing committees and the interested law enforcement officials know, is not easy to meet. Much has been done over the last years nevertheless.

The Kefauver Committee for the first time really penetrated the ancient brotherhood's armor of secrecy. The

Daniel Committee with its resulting legislation made dangerous, and precarious, one of its principal sources of income and power—narcotics. The McClellan Committee, which has earned the respect and attention of Congress, is slowly but methodically attacking the mafiosi from the other flank. Legislation is being devised that will eventually make labor racketeering and other Mafia specialties almost as dangerous and precarious as narcotics trading. This will probably take several years. But the groundwork has been done. Other legislators, federal and state, will be able to build on solid knowledge—names, connections, methods of operation. Congress can never legislate specifically against the Mafia. But, by legislating against organized crime, it hits first and automatically at the brotherhood. Most important of all, the public—often slow to understand basic problems but remorseless once it does—is gradually beginning to fit organized crime together with its background. When this happens, and it is beginning to happen, the brotherhood will be finished as the spine of our huge, wicked, destructive, expensive underworld. Nothing can take its place. Organized crime will never be destroyed completely; it is apparently too much a part of our society. But we will probably live to see the crumbling of the Mafia—the twilight of the greatest of the villains.

Appendix

I

The purpose of the following list is to indicate the penetration by the brotherhood into union labor and legitimate business. The list does not purport to be a complete record of the interests of any of the individuals named, nor does it show whether control of a given enterprise is outright or through a "front."

Union labor (the term as used here also covers labor-management relations) is of interest to the brotherhood because locals with closed shop contracts provide the union officers with a steady flow of funds from a captured dues-paying membership, and because unions have immunities not enjoyed by other organized groups. Extortion, bribery, shakedowns and violence are used to keep unions and industries in line. Frequently a conflict of interest occurs where a group of racketeers control a union and also the company which employs members of the union. This is particularly true in the construction business, garbage and waste collection services, and the distribution of linens and laundry.

Legitimate business is used, among other reasons, for the purpose of creating monopolies, the investment of funds from illegal enterprises, and as fronts to cover illegal activities. It is not a coincidence that many members of the brotherhood who are known to be active in the narcotics traffic also control sections of the New York waterfront and have interests in trucking companies, import-export houses, and the wholesaling of cheese, olive oil and other imported produce. This means that a kilo of heroin (about 33 ounces) placed in a barrel of olive oil or a wheel of cheese before shipment will be in "safe" hands from the time it reaches dockside in the United States until it is delivered to the buyer. Testimony before the McClellan Committee (the source for the following list) suggested a possible reason for the interest on the part of some racketeers in both the chemical and garment industries. The common chemical acetic anhydride, which is used in the manufacture and treatment of rayon, is also used in the conversion of raw opium into the morphine base from which heroin is made.

All of the men named in the following list attended the Apalachin meeting of November 14, 1957.

ALAIMO, DOMINICK
chemicals
coal companies
garment industry
union labor

BONNANO, JOSEPH
funeral homes
garment industry
import-export
linens & laundries
olive oil & cheese

BONVENTRE, JOHN
garment industry
import-export
real estate

BUFALINO, RUSSELL
automobile agencies
coal companies
construction
garment industry
jewelry & furs
union labor

CARLISI, ROY
horses & tracks
produce & markets
real estate
union labor

CASTELLANO, PAUL
produce & markets
waterfront
union labor

CATENO, GERARDO VITO
coin machines
entertainment
oil & gas leases
paper & wastepaper
real estate
restaurants & bars
trucking
union labor

CIVELLO, JOSEPH FRANCIS
import-export
olive oil & cheese
produce & markets

COLLETTI, JAMES
import-export
olive oil & cheese
real estate
restaurants & bars

CUCCHIARA, FRANK
import-export
olive oil & cheese
restaurants & bars

DE MOOCO, JOHN ANTHONY
coin machines
real estate
restaurants & bars
union labor

FALCONE, JOSEPH
coin machines
produce & markets
real estate

FALCONE, SALVATORE
horses & tracks
olive oil & cheese
produce & markets
real estate
union labor

GAMBINO, CARLO
garment industry
paper & wastepaper
produce & markets
steel tanks
union labor

GENOVESE, VITO
horses & tracks
import-export
neon signs
paper & wastepaper
real estate
restaurants & bars
steel strapping
union labor
waterfront

LA DUCA, JAMES
entertainment
hotels
retail clothing
soft drink distribution
taxicabs
union labor

LARASSO, LOUIS ANTHONY
construction
union labor

LOMBARDOZZI, CARMINE
coin machines
construction
real estate
stocks & securities
television service
trucking
union labor
waterfront

MAGLIOCCO, JOSEPH
beverage distribution
import-export
linens & laundries
olive oil & cheese
union labor

MAJURI, FRANK THOMAS
construction
union labor

MANCUSO, ROSARIO
construction
prize fighting
restaurants & bars
union labor

MIRANDA, MICHAEL
automobile agencies
coin machines
horses & tracks
insurance
jewelry & furs
union labor

ORMENTO, JOHN
chemicals
garment industry
trucking
union labor

PROFACI, JOSEPH
construction
garment industry

import-export
olive oil & cheese
union labor

RAO, VINCENT
construction
garment industry
real estate
restaurants & bars
union labor

RICCOBONO, JOSEPH
garment industry
jewelry & furs

ROSATO, JOSEPH
trucking

SCALISH, JOHN
coin machines
union labor

SCIANDRA, ANGELO JOSEPH
coal companies
entertainment
garment industry
trucking

VALENTE, COSTENZE PETER
produce & markets
restaurants & bars

ZITO, FRANK
coin machines
olive oil & cheese

II

The brotherhood uses intermarriage to promote solidarity within the organization. The names in the following list have been selected from a more extensive roster published in the hearings before the Select Committee on Improper Activities in the Labor and Management Field (the McClellan Committee) for July 1, 1958. According to testimony given before the committee, most of the men named below have police records and many of them attended the Apalachin conference. However, the only purpose of this list is to give an indication of the close (and confusing) relationships common to the brotherhood. Husbands and wives are listed in the left-hand column, and comments on relationships are supplied in the right-hand column.

	Husband / Wife	Comments
1.	ANGELO MELI VICENZA DI MERCURIO	
2.	FRANK MELI GRACE PANZICA	Brother of Angelo (1)
3.	VINCENT H. MELI PAULINE PERRONE	Son of Angelo (1) Daughter of Santo Perrone

4.	SALVATORE ANGELO MELI	Son of Angelo (1)
	DOLORES LIVORSI	Daughter of Frank Livorsi
5.	WILLIAM BUFALINO	Son of Charles Sr.
	MARIE ANTOINETTE MELI	Daughter of Frank (2)
6.	CHARLES BUFALINO JR.	Son of Charles Sr.
	TINA VOLPE	Daughter of Santo Volpe
7.	RUSSELL BUFALINO	Nephew of Charles Sr.
	JOSEPHINE SCIANDRA	Cousin of Angelo Sciandra
8.	SALVATORE FALCONE JR.	Son of Salvatore Sr.
	EMMANUELA BUFALINO	Daughter of Charles Sr.
9.	WILLIAM TOCCO	Father of Jack (10) and Anthony Joseph (14)
	ROSALIE ZERILLI	Sister of Joseph Zerilli (11)
10.	JACK TOCCO	Son of William
	ANTOINETTE MELI	Daughter of Angelo (1)
11.	JOSEPH ZERILLI	Brother of Rosalie (9)
	JOSEPHINE FINAZZO	
12.	PAUL JOSEPH TOCCO	
	JOSEPHINE ZERILLI	Daughter of Joseph (11)
13.	ANTHONY ZERILLI	Son of Joseph (11)
	ROSALIE PROFACI	Daughter of Joseph Profaci (14)
14.	JOSEPH PROFACI	Father of Rosalie (13) and Carmella (15)
	NINFA MAGLIOCCO	Sister of Joseph Magliocco
15.	ANTHONY JOSEPH TOCCO	Son of William (9)
	CARMELLA PROFACI	Daughter of Joseph Profaci (14)
16.	THOMAS DIOGUARDIA	Brother of John Dioguardia
	ROSE MARIE LIVORSI	Sister of Dolores (4) and Patricia (17)
17.	TOM ORMENTO	Son of John Ormento
	PATRICIA LIVORSI	See (16) and (4)